Learning Disabilities and Your Child

A SURVIVAL HANDBOOK

OTHER BOOKS BY LAWRENCE J. GREENE

GETTING SMARTER,
Simple Strategies for Better Grades

KIDS WHO UNDERACHIEVE

SMARTER KIDS

Learning Disabilities and Your Child

A SURVIVAL HANDBOOK

(Formerly titled *Kids Who Hate School*)

Lawrence J. Greene

FAWCETT COLUMBINE   NEW YORK

This book is dedicated to the 7,000 kids with whom I have worked over the last seventeen years. Each and every one of them tested my resources every bit as much as I tested theirs. I hope that they have derived as much from the process as I have.

Contents

CHAPTER 2

DIAGNOSIS: THE FIRST STEP TO REMEDIATION

CHAPTER 3

IDENTIFYING YOUR CHILD'S LEARNING PROBLEMS

CHAPTER 7
COMMUNICATING WITH YOUR CHILD'S TEACHER

CHAPTER 8
PARENTING THE LEARNING DISABLED CHILD

CHAPTER 9
DEALING WITH THE EMOTIONAL FALLOUT

CHAPTER 10
COMMUNICATING WITH YOUR CHILD

Index of Checklists

Author's Note

The case studies and anecdotal material that are included in this book are drawn from my seventeen years of clinical experience as a learning disabilities specialist. All of the educational data cited in the case studies is correct and accurate. Certain facts and background information have been changed, however, to protect the identities of the children and their families.

Acknowledgments

I am indebted to my exceptional staff for their support, counsel, and criticism. These dedicated people are the ones who treated the children described in this book. Without their remarkable talents, this book would not have been possible. I am especially indebted to Lorraine Koranda who diligently verified my spelling, syntax, and grammar, and to Leigh Jones-Bamman, who served as my research assistant, fact checker, and critic.

Learning Disabilities and Your Child

A SURVIVAL HANDBOOK

Introduction

He is eight years old and so far the most significant thing he has learned in school is how to fail.

He can barely read, seldom finishes a project he starts, and has difficulty concentrating. His handwriting is illegible. When his teachers speak in class, he doesn't listen. When they give instructions, he is confused. Distractible, inattentive, fidgety, overactive, each day he falls further and further behind.

His parents love him, of course, but their patience is wearing thin. They are convinced that his problems would disappear if only he would try harder. As the months pass, they become more and more desperate. His teachers are equally perplexed. Despite their efforts, they recognize that the child is not learning properly. With each passing day, the boy's self-image sinks a bit lower. School becomes intolerable, and with increasing frequency he finds refuge in his daydreams. The boy's name is Mike, and he is one of the 8,000,000 children in the United States with learning problems.

Eight years later, Mike is six feet tall. He can still barely read. Two facts have changed, however. Mike now has a probation officer assigned to him by juvenile court and attends a continuation high school on an irregular basis.

3

Mike's parents and teachers have learned to expect very little of him. His school counselor and his probation officer are happy when he simply decides to show up at school. Repeatedly disappointed, his parents have become resigned to their son's erratic behavior and unreliability.

Although Mike has made several halfhearted attempts to find a part-time job at a hamburger stand and a car wash, he has had no success convincing anyone to hire him. Any prospective boss can see that he would be a high-risk employee. No longer able to communicate with his parents, he feels like an unwanted guest in his own home. With increasing frequency, he directs his hostility inward and appears detached and distant. Irresponsible, uninvolved, and turned-off to anything that requires effort or perseverance, the sixteen-year-old is a failure in his own eyes, and his prospects, like his self-confidence, are nonexistent.

The entire process of destroying Mike's self-esteem spanned ten years. The seeds of destruction were planted, however, the day he first entered kindergarten. Unable to learn like the other children, the five-year-old quickly recognized that he was different. While most of his classmates progressed from one learning experience to the next, he progressed from frustration, to failure, and finally to despair.

This book is not written for Mike. It is unlikely that he could read it. In fact, this book is not even written for Mike's parents. Unfortunately, too much emotional and academic damage has already been done to their son. If Mike is ultimately to overcome his learning problems, he will have to make a commitment to straightening out his life, and he will have to accept help and counseling.

The goal of this book is quite basic: to provide you with the information you require to avoid a potential tragedy. As a concerned parent, however, you must do more than simply acquire information. You must become constructively involved in your child's education. This need for direct involvement is especially urgent if you perceive that your child's learning problems are not being dealt with appropriately or if your child is not making academic progress.

Your child does not have to end up like Mike. With your help, he can avoid the quicksand. But before you can play a role in the process of providing for your child's special educational needs, you must understand these needs. Only then can you intelligently evaluate your options. One fact is inescapable: You will be forced by circumstances to make some critical decisions that can dramatically affect not only the course of your child's education, but also the course of his entire life. The more information and insight you have, the better your decisions will be.

The second objective of this book is to help you seek out, evaluate, and utilize the professional resources available in your child's school and in your community. These professionals—teachers, school psychologists, learning disabilities specialists, tutors, principals, physicians—can be invaluable allies. Their knowledge and skills can help guide you through the labyrinth of choices and decisions you must make about your child's education.

Although professional guidance can be invaluable, it can also be incomplete, inaccurate, contradictory, and confusing. In time, most parents come to the realization that they must rely primarily on their own insight and intuition. Fortunately, intuition and insight are parental resources that can be developed and refined.

When properly diagnosed and treated, most learning deficiencies can be remediated. With quality remedial assistance, a child's academic skills may improve by two or more grade levels in one year. Even greater gains are possible.

Unfortunately, each year hundreds of thousands of learning disabled children do not receive the appropriate assistance because this help is not available, or because their learning problems are never properly identified or treated. Without appropriate intervention, these children are destined to become defeated learners.

America abounds with defeated learners. As children, they struggle to survive in school. As adults, they resign themselves to working at menial jobs, or they are enmeshed in careers that do not fulfill their needs. Many are in prison.

Society is not the only loser when potentially capable children do not actualize themselves. The primary victims are the children. Those who conclude that they are unable to learn are in jeopardy of suffering serious and sometimes irreversible psychological damage. The resultant loss of pride, self-esteem, and potential accomplishment need not occur. Concerned, informed, and involved parents and teachers will not permit it to occur.

CHAPTER 1

The Failure Cycle

ELENA: RETENTION WASN'T THE ANSWER

A shy ten-year-old girl with dark hair and an impish smile entered my office with her parents. Her bent shoulders and neck gave the impression that she had a spinal deformity. Because she avoided looking directly at me, establishing eye contact with her was impossible. I could see that it was going to be a difficult diagnostic evaluation, not only because of her timidity but also because her parents barely spoke English.

I knew enough Spanish to be able to communicate with the family, and I was able to piece together the girl's background. Her name was Elena, and she attended an inner-city parochial school. The family spoke exclusively Spanish at home. Although the child had been retained twice, she could still barely read. Despite her chronically poor posture, Elena's parents reported that their daughter had no significant medical or congenital problems. They also reported that she was not progressing in school. On her teacher's recommendation, she had been retained in kindergarten. After she completed first grade, her teacher and parents decided to retain her again because she was still not progressing. Now ten years old, Elena was only in second grade. Embarrassed by her height and age, she had begun to bend her head and shoulders forward in an attempt to camouflage her height. At the tender age of ten, she was already lying about how old she was.

The second retention had not solved Elena's learning problems, and the school began to suspect that the child was retarded. Although fluent in both Spanish and English, she seemed incapable of deciphering written words. The evaluation form completed by her teacher indicated that the ten-year-old was highly distractible, noncommunicative, and chronically shy. Although Elena was never a behavior problem in class, she nevertheless exasperated her teacher because she was unable to keep up with the other students. Realizing that a third retention was out of the question, the principal had referred the family to our center for testing.

At first, communicating with this withdrawn little girl was difficult, but as Elena began to feel more at ease, she responded to my questions in a most distinctive way. In her impish manner, she would answer a question and then make a little joke or even a pun. As she described her day in school or her teachers or her friends, her wit became very apparent. There was no question that she was bright, perhaps even gifted. My tests confirmed that she had a serious learning disability and that her problems were not simply the result of the fact that the family spoke a foreign language at home.

When I finished testing Elena, I told her parents that their daughter had significant learning problems. I explained that she had difficulty seeing words accurately when she read and that she had difficulty remembering words that she had previously struggled to "sound out." Each time she saw a word that should have been familiar, it was as if she were seeing it for the very first time. Reading required continuous effort, and the ten-year-old was clearly becoming demoralized by the struggle. Unless she quickly received learning assistance, she would soon give up trying. Unfortunately, the specialized help she desperately required was not available at her parochial school.

Despite the seriousness of her learning problems, I felt that Elena's deficits could be remediated. Her superior intelligence considerably improved the prognosis. It was absolutely critical, however, that help be provided before any more damage was done to her already fragile self-concept.

I wish I could report that the story had a happy ending, but I cannot. Unfortunately, I was not successful in persuading Elena's parents to let us work with her at our learning disabilities center. When I finished explaining the results of my tests, Elena's parents told me that they wanted to discuss the matter privately. They agreed to call me and let me know if they wished to enroll their daughter in a specialized learning assistance program at our center. The call never came. I don't believe that the cost of the program was the deciding factor because I had carefully explained to the parents that scholarship assistance was available.

When I said good-bye after the diagnostic conference, I already sensed that the parents would never contact me. I felt like a physician must feel when a critically ill patient refuses treatment. If Elena were to be spared further emotional damage, her parents would have to find help for her somewhere. Her learning problems would not "go away" of their own accord. Elena would fall further and further behind in school, with devastating psychological consequences. A superior human being stood an excellent chance of being permanently scarred by a problem that was correctable. Elena's self-image had already been seriously damaged, and the damage would soon be irreversible.

QUITTING VS. STRUGGLING

Imagine a real estate salesman who works in an office where everyone is selling houses—except him. Each day he goes to work and hopes to sell a house, but in spite of his efforts, he fails to make any sales. After a month of no success, he begins to experience self-doubt and feelings of insecurity. His enthusiasm disappears, and he dreads going to work. With increasing frequency, he arrives late at the office and finds excuses for leaving early. One evening on the way home he stops for a drink, and the next morning he calls in sick. The prospect of facing another day of failure and rejection depresses him, and he finds himself feeling resentment toward the other more successful people in the office. The ritual of a single after-work drink soon becomes a ritual of several after-work drinks. The man starts losing his temper with his children over minor things, and he becomes gruff with his wife. They begin to argue more frequently. Each new day without success causes his self-confidence to erode further. Finally, he quits.

Having the option to quit is one of the privileges of being an adult. The unsuccessful real estate agent can decide to open a restaurant or become an accountant. A child does not have similar options. Legally, he is required to attend school until he reaches sixteen. But he can decide to give up and for the next ten years simply go through the motions of being educated.

Instead of a real estate agent, imagine a child of five. On the first day of school he appears to be just like the other kindergarten children. Excited, apprehensive, perhaps a bit bewildered, he arrives in the classroom that first day to begin the process of acquiring the educational tools that he will need to succeed in a complex, competitive world. During the next 180 days he will be taught to obey rules, follow instructions, and interact with other children. He will be taught how to cut and to trace and to draw and to color within the lines. He will learn to raise his hand when he has to go to the bathroom. He will learn to participate in a group and make the transition from "fun time" to "work time." After a few months, he will be taught to blend the sounds of letters to make simple words. The child will be on his way to mastering the most essential skill that is taught in elementary school. He will be learning to read!

But imagine if the child is unable to conform to this script. He has difficulty obeying the rules, following instructions, and interacting with the other children. Overactive and easily distracted, he finds it impossible to keep up with the other children. He can't cut and trace and draw and color within the lines because his fingers don't seem to work right. Although he is shown the letters of the alphabet and is taught how to pronounce them, he can't remember the names of the letters or the sounds that they make. The task of putting the sounds together to make simple words is overwhelming.

The child looks around at the other children in the class. They understand what the teacher wants them to do, and they are able to do what she asks. Their drawings have fingers and ears and clothes, and the teacher likes their work. They are able to write their names on the line, and they remember to put in all the letters and spell their names correctly. They also remember all the words in the songs that are sung in class, and they remember to raise their hands when they have a question or when they have to go to the bathroom. Unlike our hypothetical child, they can sit quietly in the circle without hitting other children or making noise. They can recognize the letters that the teacher holds up, and they can remember the sounds that those letters make. Realizing that he cannot do these things, the child concludes that there is something very wrong with him. He must be stupid.

The child learns to cope as best he can. In an attempt to camouflage his deficiencies, he may become shy or act out. Although he may persist in trying to learn, he will most likely simply give up and accept his limitations. Once he accepts his fate, the child has begun the process of learning to be a failure. Although he may not be able or willing to express his innermost feelings, he knows that he is incompetent. No evidence suggests any other possible conclusion. Because he receives no acknowledgment of his efforts, no affirmation, and no happy faces on his papers, he begins to hate school and himself.

Despite the turmoil the struggling child experiences each day in school, his parents and teachers expect him to continue working, trying, and behaving. He is not permitted to express openly his frustration or his anger in school nor, perhaps, even at home. On the contrary, he is expected to show up in school each day and to learn, or at least to go through the motions of learning. If he is unwilling to adapt to this script, he will be labeled a behavior problem. If he does conform, he has no alternative but to turn his anger and frustration inward where it will seethe and fester. Unless there is intervention, the child will suffer through this process for eleven more years. Naively, his parents and teachers continue to hope that he will somehow magically emerge from the educational production line emotionally and educationally intact.

Unlike the real estate agent, a child cannot start coming to school late. Nor can he call in sick when he's really not sick. Although Mommy may be fooled a couple of times by tummyaches, she quickly learns to detect when he's faking. Not getting ready for school on time doesn't work either. Everyone gets angry, and he still has to go to school. Losing his temper or having a tantrum is a sure guarantee of punishment and possibly a spanking. Although he may want to quit, he cannot—at least not until he reaches sixteen. Having no other options, the child begins to build a wall around himself that is designed to protect him from defeat, frustration, and pain. To the outside world, this wall will assume the form of irresponsibility, misbehavior, listlessness, or daydreaming. Even if the school authorities and the child's parents decide to retain him, he will ultimately be promoted from one grade to the next, regardless of whether or not he has acquired the required skills.

There are few safety valves for the academically troubled child. If he does not receive effective learning assistance, he has five basic choices:

1. He can give up.
2. He can act out.
3. He can withdraw into himself.
4. He can develop alternative areas in which he can succeed.
5. He can persevere.

Few struggling children select option five. The majority simply resign themselves to seven hours a day of frustration and learn to cope as best they can.

Despite the fact that a learning disabled child may be only six years old, doors to potential careers and professions are already beginning to close. Unless his learning problems are resolved, these problems may ultimately reduce the child's future potential earning capacity by as much as 75 percent. To insulate himself from feeling inadequate, the child will probably begin to develop a complex system of coping mechanisms, compensatory behaviors, and rationalizations which his parents and teachers will perceive as irresponsibility, unreliability, laziness, and immaturity.

When faced with the prospect of a seemingly endless and unwinnable struggle, most learning disabled children choose options one, two, or three. Although a child is not permitted by law to quit, he can give up. He may not be permitted to scream, "I've had it. I'm not going back to that horrible school anymore!" He can, however, begin to devise a system of behaviors that will help him to cope with the frustration and failure that he is forced to experience each day. The child may become shy or disruptive. Or he may become a clown or a bully. If he is clever, he may realize that he has other talents that he can use to compensate for his learning deficiencies. He may realize that he possesses natural charm, athletic ability, or wit. Or he may discover that he is good at working with his hands or his fists. If he is smart, he will select compensatory behaviors that will help him survive emotionally. If he is not clever, he will select compensatory behaviors that will magnify his deficits.

By the time the learning disabled child becomes a teenager, whatever coping system he has developed will probably be operating at full throttle. His defenses against feeling inadequate will be all but impregnable. Repeated negative life experiences will produce negative attitudes, behaviors, and self-esteem. Although the teenager's sense of self can be redefined with learning assistance and counseling, the process is arduous and problematic. Usually the teenager must first experience a sense of desperation and hopelessness before he would be willing to begin the sometimes painful, self-confrontive process of remediation. This same desperation and hopelessness could also have the opposite effect. It could cause the teenager to shut down emotionally and academically.

Parents of an older learning disabled teenager must resign themselves to the fact that they cannot force their child "to work on his problems." At this stage of their child's life, the most they can do is provide support for their teenager and encourage him to avail himself of potential resources such as private tutoring, counseling, and special learning assistance programs offered at many local community colleges.[1]

FAILURE IS HABIT-FORMING

Children learn to fail in much the same way that they learn to read—through practice and experience. Those who are forced by circumstances beyond their control to fail repeatedly often begin to anticipate, accept, and accommodate themselves to inevitable defeat. This acquiescence can be addictive. Habitually failing children may become so accustomed to defeat that they reject the possibility of success.

Subjected to demands they cannot meet and to feelings of hopelessness and inadequacy, struggling children may find a sanctuary in defeat. Failure begins to provide them with an identity. They are the class clowns, the worst readers, or the poorest athletes. In time, the pattern of failure may become such an integral part of their personalities that they may find the prospect of giving up their failure habit emotionally unsettling.

Like the chronically obese person who continues to eat the wrong foods because he is unconsciously intent on remaining obese, the chronically failure-oriented child may do the very things that ordain his continued failure. He may, for instance, choose not to complete his assignments, or he may submit his reports late. He may forget to bring home his textbooks before an exam, or he may hand in a report that is sloppy or illegible. Although the source of the child's struggle may involve specific learning deficits, the child's deficiencies may be magnified by his need to structure his own failure. When faced with the prospect of succeeding, the failure-habituated child may experience distress and anxiety. Unless the habits are broken, they can dictate the entire course of the child's life.

CONFLICTING RECOMMENDATIONS

Watching a child suffer in school is an excruciatingly painful experience. Parents may sense intuitively that their child is not learning properly, and

[1]See Chapter 11, "Dealing with Learning Disabled Teenagers."

they may know that something urgently needs to be done to help. Nevertheless, they may feel powerless. Perhaps they hesitate to become involved because they feel that they lack the expertise to know precisely what needs to be done. Their confusion may be compounded by the sometimes conflicting information and recommendations of friends, pediatricians, teachers, and psychologists. They may feel like the person who knows nothing about cars and is told by one mechanic that his engine needs an overhaul and by another that all he needs is a new carburetor.

Usually the parents of a learning disabled child must rely on their child's teacher and/or the school psychologist to suggest the appropriate remediation strategy. Sometimes the appropriate course of action is obvious, and all of the professionals involved are in agreement. Unfortunately, this is not always the case. It can be confusing and disconcerting when the teacher, the school psychologist, the resource specialist, and the pediatrician do not agree on a strategy, or when the remedial program appears to be failing. Parents can easily become overwhelmed by feelings of hopelessness and helplessness. If sufficiently discouraged and confused, these parents may erect their own emotional defenses to keep from having to confront and deal with their child's problems. Essential remedial treatment may be delayed, and the psychological and academic effects of this delay may be disastrous.

PARENTS' RATIONALES

Learning problems cannot be resolved without some key commitments by parents, teachers, and children. Parents must be willing to commit themselves to finding appropriate help for their child—either within or without the public school system—and to providing ongoing support for the child and his teacher during the remediation process.

The child must also make a commitment to the remediation program. Although he may not be ecstatic about the prospect of receiving learning assistance, he must be willing to work at resolving his problem, and he must persevere, even when quitting may seem very appealing.

The final commitment must come from the professionals offering the learning assistance. These reading, resource, and learning disabilities specialists must be willing to dedicate themselves to offering the best remedial program that they are capable of providing.

Unfortunately, these essential commitments are not always made. To justify their own unwillingness to commit to the remediation process, parents often employ a wide spectrum of rationales, including:

Laziness:	There's nothing really wrong with my child. He's just lazy.
School's Responsibility:	I pay taxes for education. The school should take care of my child's problems.
I Suspected a Problem:	I knew there was something wrong back in first grade. The school assured me that there was no problem and told me not to worry.
Immaturity:	The teacher said my child was just immature and that if we had him repeat first grade everything would be OK.
Confusion:	We didn't know what to do. So we didn't do anything.
I Made It!:	I had the same problem in school, and I'm OK. (This comment usually comes from fathers.)
Patience:	He'll outgrow it.
Inconvenience:	It's too far to drive to the learning center.
Cost:	Private learning assistance is too expensive.
Discipline:	My husband (or wife) thinks it's a behavior problem and that we are not strict enough.

Parental attitudes about learning assistance often have a direct impact on the outcome of the assistance program. Those parents who are unconvinced about the need for remediation, skeptical about their child's assistance program, or uncommitted to providing assistance will either intentionally or unintentionally communicate their feelings to their child. The child in turn will become unconvinced, skeptical, and uncommitted and will probably resist the remediation process.

Negative expectations on the part of the parents have a disturbing tendency to become self-fulfilling. For example, skeptical and resistant parents might elect to withdraw their child from the learning assistance program before he has completed the process. In so doing, they are unwittingly engineering another defeat for their child. Although parental rationales may not represent an intentional effort on the part of parents to deny their child help, these attitudes can seriously interfere with the child receiving much needed assistance. Because of their serious implications, these rationales merit a response.

Laziness:	Children are *not* lazy by nature. Laziness is a learned behavior and usually functions as a

psychological defense mechanism. By not trying, children may delude themselves into believing that they haven't really failed.

School's Responsibility: Yes, the school *should* provide quality learning assistance. Unfortunately, schools do not always do so. Parents must still pay their taxes, whether or not their child is provided with the appropriate help. The responsibility for monitoring the child's progress and guaranteeing that his academic needs are being met rests firmly on the shoulders of the child's parents.

I Suspected a Problem: When parents are convinced that their child is not learning properly, they must begin to ask penetrating questions and demand penetrating answers from the professionals who are teaching and testing their child. If they are intuitively convinced that their child is struggling because of an undiagnosed problem, they should trust their intuition.

Immaturity: Relatively few children are actually physiologically immature. Teachers often use this catchall term to describe behaviors they cannot understand or accurately identify. Parents who doubt that their child is immature are advised to request an assessment of their child's specific deficits. They are also advised to consult their pediatrician.

Confusion: Parents who are confused or unsure should seek professional advice. They should discuss their concerns or confusion with their child's pediatrician. They can also seek out other parents whose children have a similar problem. If there is a university in their town or city, they may be able to discuss their concerns with a faculty member in the education department there. (Please note: There may be a fee for a formal conference.) They may also request from their child's school or physician a referral to an appropriate outside agency. They should inquire if there is a learning disabilities lab associated with a local university or college. As a last resort, they can look in the phone book for a private agency.

I Made It!: Parents may have successfully survived their own learning problems, but that does not necessarily mean that their child will survive his problem. Without assistance, the learning disabled child who is not helped may become psychologically crippled by his learning problems.

Patience: Children do not generally "outgrow" learning problems. They do outgrow school, however, and if they suffer too severely, they may ultimately decide to drop out. Children also outgrow acne, but if the condition is not treated, they can become badly scarred in the process of "outgrowing" it. Untreated learning problems can severely damage a child and warp his perceptions about himself.

Inconvenience: It may be an inconvenience to procure learning assistance for a child, but the ultimate inconvenience will be far greater if the child's learning problems are not resolved. Private tutoring may be the parents' only recourse, if quality learning assistance is not available in a child's school. Providing remedial help for a child is analogous to taking out an insurance policy. This help could well prove to be one of the wisest investments parents could possibly make in their child's future. To survive in a competitive world a child will require at least eighth-grade reading, writing, and math skills. The requirements for college admissions are, of course, much higher. There is no guarantee that special help will totally eliminate a child's learning difficulties, but the alternative is to do nothing and hope that the problems will magically disappear. The risks involved in waiting are simply too great.

Cost: At issue are a family's priorities. If the program available to a child in his public school is inadequate, parents must decide the extent of their commitment to resolving their child's learning problem. Although private assistance can be expensive and may cause economic hardship, such assistance can pay for itself many times over in the child's ultimate increased income potential.

Discipline: Providing discipline is a clear parental mandate. Discipline can build character, but discipline alone will *not* correct a learning problem.

CHILDREN'S RATIONALES

Children with learning problems often have their own unconscious system of justifications and rationalizations for not committing emotionally to a remediation program. Kids can obviously find lots of things that they would prefer to do than spending extra time and effort on spelling, reading, or math. Struggling children with a long history of learning problems may be especially resistant to receiving learning assistance. Because of their often painful associations with school, they will naturally recoil from the source of their discomfort. Making a commitment to resolve their learning problems involves taking some risks. They realize that they are exposing themselves to potential frustration and possible failure. To protect themselves, they may construct elaborate psychological defense mechanisms. Ironically, this resistance often disappears once struggling children begin to experience success at school.

Children tend to be myopic about the consequences of the choices they are making about their lives. Their lack of perspective and experience increases the risks of distortions in perception. The frustrated, insecure learning disabled child may pretend that his learning problems do not exist or that the problems will somehow disappear. He may delude himself into believing that he can handle things without help, or he may argue that his assistance program is not working. Until the child matures and develops perspective, he must rely on his parents to guide him so that he makes choices that are in his best interests.

Most children, for example, would choose not to go to the doctor for an injection, even if they were sick and needed one to get better. During the formative years, parents must make the decisions involving such important issues as health care for their child. These decisions may occasionally make the child unhappy, and although parents do not enjoy causing unhappiness, sometimes they must. For instance, a child may cry because he is being punished for playing with matches. Were his parents not to punish him for fear of making him cry, they would be remiss in fulfilling their responsibility as parents. Any temporary upset that the child experiences must be weighed against the potential tragedy that could occur if the child does not learn how dangerous playing with matches can be. The unpleasantness of the child's temporary upset about being enrolled in a learning assistance program must be weighed against the potential damage to his life and self-esteem if he is allowed to forgo such assistance.

PROFESSIONAL RATIONALES

Teachers and school district officials may also have well-formulated explanations about why it is difficult or impossible for them to provide for certain children's special learning needs. With justification, many of these teachers contend that they are overwhelmed with too many children in their classrooms and too many responsibilities. Some classroom teachers frankly admit that they lack the specialized skills to provide for the needs of the learning disabled child. Other teachers point out that vital learning assistance programs have been eliminated because of cuts in school budgets. Some teachers will even acknowledge that they are simply burned out after too many years of teaching. Their depleted energy level will directly affect the quality of their teaching and the intensity of their commitment to the educational process.

The levels of concern, awareness, and sensitivity of teachers about the plight of the learning disabled child varies significantly from school to school and from district to district. Some teachers are far more acutely aware of the behavioral and psychological implications of learning problems than others. Although a dedicated teacher may recognize the potentially disastrous emotional consequences of an unresolved learning disability, this recognition does not assure that a child's learning problems will be appropriately treated and resolved. The typical classroom teacher has approximately thirty children in his class. Theoretically, each student should require no more than three to four percent of his time and energy. A student who requires twelve percent of the teacher's times creates an imbalance in the classroom. Were the teacher to give the child twelve percent of his time, he would be doing a disservice to the other children. The most obvious solution to this dilemma is to provide quality specialized learning assistance programs for all children who need them. Unfortunately, economic realities would seem to preclude such an ideal solution. Most school districts have sufficient funds and personnel to provide only for the most seriously learning disabled children.

TO INTERVENE OR
NOT TO INTERVENE

Once parents become convinced that their child requires learning assistance that is not being provided, they are faced with an important decision. They must decide whether or not they want to become actively involved in seeking alternative learning assistance for their child.

For many parents, the prospect of becoming involved in their child's education is frightening. As nonprofessional educators, they may lack confidence in their insights and intuition about their child's educational needs. Other parents may be reluctant to intervene because they recall being intimidated as children by authority figures such as principals and teachers. They may feel that they have no right to meddle or may conclude that the professionally trained teacher or school psychologist *must* know what is best for their child.

Despite good intentions and training, professionals do not always know what is best for a child. Although they may be able to identify a child's specific learning deficits, they may not have the resources to remediate those deficits. Often the diagnostic capabilities of a district exceed its remediation capabilities. Testing a child and identifying his blatant learning deficiencies is considerably easier than correcting those deficiencies.

In this era of budgetary cutback, learning assistance programs are usually filled with children who have serious learning problems. These programs may not have room for children with less severe learning disabilities. Other school districts may simply lack an adequate learning assistance program.

Quite often, nonprofessionally trained parents who trust their intuition have a far better sense of their child's educational needs than the professional does. Parents should not discount their intuition. It is one of the highest forms of human intelligence and represents the distillation of a person's life experiences. As parents acquire more information and insight about learning disabilities, the accuracy of their intuition invariably improves.

Intuitively, parents should know whether their child's educational needs are being met. This same "instinct" will tell them whether or not retention appears to be a viable solution to their child's learning problems. Their intuition will also help them decide if their child needs an extensive diagnostic work-up and if their child would benefit from placement in a specialized program. Having access to objective data and test scores which indicate a child's level of academic performance is an essential component in the decision-making process. Although the input and recommendations of professionals are vitally important, in the final analysis, it is the parents who must decide what is best for their child.

The following checklist is designed to help parents decide whether or not they need to intervene and take a more active role in their child's education.

PARENTAL INVOLVEMENT CHECKLIST

	YES	NO
Do you feel that your child has a learning problem?	☐	☐
Do you feel that you child's learning deficits have been accurately identified by his/her school?	☐	☐
Do you feel that adequate diagnostic testing has been administered?	☐	☐
Do you feel that you understand the results of the tests that have been administered?	☐	☐
Do you feel that your child requires further testing?	☐	☐
Is your child receiving special learning assistance for any learning deficits that may have been identified?	☐	☐
Are you pleased with your child's assistance program?	☐	☐
Is your child responding positively to this assistance?	☐	☐

Interpreting the Checklist

A pattern of "yes" answers would suggest that a child's educational needs are being met. A pattern of "no" answers is indicative of a potential educational problem that requires parental intervention. Parents who suspect that their child's educational needs are not being met must decide whether or not they want to intervene. If they do choose to participate actively in procuring appropriate learning assistance, they must then determine how they can make the most effective contribution.

Logic would dictate that if a child is struggling in school, he should be tested immediately so that his problems can be identified and remediated before he falls seriously behind. Unfortunately, this logical procedure is not always followed. There may be too many children waiting to be tested and too few school psychologists to test them. Or there may be too many children in the district who need special help and too few places available in the special programs.

In the event that a child's school does not voluntarily recommend testing, it may be necessary for parents to request a diagnostic evaluation. Denial of this request or a determination on the part of parents that quality remedial assistance is not available at their child's school would force parents into another decision-making mode. Parents have three options: They can choose to do nothing and hope that their child's learning problems correct themselves; they can continue to monitor the situation; or they can look outside the district for private learning assistance.

CHAPTER 2

Diagnosis: The First Step to Remediation

JOSH: A MANAGEABLE TORNADO

Josh zoomed around the classroom knocking over chairs and pulling things out of drawers. The other five-year-olds stared at him wide-eyed with perplexed looks on their faces.

When the principal called Josh's mother and asked her to pick up her son, he explained that her child was out of control and was disturbing the other children. Both the principal and the kindergarten teacher felt that the five-year-old was not yet ready for kindergarten.

With reluctance, Josh's mother agreed that perhaps her son did need time to mature. She consented to keep him home for another year.

The following September Josh's mother once again took her son to his assigned classroom. And once again she received a call from the principal. He informed her that Josh's behavior had not improved and that he was still out of control. He suggested that Josh be held out of kindergarten for another year. Although Josh's mother strongly objected, the principal was adamant. He would not permit the child to attend his school.

Determined to find a school for her son, the woman began visiting other schools in the district. She did not deny that Josh was hyperactive, but she felt that the school district was responsible for educating her son. If the local school would not agree to provide this education, she would find another school in the district that would.

Each time that Josh's mother did find a school willing to accept her child, she would invariably receive a call from the school's principal informing her that, upon further consideration, they had decided her son could not be admitted into the kindergarten program. It became clear that the principal of Josh's original school was advising the other principals in the district not to accept Josh into their kindergarten program.

In desperation, the woman began to visit schools in other districts. When she found a strong kindergarten teacher or a program that was highly structured, she would request an interdistrict transfer. Invariably, the request would be denied by her own district.

After months of frustration, the woman discovered a remarkable teacher who taught in a school that was a considerable distance from her home. Despite being forewarned by the mother about Josh's hyperactivity, the teacher agreed to have the boy in her class. Josh's mother then informed her local school district that if they attemped to block the transfer in any way she would consult an attorney. The transfer was approved.

The kindergarten teacher at Josh's new school employed a novel technique for helping Josh to control his hyperactivity. She taught this "unmanageable" six-year-old yoga. When Josh sensed that he was becoming excited, he was sent to a certain spot in the classroom where he could sit down unobtrusively, assume the traditional yoga position, and quietly chant his own personal mantra until he calmed himself down.

The teacher also worked out a private communication system with Josh. If Josh was unaware that he was becoming hyperactive, she would alert him with a signal. This signal told Josh that it was time to get himself under control. A second signal would indicate that he was to go to his special "spot." The system worked perfectly. The teacher taught Josh to take responsibility for his hyperactivity. Once the six-year-old learned how to control himself, he could begin the process of acquiring an education.

RECOGNIZING AND INTERPRETING THE SYMPTOMS

The proper identification of a learning problem is only the first step in the remediation process. Before the data obtained from testing and from subjective observations can have prescriptive value, it must be properly interpreted.

Although the principal of Josh's local school had accurately identified Josh's problem, his proposed "solution" to the problem was to do nothing. By insisting that Josh be held out of school, he was avoiding his responsibility to deal with Josh's hyperactivity and to provide the child with the specialized help he needed in order to learn.

Contrary to popular opinion among many teachers and some parents, hyperactivity is not the result of immaturity, and the problem is seldom resolved by giving a child time to "outgrow" the condition. Although hyperactivity may become less problematic as children mature, it does not necessarily disappear when children reach adolescence. Some hyperactive children never outgrown their hyperactivity. They simply become hyperactive adults.

Hyperactivity is a physiologically based phenomenon characterized by excessive firing of the motor neurons. The condition may be triggered by neurological, emotional, dietary, and/or environmental factors. Hyperactivity encompasses a wide range of behaviors. Children at the subtle end of the spectrum may have only occasional episodes of hyperactivity. In the middle of the spectrum are the children who might best be described as moderately overactive. At the severe end of the spectrum can be found the children like Josh who are chronically frenetic and distractible.

Although the phenomenon of hyperactivity is not completely understood, the condition can be controlled in numerous ways. Methods which have proven successful include behavior modification, perceptual-motor training, disciplined athletic conditioning, yoga, meditation, special diets, and medication.

Holding a child out of school until he "matures" does not cure hyperactivity, nor does retaining the child so he can repeat the school year. Despite the fact that some of the overt symptoms of hyperactivity often become less obvious when a child reaches adolescence, the child must nevertheless be educated while he is waiting to "outgrow" his problem.

Fortunately, the manner in which Josh's school district responded to his hyperactivity is atypical (and illegal in the state of California). The widespread practice of labeling hyperactive children as "immature," however, is quite typical. Far too many learning disabled children are misdiagnosed simply because no one has bothered to identify their precise learning deficits.

Relatively few children are actually physiologically immature. When the term "immaturity" is used by teachers or administrators to describe hard-to-define behaviors, the description offers little insight into the source or the specific symptoms of a child's problem.

Although diagnosed as unmanageable, Josh was actually capable of learning once he was placed in the appropriate learning context. Like many children who are out of control, the child required a highly structured program, a strong and creative teacher, and a well-conceived behavior modification system that could train him to take responsibility for his own behavior.

It was fortunate that Josh's mother was a determined lady. If the six-year-old had been kept out of school for another year, he would have undoubtedly concluded that there was something profoundly wrong with him, and he probably would have begun to act as if he were defective. In time this self-perception most likely would have become an integral part of his personality.

LEARNING VS. NONLEARNING

Nature has genetically programmed into human beings a compelling need to learn. From an early age, children are consumed by a need to understand how they and the world around them "work."

A four-month-old infant, for example, will gaze with rapt attention at his hand. Staring at his fingers as they open and close, the child discovers that he is the one who is controlling his hand. This realization will have a profound impact upon the child's evolving appreciation of the process of cause and effect. This process is the cornerstone of all knowledge.

As a newborn, the infant soon learns that when he cries, he will be fed, cuddled, or changed. Unconsciously, he begins to recognize that he has the power to influence, affect, and, to some extent, control his environment. Once he discovers this power, he will begin a process of assuming and asserting increasing control over his life. This process will ultimately lead to his becoming an independently functioning young adult.

By means of trial and error, the infant begins to build a vast storehouse of data. He realizes that the more he understands about his world, the more power he has. Everything he touches or puts into his mouth helps him identify, distinguish, and remember objects and classify experiences.

When the infant turns over and begins to crawl, he discovers that he can expand his world by simply moving from where he is to where he isn't. As he crawls from one place to another, he learns to judge the distance. He also learns how long it takes to get from point A to point B. In this way, the infant begins to integrate the concepts of time and space. These concepts are essential building blocks for the subsequent mastery of analytical problem-solving skills.

As the child becomes increasingly mobile, he realizes that although his mother remains the center of his universe, there is a new and exciting world out there waiting to be explored. His sensory systems are assaulted by countless new objects that need to be examined and countless nooks and crannies that need to be investigated. Like a computer, he voraciously consumes and files the new information that he is continually acquiring about his world.

The child is instinctively compelled to expand the boundaries of his understanding. He learns how to use his fingers to open a drawer or to lift the lid on a pot. Enthralled with wonder and curiosity, his brain absorbs this new data and cross-references it with previously stored information. With rapture, the child discovers that all he has to do is open the door to the cabinet under the sink, and a whole new universe of potential experiences unfolds before his eyes!

Parents are justified in feeling anxiety when their child does not want to learn. Equally alarming is a situation in which a child enters school anxious to learn and then loses this desire. The child who fails to develop curiosity about himself and his world is at risk of becoming intellectually anesthetized. Unless there is intervention, his reluctance to learn may develop into an aversion to learning. Such an attitude can have disastrous educational, psychological, social, and vocational consequences.

Six major elements comprise the equation that produces academic achievement: intelligence, stimulation, desire, effort, academic skills, and encouragement. The risk of a child developing learning deficiencies increases significantly whenever any of these elements is missing.

Before parents can help the child who is not learning properly, they must identify the missing element or elements in the learning equation. They must determine if their child is not being adequately taught or if their child has academic deficits directly attributable to underlying learning problems. They must also examine objectively their own respective roles and determine if they are providing their child with adequate encouragement and support.

Each element in the learning equation can be affected by a wide range of emotional and environmental factors. Psychological or family problems, peer pressures, language difficulties, puberty, and the frequent changing of school are but a few of the many conditions that can undermine a child's ability or desire to learn.

REBECCA: A VICTIM OF NEGLECT

Rebecca never made it to the center for the initial appointment. The night before we were to meet she had gotten angry with her parents and had run away. When the fourteen-year-old finally did come in one week later, she was friendly and responsive.

The daughter of a dentist, Rebecca had a long history of learning disabilities. Her parents had become so disillusioned with her academic progress that they had decided to take her out of school and hire a private tutor to educate her. This had proven unsuccessful, and recent tests indicated that the eighth grader was functioning at a beginning fourth-grade level in most academic areas.

Rebecca's father explained that his daughter had been badly mistreated by his ex-wife whom he had divorced one year after Rebecca's birth. The court had initially awarded the mother custody of Rebecca. According to the father, a pattern of mistreatment then ensued. The mistreatment consisted of neglect rather than outright physical abuse. Restricted to her crib, the child was not permitted to crawl and explore her world. After two years, the court decided that the mother was unfit and granted the father and his new wife custody of Rebecca.

Given the sensory deprivation she experienced as a child, it was easy to understand why Rebecca was not struggling academically. She had been denied vital attention and stimulation during a critically important developmental period in her life. From my observations of the teenager's reactions, I was certain that the trauma of her childhood had caused emotional scars that were contributing to her learning problems. Although she appeared affable, she also appeared to be repressing a great deal of emotion. She would frown or clench her teeth when her parents said anything that was even mildly critical. It was clear that a very strained relationship had developed between Rebecca and her father and stepmother. Her parents had fallen into the trap of nagging her continually about her studies and her irresponsibility. Rebecca responded to their criticism by blocking them out and by becoming even more irresponsible.

The situation had reached the crisis point. Rebecca had developed a phobia about everything related to school. Unless her parents refrained from continually expressing displeasure and unless she received intensive learning assistance, I feared that the teenager might run away for good and disappear into the back streets of San Francisco.

During the initial session, I succeeded in getting Rebecca to express to her father how she felt when he "put her down." At first, she refused to acknowledge that she was angry, but after a few minutes she finally managed to tell her parents, with tears in her eyes, how much their constant criticism hurt her.

By the end of the conference, Rebecca's parents conceded that they needed help in learning how to express their feelings to their daughter in a nonderogatory way. They agreed to seek family counseling, and Rebecca consented to come to the center for three hours of learning therapy and tutoring each week.

I knew that if Rebecca were to prevail over her learning problems and family problems, she would have to commit to the counseling process *and* the academic remediation process. From my observations, I had serious misgivings about the fourteen-year-old being capable of making even a partial commitment to a learning assistance program that would extend for a minimum of twelve months. Because I was convinced that she was not yet ready emotionally to respond to learning therapy, I recommended that family counseling be the immediate priority. Each member of the family needed to examine how he or she was relating to the others in the family, and each needed to learn how to communicate without pressing "hot buttons." The anger and frustration would have to be defused before Rebecca could begin to derive benefit from her learning therapy.

THE CAUSES OF
LEARNING DISABILITIES

Learning disabilities can defeat the efforts, destroy the desire, and undermine the confidence of even the most diligent student. Factors which can cause or contribute to a learning disability include:

1. Low aptitude or intelligence
2. Emotional problems
3. Poor teaching
4. Neurological disorders (e.g., a brain injury)
5. Sensory impairment (e.g., a hearing or vision loss)
6. Perceptual dysfunction (e.g., poor visual memory)
7. Language deficiencies (e.g., English is not the native language)
8. Language disorders (e.g., speech impediments or difficulty with oral expression)
9. Cultural or environmental influences (e.g., academic achievement is not reinforced by the family or subculture)

Before parents, teachers, school psychologists, and learning disabilities specialists can determine if a child has a learning disability, they must first determine what the child knows and doesn't know. Testing can provide this data, assuming the tests are properly selected, administered, and interpreted.

DETERMINING A CHILD'S LEVEL OF ACHIEVEMENT

Three criteria are generally used to determine a child's academic achievement: standardized or normed tests such as the Stanford Achievement Test, teacher-designed tests and assignments, and the subjective impressions of teachers.

Standardized Tests

Standardized tests are administered to large numbers of students throughout the country. They are designed to determine a child's level of achievement relative to other children of his age and grade level.[1] By statistically comparing a child's performance on a nationally normed test with the

---

[1]See Glossary of Testing Terms for definitions of terms used in this section. Also, see Testing Appendix for a description of many of the diagnostic and achievement tests that are commonly administered.

performance of other children at specific grade level and chronological age who have taken the same test, educators can establish achievement norms for children. This process of establishing national norms is called standardization. The following is a facsimile of the typical comparative performance data produced by standardized achievement tests.

FACSIMILE TEST RESULT REPORT

	Raw Score	*Stanine*	*Percentile*	*Grade Equivalency*
Reading Comprehension	27	4	46°	3.7
Vocabulary	32	5	48°	3.9

The facsimile test result report presented here records a hypothetical fourth grader's scores on a standardized reading test. The child's raw scores (27 in reading comprehension and 32 in vocabulary) represent the total number of his correct answers on the test. The stanine scores (4 in reading comprehension and 5 in vocabulary) are a statistical representation of the child's correct answers on a scale from 1 to 9. The scores indicate the child's performance relative to the other hundreds of thousands of children who took the exam.

The percentile score in reading comprehension (46°) is another way of statistically ranking the child's performance relative to other children taking the test. In the hypothetical test result form above, out of every 100 children of the same age and grade level taking the test, the child scored higher than 45 children and lower than 53 children. (The ninety-ninth percentile is the highest statistical score that one can receive on a standardized test.)

The percentile score can offer valuable comparative information. For example, a fourth grader takes a standardized exam on October 3 (the second month of fourth grade). He receives a raw score of 23, which statistically translates into a grade-level equivalency score of 3.2 (third grade, second month). If the child were reading at grade level, he should have tested at 4.2. His score of 3.2 indicates that he is one year below grade level.

The child scoring below the norm on standardized tests is evidencing a potential academic deficiency. Although test scores can be skewed by such factors as test anxiety and/or distractibility, the scores generally offer a relatively accurate profile of the child's level of skills. The child who is testing below grade level, receiving poor grades on teacher-designed tests, and manifesting poor performance in class should immediately be targeted for diagnostic testing to determine if there is an underlying learning disability.

Teacher-Designed Tests

Teacher-designed tests and assignments utilize more subjective criteria for determining a child's level of achievement than do standardized tests. This lack of statistical objectivity, however, does not reduce the validity of teacher-designed tests. Such tests are, in fact, the cornerstone of the academic grading process.

Most teacher-designed tests are "criterion referenced." This means that the content of the test is directly linked to the specific material contained in the child's textbooks and to the material that the teacher is teaching in class.

Although teachers are responsible for covering the material designated in the school district's curriculum, they are generally given some latitude in choosing their academic priorities and teaching methodology. When developing curricula, lesson plans, and performance standards, one elementary school teacher may choose to emphasize writing and language arts skills, while another, who teaches at the same grade level, may feel that reading comprehension, handwriting, and spelling are the priorities. The choices that the teacher makes about course content, teaching methods, and standards will reflect his training, educational philosophy, and classroom experience.

The inevitable variations in course content and performance standards from teacher to teacher necessitate teacher-designed tests. If the teacher's tests are fair and properly designed, they will provide important information about the child's academic skills and learning proficiency. Poor skills and poor proficiency usually manifest themselves in poor performance on teacher-designed tests.

Unless they have evidence to the contrary, parents must assume that the teacher's criteria for evaluating students are fair and valid. Poor grades on tests should be considered a primary indication of a possible learning disability. Warning bells should go off when poor grades are confirmed by low scores on standardized tests. Children who do poorly on both types of tests should be screened for a learning disability.

In the process of identifying a child's learning disability, parents and teachers must consider other factors besides a child's grades on teacher-designed tests and his scores on standardized tests. These factors are examined here.

INTELLIGENCE

Intelligence: The capacity to learn from experience and from mistakes and the capacity to use the knowledge gained to solve problems, to understand concrete and abstract ideas, to perceive relationships, and to identify and retain relevant information.

Virtually every voluntary act performed by human beings requires intelligence. The spectrum of tasks that humans are capable of performing is extensive. These tasks range from brushing one's teeth to solving a highly complex problem involving the use of differential calculus. Whereas most human beings have the requisite intelligence to brush their teeth, relatively few are capable of solving a problem involving the use of differential calculus.

Many of the tasks that a human being performs in a perfunctory manner actually demand intelligence and skills far beyond the capabilities of all other species. The ability to perform these tasks is generally taken for granted. Even such a mundane undertaking as driving a car requires co-ordination, spatial judgment, analytical thinking skills, memory skills, visual discrimination skills, and reading skills. Without minimum average intelligence, a person could not perform the requisite subtasks. As a general rule, the more complex the endeavor, the greater the intelligence that is required.

Because the learning disabled child often has difficulty mastering skills that his nonlearning disabled counterparts can master with facility, he may be inaccurately perceived as lacking intelligence. Learning disabilities can affect children across the entire intelligence spectrum. Children who are brilliant, of average intelligence, or of below-average intelligence are equally susceptible. The behaviors and deficits associated with learning disabilities can so completely undermine the child's academic performance that they can cause the child with average or even superior intelligence to appear unintelligent, not only to his classmates, but also to himself. The psychological consequences of this distortion in perception can have a negative impact on all aspects of the child's life.

Learning is a sequential process. When a person learns, he adds to what he already knows. In this way, he is able to do increasingly more demanding and complicated tasks. For instance, a student who wants to play tennis well or learn a foreign language must first learn the basics of the game or the language. As she learns these new skills, she will inevitably make mistakes. Her capacity to learn from these mistakes is an essential characteristic of intelligence. The more intelligent the person, the less likely he is to repeat the same mistakes.

The ability to perceive relationships and to associate new material and information with what has already been learned is another primary characteristic of intelligence. A student is demonstrating intelligence when she perceives that the method that she has already used to solve one equation can be used to solve a similar equation.

Speed of response to stimuli is another primary manifestation of intelligence. This quickness manifests itself not only as a facility to master new material, but also as wit, humor, insight, artistic creativity, and intuition.

The learning disabled child who is not processing sensory data efficiently, and who is chronically distractible, sloppy, and overactive, seldom responds efficiently to stimuli. Because of this neurological inefficiency, the child may not manifest the wit, humor, insight, artistic creativity, and intuition that are typically associated with intelligence. Thechild, however, may actually be very intelligent, and perhaps even brilliant.

APTITUDE

Aptitude: A specialized facility to learn or understand a particular skill, which manifests itself in a specific ability, capacity, or talent.

An important differentiation must be made between general intelligence and specialized intelligence. The latter is more precisely described as aptitude. A person who is adept at taking engines apart and putting them back together probably is manifesting good mechanical aptitude. This same person, however, may not have a great deal of general intelligence.

Some people have superior general intelligence as well as superior aptitude in a specialized area. The person who can design a computer program and play the cello well has both types of intelligence. She will require generalized intelligence to understand how to control the many variables involved in writing a complex mathematically based program, and she will require musical aptitude to read music and play her cello. At the same time, this person may lack (or think she lacks) the requisite mechanical aptitude to rebuild the engine in her car.

There are many highly intelligent people who lack, or are convinced that they lack, specific aptitudes. A brilliant novelist may not be able to set up his word processor, and a brilliant physicist may not be able to paint a mural.

MEASURING INTELLIGENCE AND APTITUDE

IQ (intelligence quotient) tests were designed to predict academic success. Theoretically, the higher a child's IQ score, the better his chances of doing superior work in school. Although an IQ test is intended to measure a child's potential, it does not always do so accurately. Many children who have high IQ scores do not become academic achievers. Conversely, many children who have average IQ scores graduate from college, go on to graduate school, and become highly proficient and successful in their chosen professions.

The results of an IQ test are not sacred. Before parents draw any conclusions about the results, they should have the test scores professionally interpreted. Mitigating factors such as stress, hyperactivity, distractibility, and poor rapport with the examiner must be taken into consideration. An inconsistency between a child's IQ and his school performance raises important questions which must be examined by the child's parents and the appropriate school personnel. Several common inconsistencies are examined here.

High Test Scores and Poor Class Performance

This type of discrepancy suggests that the child has some type of learning, attitude, family, or emotional problem. A significant discrepancy between the child's verbal score and his performance score on an IQ test (the

WISC-R is usually administered in most schools; see Testing Appendix for a description of this test) suggests the possibility that the child has an underlying learning problem. It is also possible that the child with high test scores and poor performance in class is simply bored. The unstimulated child rarely functions at a level commensurate with his ability, and the quality of his work generally reflects his lack of active involvement in the learning process. Although the child may test well on standardized tests, he may do poorly in class and on teacher-designed tests.

Low Test Scores and Average or Better Class Performance

The child with a low IQ score who performs well in class may be an overachiever who tries to compensate for average general intelligence by working diligently. If the test scores are skewed by emotional factors, distractibility, or poor rapport with the examiner, the scores may not provide a valid indication of the child's true ability. The child may actually be more intelligent than the tests suggest.

Low Scores and Superior Performance

When the child's IQ scores are low and his performance level is high, the scores are highly suspect. The child may have been upset when he took the exam, or he may have been so distracted or inattentive that the results of the tests were artificially deflated. In other cases, the test results may have been distorted by language and cultural factors.

When properly interpreted, aptitude and intelligence tests can be important diagnostic, predictive, and prescriptive tools. The scores can help educators identify a child's strengths. For example, a child who demonstrates high intelligence can be placed in gifted classes where he can be challenged and stimulated. At the same time, IQ tests and aptitude tests can work at cross-purposes with a child's development, especially when they are misinterpreted, inadequately administered, or used to label and catalog a child for the purposes of gratifying his parents' egos.

IQ test scores can also be used as a rationale for excluding academically struggling children from receiving learning assistance. In many school districts, a child with a low average IQ who is functioning below grade level may not qualify for special help. Although remedial support might improve the child's skills, this support is denied because the child has below-average intelligence and no specific learning disabilities. The school authorities may conclude that it is unrealistic to expect that learning assistance would produce better school performance.

STUART: HE WASN'T REALLY RETARDED

The ten-year-old's face was impassive as I discussed with him the new learning assistance program he was about to begin. I couldn't tell if Stuart didn't understand or simply didn't care. At first, I suspected that Stuart might be retarded. When I looked at the mother, however, I could see the same placid, passive look. Although her questions indicated that she was intelligent and concerned about her son, she showed no visible response to any of the information I attempted to communicate to her. The lack of affect appeared to be a family trait.

Despite remedial assistance in school, Stuart had made little academic progress during the preceding two years. My tests revealed that the fifth grader was functioning at the third-grade level in reading and math and that he had a relatively severe learning disability.

After six months of learning assistance at our center, Stuart began to make some modest improvement. His classroom teacher at school confirmed our clinical impressions. She reported that Stuart was making slow but steady gains and was beginning to catch up with his classmates.

Stuart's pediatrician had also noted the child's lack of visible emotional response. He recommended that the child be given an IQ test by a clinical psychologist on the staff at the medical center where he practiced. The psychologist reported that Stuart's IQ was 65, and he recommended that the child be placed in a class for the retarded. The physician called me and asked me to encourage the parents and the public school authorities to place the child in an EMR class (educably mentally retarded).

My staff would not accept the results of the test. They had worked extensively with Stuart and had observed that he could grasp math concepts, perform math computations, draw inferences, and read with comprehension. Although he did not grasp new material quickly, he could learn with the appropriate support. They concurred that Stuart's intelligence was probably in the low-average range and that he had serious learning problems, but they would not concede that he was retarded. His performance at our center and in his regular classroom raised serious questions about the validity of the test. Everyone, including Stuart's classroom teacher, was categorically opposed to placing the child in a class for the retarded.

I also felt that the test results were suspect, especially when his parents reported that Stuart had been so frightened by the psychologist administering the test that he couldn't concentrate. To verify the test results, I asked the school psychologist on my staff to retest the child. She gave Stuart a different IQ test than the one originally administered because she felt that this test was less biased against children with learning problems. Recognizing Stuart's apprehensions about being tested and his insecurity with strangers, the psychologist, a gentle and sensitive woman in her sixties, spent thirty minutes chatting with him before beginning the test. This conversation so allayed his fears that he actually began humming during "easy" portions of the test.

Stuart's IQ level on this second test was 92. His score represented an increase of 27 points, and the results placed him within the low average range of intelligence.

Had Stuart's parents followed the advice of the pediatrician and the psychologist, and had they placed him in a class for the retarded, they unwittingly would have done their son a grave injustice. Labeling any child poses serious risks. The academic and psychological implications of affixing an incorrect label to a child can be disastrous. The child who is misclassified as retarded—even borderline retarded—may never be able to shed this classification despite subsequent evidence that he is of normal intelligence. In virtually every state, children identified as retarded have later been identified as having neurological, developmental, emotional, or language problems. Because of underlying problems not directly related to intelligence, these children tested poorly on IQ tests and demonstrated behaviors that might be associated with retardation. Despite this supposedly conclusive evidence, these children were actually far more intelligent than the tests and behaviors indicated. In some particularly horrific cases, children incorrectly diagnosed as retarded have actually been institutionalized.

Once a child's parents and teachers accept that he is retarded, their inclination is to expect less from him. The child will most likely respond to their lowered expectations by lowering his own level of expectation.

His subsequent achievement and performance will reflect his acceptance of the fact that he is retarded. (See pages 112–15 for a more complete discussion of retardation.)

Stuart is currently in junior high school and is a solid C student. He is able to keep up with his class, and he is able to do all of his assignments. Although he no longer attends our center, he continues to receive limited remedial support each day from the school resource specialist. His ambition is to become a professional fisherman and to own his own boat.

FACTORS THAT CAN AFFECT IQ SCORES

Testing a child's IQ is in some respects akin to walking through a mine field. Because of the many factors that can distort a child's scores, the process of achieving an objective, fair, and meaningful assessment of a child's abilities can be perilous.

The results of any evaluation procedure administered to an anxious or distressed child are especially suspect. Emotional stress or poor rapport with the examiner can so undermine the validity of the test that it becomes meaningless.

If a child has negative associations with school, with tests, and/or with test givers, he may be convinced in advance that he will do poorly on the test. This negative mind-set can undermine the child's mental efficiency and test performance. He may become confused, inattentive, or disoriented, and may have difficulty understanding questions, recalling information, and applying skills that he has mastered. As his anxiety level mounts, the child may "shut down" and become nonfunctional. Under such conditions, it is improbable that the child could function at a level commensurate with his true potential. A child's performance on an IQ test can also be affected by the type of test selected and the personality of the examiner. Stuart's reaction to the psychologist who examined him clearly illustrates this effect. Tiredness, a headache, or a bad cold could also skew the test results.

Cultural bias inherent in the test can also distort a child's scores. A test question might read:

Manager is to baseball team as _____ is to orchestra.
a. violin   b. opera   c. stage   d. conductor

The child living in a ghetto might not be able to relate to this analogy because violins, conductors, and operas may not be part of his life experiences. Making judgments, pronouncements, and predictions about the child's ability on the basis of such questions would be a travesty.

Because of the potential for distortions, intelligence tests must be cautiously and conservatively interpreted. Environmental and psychological factors must be considered if the test scores and the testing process are to have meaning.

Educational research has demonstrated that a teacher's academic expectations of his students can be strongly influenced by knowing a child's IQ scores. Teachers who are aware that a child's IQ scores are low tend to expect less from him than teachers who have no knowledge of his scores. Conversely, teachers who are aware that a child's IQ scores are high tend to have higher expectations and may put forth greater effort to teach the learning disabled child who has been identified as bright.

A teacher's expectations are often self-fulfilling. A child who realizes that his teacher has little confidence in his ability to achieve probably will conform to the teacher's level of expectations and produce poor to marginal work. On the other hand, the child who senses that his teacher has positive expectations and is supportive will generally respond by working conscientiously and by producing higher caliber work.

The inherent danger of inadequate interpretation of IQ test scores by parents and professionals has caused many school districts to use these tests selectively. Only those children considered to be possibly retarded, learning disabled, or gifted are now being tested in California school districts. Even selective testing, however, can be dangerous. A gifted child may have a slight fever and perform poorly when tested. As a consequence, he may be denied admission to enrichment programs limited to children with high IQs.

DIAGNOSTIC TESTING: A MEANS TOWARD AN END

The ability to process data is the cornerstone of all learning. The primary function of diagnostic testing is to determine why a child is unable to learn and, specifically, if he is unable to process information efficiently. This process is a prerequisite to providing appropriate remedial assistance for the learning disabled child.

On the most basic level, the processing of information requires that students be able to decipher or decode written and spoken words and symbols. The capacity to decode these symbols is integral with attaining such higher-level academic skills as drawing inferences, perceiving analogies and relationships, and using symbolic logic.

The wide range of causes and symptoms of learning problems necessitates a correspondingly wide range of diagnostic testing options. Many highly accurate and reliable diagnostic procedures are available that permit school psychologists, reading specialists, and learning disabilities specialists to identify a child's specific symbol-processing deficiencies with a high degree of accuracy.

Diagnostic procedures can range from quick screening tests to comprehensive diagnostic evaluations. The nature of the child's problems and the testing orientation of the school district will determine the appropriate testing procedures. Complex, atypical, severe, or enigmatic learning problems usually require an extensive diagnostic work-up to identify the child's specific learning deficits. Straightforward learning problems involving blatant symptoms may necessitate only an abbreviated diagnostic screening.

Diagnostic tests measure a wide spectrum of skills and abilities including aptitude, perceptual processing efficiency, word recognition, reading comprehension, inferential skills, math computational skills, memory skills, visual-motor skills, and motor coordination.[2] As the first step in the remediation process, these tests are designed to identify specific deficits. The data obtained can be used by the learning disabilities specialist to create an individualized remediation program and to define educational objectives.

In California school districts, certain diagnostic tests are administered by learning disabilities specialists and others are administered by school psychologists. The test results provide important information for parents, learning disabilities specialists, reading specialists, resource specialists, and classroom teachers. Because the test reports may contain a great deal of technical data and jargon, they will probably need to be interpreted for parents. The school psychologist or learning disabilities specialist administering the tests has a responsibility to explain the results in terms that can be understood. He also has a responsibility to make sure that the

[2]See Glossary of Educational Terms for a definition of these terms. Also see Testing Appendix.

child's classroom teacher, who may not have received any formal training in the diagnosis or treatment of learning disabilities, fully understands the child's learning strengths and weaknesses. Incomprehensible reports defeat the intent of the testing process. If parents and teachers are to be supportive, they must be able to understand why the child is struggling and what needs to be done to help him.

The diagnostic report can be an invaluable prescriptive tool for the trained specialist. Once the student's learning deficits have been identified by the diagnostic test, the appropriate specialists (l.d. teacher, resource specialist, speech therapist, and school psychologist) can work together to design an individualized education plan (IEP). Specific remediation goals can be targeted, and these goals will provide the remediation process with focus and direction.

Specialized tests might reveal that a particular child is having difficulty with reading comprehension or vocabulary because of visual memory deficits. Although able to read grade-level material, the child may not be able to remember the content of what he has read because of visual memory deficits. Such a child is also likely to have difficulty with spelling, inasmuch as good spelling skills require the ability to remember the letters that make up a word. He will probably also have problems reading nonphonetic words (words that cannot be sounded out). Insight into the child's specific deficiencies will permit the specialists to design a carefully conceived remediation strategy.

THE MARGINALLY LEARNING DISABLED CHILD

As a general rule, children with severe and obvious learning problems have a much better chance of being identified and receiving learning assistance than children with subtle learning problems.[3] Whereas the academic performance and the behavior of the disruptive, hyperactive, learning disabled child demands attention, that of the shy, hypoactive (lethargic), learning disabled child usually does not. Learning problems such as dyslexia are more likely to be recognized and treated than more nebulous

[3]See *Kids Who Underachieve* by Lawrence J. Greene (Simon & Schuster, 1986).

learning problems characterized by disorganization, impulsivity, and poor study skills.[4]

Economics have forced many American schools to adopt the mentality of a battlefield hospital where only the most severely wounded casualties are treated. The "slightly wounded" are sent back to the front lines without treatment or, at most, with a bandage over their wound. In many instances, school districts have either chosen or been forced to disregard the needs of the marginally learning disabled child.

At the present time, many California school districts require that a child test a minimum of two years below grade level in order to qualify for learning assistance. Because children with subtle to moderate problems are generally considered to have far less urgent needs than severely learning disabled children, they are seldom even evaluated. As a general rule, learning assistance is reserved for those with significant deficiencies.

Denied help, the child with marginal or moderate learning problems will probably continue to perform at a level below his ability throughout his education. One of the unfortunate consequences of this situation is that the child's marginal performance may be construed by parents, teachers, and the child himself as evidence of marginal ability. This can lead to a lowering of expectations by the adults and the child. Perceiving himself as unable to achieve, the child will begin to function at a level commensurate with this negative perception of his own capabilities and potential.

Children with subtle to moderate learning problems (one year or less below grade level in an academic subject) may represent as much as 25 percent of the students in our schools. These children are typically expected to fend for themselves. Some will muddle through school with grades that are barely passing, others will fail. Occasionally, marginally learning disabled students with exceptional grit and determination are able to prevail over their problems despite the fact that they are denied help.

With only minimal assistance, the majority of students with subtle learning problems could quickly catch up with their classmates. Without this assistance, most are destined to remain underachievers.

The parents of marginally learning disabled children must become involved in their child's education. This responsibility is every bit as com-

[4]See *Getting Smarter: Simple Strategies for Better Grades* by Lawrence J. Greene and Leigh Jones-Bamman (David S. Lake Publishing, 1984).

pelling as that of the parents of more seriously learning disabled children. If the child's school does not have the resources to provide appropriate diagnostic testing and assistance, the child's parents may be forced to seek help privately.

A word of caution, however, is in order. Some parents become excessively concerned and go overboard in their desire to seek help for their child. The parents of the child described here are a case in point.

ERIC: TOO MUCH TESTING

My initial impression of Eric was that he was a bright child with a moderate learning problem. The diagnostic evaluation revealed that the nine-year-old had minor motor-coordination and reading deficits. He was having an especially difficult time differentiating between right and left, and this poor sense of directionality was directly related to his letter reversals when reading and writing.

The checklist completed by the classroom teacher confirmed that the third grader was reversing letters when he read and wrote. (See page 56 for a copy of this checklist.) *B*s were seen as *d*s and *q*s as *g*s. The teacher also indicated that the nine-year-old was struggling to keep up with his class. She reported that he was easily distracted and tended to daydream. Although he had not been given any standardized reading tests during the previous six months, she estimated that he was reading in class at least one year below grade level. My own assessment confirmed her estimate.

After evaluating the results of the diagnostic test and the input provided by the classroom teacher, I concluded that Eric had a moderate learning problem, and I recommended that he receive two hours per week of intensive learning assistance. The first hour of the weekly program would focus on correcting his motor-coordination, directionality, and concentration deficits, and the second hour would stress remedial reading assistance.

Eric's parents agreed to the proposed strategy, and their son was assigned to one of our learning disabilities specialists. A battery of standardized academic tests was scheduled to provide the teacher with more information about Eric's specific academic strengths and weaknesses.

At this point Eric's father informed me that the family physician had recommended that he have his son comprehensively evaluated at a medical center. The tests would include a psychiatric and neurological work-up as well as an extensive academic assessment. The father asked if I felt that it would be advisable to go ahead with the evaluation, and I responded that there was value in seeking another opinion. I stated, however, that I was confident that the results of the work-up would confirm my diagnosis. Given the moderate nature of Eric's deficiencies, the extensiveness of the proposed work-up seemed excessive.

Although Eric's motor coordination was deficient, the deficits were quite subtle. He could skip, hop, and coordinate both sides of his body, and this suggested that the likelihood of organic neurological damage was slight. It is standard procedure for pediatricians who detect significant motor-coordination deficits and/or other neurological symptoms ("hard" symptoms) to refer the child to a pediatric neurologist who, depending on the presenting symptoms, may perform an EEG (electroencephalo-gram). In this procedure, electrodes are attached to the child's head, and brain waves are measured. Irregularities or deviations from normal neuro-logical patterns may indicate organic brain damage. Relatively few subtle to moderately learning disabled children actually have organic, measurable brain damage. Although it is relatively common for children with perceptually based learning problems to have motor-coordination deficits, these "soft" symptoms are rarely caused by organic brain damage. (See "minimal brain damage" and "minimal brain dysfunction" in the Glossary of Educational Terms.)

Eric's parents elected to go ahead with the comprehensive testing battery. The nine-year-old was evaluated by a staff pediatrician, a psychiatrist, a neurologist, a clinical psychologist, a social worker, an educational psychologist, a speech therapist, and a learning disabilities specialist. Each professional submitted a report. The report totaled twenty-four pages and the fee for the procedure was $1,900. The results of the tests are summarized here.

1. Eric had no neurological damage.
2. Eric's IQ was in the high-normal range.
3. Family counseling was recommended. (Both parents were already in psychotherapy.)
4. Eric had a moderate learning disability. (The specific learning deficits were enumerated in the report.)
5. Subtle coordination deficits were observed and specific perceptual-motor activities were recommended.

6. Remedial learning assistance was recommended.
7. It was recommended that Eric reduce the amount of sweets he consumed, as he was approximately fifteen pounds overweight.

Eric's parents were presented with a precise, well-crafted diagnostic report. Although far more comprehensive than my diagnostic procedure, the evaluation confirmed my assessment. Nineteen hundred dollars was a substantial amount of money to pay for the confirmation of a moderate learning problem. In fact, the diagnostic procedure turned out to be far more costly than the remediation program we designed for Eric.

THE ADVANTAGES AND DISADVANTAGES OF DIAGNOSTIC TESTING

Testing overkill can be very expensive and is often unnecessary. In certain cases, extensive, multidiscipline work-ups may be advisable. Such an assessment is especially useful when a child has a severe, enigmatic learning disability, or when a child is struggling with several overlapping problems. A comprehensive work-up may also be advisable when a child does not respond to learning assistance. The input of highly trained professionals representing a wide spectrum of related disciplines can help the learning disabilities specialist select an alternative and, ideally, more effective remediation strategy.

Relatively few learning disabled children require the comprehensive, multidiscipline diagnostic evaluation that Eric received. The objective of any testing procedure is to obtain the information essential to designing a well-conceived learning assistance program. If this information can be obtained quickly and inexpensively, so much the better. Once the resource specialists have obtained the relevant data, they can then devote their energies to remediation.

CHAPTER 3

Identifying Your Child's Learning Problems

KRISTIN: STRUGGLING TO CATCH A MOVING TRAIN

The little girl's parents were upset and confused. They had just learned that their five-year-old daughter would not be allowed to progress from the preschool program into the academic kindergarten at her private school. The kindergarten teachers at the school had decided that Kristin was not yet developmentally ready to participate in their highly academic program.

The policy at this particular private school was to screen all "candidates" for kindergarten to determine the level of their learning readiness skills. The kindergarten program was very accelerated, and five-year-olds were expected to be able to read at the upper first-grade level by the time they completed kindergarten. Because of the school's clearly defined admissions criteria, the teachers on the screening committee had become highly proficient at identifying and rejecting those children who would probably have difficulty handling the curriculum. The parents of children not accepted had the option of reapplying the following year. In the interim, they could enroll their children in a less demanding kindergarten program or have them repeat the developmental preschool program.

Kristin's scores on the screening test had not met the entrance requirements. The motor-coordination section of the test confirmed the preschool teacher's observation that the child's gross-motor and fine-motor skills were deficient (see Glossary). The screening committee also factored into their decision other important input provided by Kristin's preschool teacher:

1. Kristin was socially and developmentally immature.
2. She needed the constant attention of the teacher.
3. She was chronically inattentive.
4. She had difficulty participating in group activities.

When informed that their daughter had not been accepted into the program, Kristin's parents were shocked. Their oldest child had successfully completed the program and was currently doing well in second grade. They had assumed that Kristin would follow in his footsteps. Kristin's father, a very successful attorney, appeared to be particularly offended by this rejection of his daughter.

Kristin's parents had refused to accept the results of the screening test, and the headmaster had referred the family to our center for an independent evaluation. After testing the child and reviewing the evaluation form completed by the preschool teacher,[1] I concurred with the committee's conclusion: Kristin was not developmentally ready to adjust to the school's kindergarten program.

My diagnostic tests indicated significant perceptual processing deficiencies. Kristin had difficulty decoding visual information. She could not, for instance, identify or distinguish between geometric shapes, nor could she recite the alphabet or identify any written letters. The tests also uncovered specific deficits involving coordination, visual memory, auditory discrimination, and spatial concepts. In almost every area, Kristin's level of functioning was approximately one year below the norm for her chronological age. The developmental maturity of her draw-a-person was that of a four-year-old. Although she could identify colors and primary body parts (e.g., her knee), she could not identify secondary body parts (e.g., her jaw). She could count to ten, but she could not recognize any written numbers. Given her perceptual deficits and lack of reading readiness skills, it was quite clear that the five-year-old would not be able to keep up with the accelerated curriculum.

I was very familiar with the curriculum at Kristin's preschool, and I

[1]You can find a copy of this teacher evaluation on page 144.

knew that her teacher had taught her the learning readiness skills that she lacked. I could only infer that her inability to master these skills was attributable to her perceptual processing deficits and distractibility.

During the diagnostic evaluation, I observed that Kristin was very emotionally dependent upon her mother. She constantly looked to her for reassurance and repeatedly complained that she was getting tired. It was an effort for the five-year-old to concentrate on any task for more than a few seconds.

Kristin's parents had been present while the tests were administered. They had seen firsthand how difficult it had been for her to do basic developmental tasks. When I shared the results of my evaluation with them, I sensed that they were willing to examine the data with open minds. I explained that Kristin's difficulties were attributable to a moderate perceptual dysfunction (this phenomenon will be examined in detail later in this chapter). Although some of her deficits might disappear as she matured, others were more problematic and required specialized treatment.

I recommended that Kristin be placed in a ninety-minute weekly learning assistance program specifically designed to help her develop more efficient perceptual processing skills. I assured her parents that the early identification of Kristin's developmental deficits had significantly improved the prognosis for her overcoming these deficits.

Kristin's parents were finally able to accept that their daughter would do better in a nonpressured, nonaccelerated kindergarten program, and they enrolled her at the local public school. A remarkable transformation occurred. With the help of the learning assistance program and the support of an excellent kindergarten teacher, Kristin quickly caught up with her classmates. All symptoms of developmental delay disappeared. Twelve months later, Kristin scored at an advanced first-grade level in both reading and math. She had become one of the best readers in her class. Now in third grade, Kristin is on the honor role at her local public school.

DEVELOPMENTAL DELAY

Children do not proceed along the developmental production line at the same rate. For reasons that are difficult to explain, some children of normal to superior intelligence develop learning and motoric skills more slowly than others.

Although intense, highly academic kindergarten programs may be beneficial and stimulating for certain children, such programs may be psychologically harmful to children who are not developmentally ready to handle the challenge. Forcing a child to endure a year of frustration and defeat does *not* build character. It simply undermines self-esteem. Fortunately, Kristin was saved from this plight. The teachers at her school wisely realized that her self-concept would have been damaged had she been pushed into an accelerated kindergarten program.

The sources of developmental delay are often difficult to pinpoint. Although children pass through predictable developmental stages, these stages are not bound by an absolute timetable chiseled in stone. A wide spectrum of biological, metabolic, environmental, and genetic factors can influence the acquisition of learning readiness skills, and any attempt to identify the reasons why a child is lagging behind must take into consideration all of these factors.

Whatever the source of developmental delay, the attendant motoric deficits and perceptual processing deficiencies can undermine the child's ability to function efficiently in school. Significant developmental lag is a warning signal. To disregard this signal is to put a child in a no-win situation that might ultimately place his mental health in jeopardy.

In many cases, developmental delay can be identified in preschool. The ability of educators to recognize this phenomenon is largely attributable to the meticulous work of the Swiss psychologist Jean Piaget. Years spent minutely observing how children learn allowed him to identify major developmental milestones. Using Piaget's observations as a frame of reference, educators have been able to create specific teaching methods and systems that are designed to stimulate developmental growth in children who are progressing atypically. Because of these programs, young children who might otherwise develop learning problems are now being spared the demoralizing effects of academic failure.

THE DIFFERENT TYPES OF LEARNING PROBLEMS

There is no universally acceptable and applicable definition of the term "learning problem," for no single definition could possibly encompass all of the associated symptoms. The gamut of symptoms characteristic of a learning disability is broad, and the nature of the symptoms will vary greatly from child to child. Despite this diversity, one characteristic serves as a common denominator in virtually all learning disabilities: perceptual inefficiency. Because the processing of sensory data in the form of words and symbols is central to all learning, perceptual inefficiency must be included in any meaningful definition of "learning problem." The following definition does so.

> **Learning Problem:** *a response pattern to sensory data that is inefficient and that interferes with the ability to understand, remember, apply, or integrate the material being taught.*

Learning problems are usually attributed to one of the following sources (all of these sources will be examined here and in following chapters):[2]

1. Neurological damage
2. Perceptual dysfunction
3. Sensory impairment
4. Language disorders
5. Mental retardation
6. Cultural deprivation
7. Language deficiencies
8. Emotional problems

Although each category of learning problem has its own characteristics, the symptoms often overlap several different categories. The hyperactive child, for instance, may have neurological damage, a perceptual dysfunction (see the next section for a discussion of this phenomenon), or an emotional problem. He may also be allergic to something that is causing or contributing to his hyperactivity.

Some symptoms of a learning problem may be so subtle that only a trained professional may be able to recognize them. More obvious symptoms can generally be identified by classroom teachers or parents. Blatant

---

[2]The terminology used to describe the different types of learning problems may vary from region to region.

indications include poor reading, spelling, handwriting, language arts, math, and study skills. Other common deficits may involve deficiencies in the areas of communication, concentration, following instructions, hyperactivity, keeping up with the class, and disorganization.

A child's learning problem may involve both blatant and subtle indications. For example, a child may have obvious difficulty following instructions and be highly distractible. The same child may have difficulty crossing the midline (coordinating both sides of his body) and may perseverate (repeat the same mistake over and over again as if he were locked into a response pattern). Although the latter symptoms might not be identified by the classroom teacher, they are, nevertheless, indicative of a possible perceptual dysfunction or neurological disorder. The child manifesting such characteristics should be evaluated by a pediatrician and a school psychologist.

Learning deficits and behaviors that overlap more than one category can make the identification process more challenging. A comprehensive diagnostic work-up may be required in order to pinpoint the sources of the child's specific disability.

A learning disabled child may manifest a wide range of symptoms or only one or two specific symptoms. For instance, the child with a perceptually based learning problem will often have difficulty reading. Some children with perceptual processing problems, however, are excellent readers and have difficulty primarily with math. Other children with perceptual problems may have no academic deficits at all. Their primary deficiencies may be in the area of motor coordination.

The following descriptions of the different types of learning deficiencies are intended to help parents understand and identify their child's specific problem. Parents are advised to be cautious about jumping to conclusions. Whenever feasible, the responsibility for the diagnosis of a learning disability should be left to trained professionals. Parental insight and understanding, however, serve several vital functions. Parents who are informed and knowledgeable can feel more confident when they target their struggling child for testing. Because of their insight they can also provide better support for the child and the teachers once the remediation process begins.

PERCEPTUAL IMPAIRMENT VS. PERCEPTUAL DYSFUNCTION

A very important distinction must be made between a perceptual (or sensory) impairment and a perceptual dysfunction. A perceptual impairment is caused by organic damage. The impairment may manifest itself as a defect in one or more sensory receptors (such as the eyes or the ears) or as brain damage due to complications during gestation or birth. Head injuries, near-drowning, and illnesses involving very high fever can also cause organic brain damage.

A child, for example, who is farsighted or nearsighted has a visual impairment. Once the ophthalmologist or optometrist identifies the child's visual impairment, he can then usually prescribe glasses to correct the deficiency. Hearing impairments can also be identified and precisely measured. Once diagnosed, it may be possible to correct or reduce the effects of the impairment with a hearing aid. Organic brain damage is another example of a perceptual impairment, and this subject will be examined in the last section of this chapter.

Perceptual dysfunctions are usually attributable to subtle, hard-to-define neurologically based deficiencies. The dysfunctions are rarely the result of organic, measurable neurological damage. Although professionals representing different fields of expertise may use different semantics, most physicians, educational psychologists, and learning disabilities specialists are careful to differentiate between a perceptual dysfunction and a perceptual impairment.

A perceptual dysfunction occurs when the brain is unable to decode sensory data properly. Examples include deficiencies in the areas of memory, concentration, motor coordination, and reading. Severe problems in any of these areas may also be symptomatic of organic neurological damage. Because of the potential for overlapping symptoms, parents should always allow the professional to make the diagnosis.

It is not totally clear why children develop perceptual dysfunction, nor is it totally clear why some children learn how to compensate for their perceptual processing deficits more effectively than others. Many renowned people, including Albert Einstein, George Patton, Thomas Edison, Nelson Rockefeller, and Bruce Jenner, have prevailed magnificently over their perceptual learning problems. Unfortunately, countless other potentially capable people never compensate for their learning problems. These people are rarely included among the ranks of the illustrious.

At one time or another, everyone has experienced temporary perceptual dysfunction. For instance, a person may be sleepy or distracted when being given instructions. Although under normal conditions he might be able to follow or remember the instructions, he finds himself asking that the instructions be repeated.

A hypothetical scenario illustrates how data is perceived and processed by the brain. Imagine that someone from San Francisco is visiting Los Angeles. After attending a party, the person decides to begin driving home that evening. She asks how to find the freeway to San Francisco. It is late, and because she is a bit tired, she has difficulty following and remembering the instructions. To compensate for her temporary auditory processing deficits, she decides to write down the directions. Several blocks from the house, she sees a sign for the freeway. After driving a few minutes on the freeway, she sees another sign and realizes that the original sign must have said San Fernando, not San Francisco. Because of her fatigue, her brain has inefficiently processed both the original auditory information and the subsequent visual information. The woman's difficulty in remembering the verbal directions can be traced to a temporary auditory memory dysfunction, and her difficulty in decoding the letters on the sign reflects a temporary visual discrimination dysfunction.

When the human brain is not fatigued or affected by alcohol or emotional stress, it usually functions like a highly efficient computer. The "computer" receives information in the form of sensations (touch or smell), visual or auditory symbols (spoken or written language), and data (facts, thoughts). This information is instantaneously processed. Input (spoken or written language) will usually elicit output (spoken or written responses). Examples of input that will usually trigger immediate responses in the form of language or actions are:

Turn right at this corner.
Please print.
The discount is 10 percent.
Answer only the odd-numbered questions.
List the dates chronologically.
How do you spell "receive"?

Human beings tend to take their brain/computer for granted. When a person is cold, his brain tells him to button up his coat. When he receives change at a supermarket, he does a quick subtraction to verify that the clerk is correct. Only when he is sleepy, dizzy, distracted, or ill does he realize that his computer is not functioning efficiently. In a sense, the brain is like the family car. We seldom appreciate its value until it breaks down on a cold, rainy night. At this point, we recognize how dependent we are on the car (or the brain), and we begin to appreciate how well it normally functions.

In most instances, the brain can process information with remarkable speed. Within a millisecond the instruction ''turn right'' will result in an immediate association with the right side of the body, assuming of course that the brain knows the difference between right and left, and with the meaning of the word *turn*. A simple diagram can describe the process.

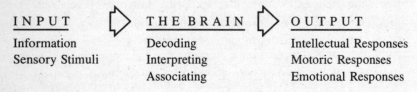

INPUT	THE BRAIN	OUTPUT
Information	Decoding	Intellectual Responses
Sensory Stimuli	Interpreting	Motoric Responses
	Associating	Emotional Responses

In addition to producing output, the brain also monitors it. When the brain recognizes that it has made a mistake, such as incorrectly directing a person to turn left instead of right, it has the capacity to correct the mistake immediately.

The human computer does have limitations. If the brain is given directions by someone with a very pronounced accent or if the directions are in a technical language that it has not been trained to understand, it may not be able to decode the information efficiently. The brain invariably has difficulty computing input when it encounters variables that have not been programmed into it. The instruction ''tournez à droite'' will mean nothing to a person who has never learned French.

A child in school is expected to process a wide spectrum of sensory data and to perform an equally broad array of sensory-based tasks. These include recognizing symbols (e.g., *b* or +), following directions (e.g., ''Open your science book to the exercises at the end of Chapter 6''), remembering information (e.g., ''When adding mixed fractions, you must remember to find the common denominator''), discriminating information (e.g., ''Find the word *influx* in the second paragraph''), associating information (e.g., ''If thin is the antonym of fat, what is the antonym of tall?''), and organizing information (e.g., ''Plot on your graph all of the information you derive from the chart''). In order to process properly these verbal and written cues, a child must first be able to decode the sensory data. The symbol for the letter *b* is written in a code that children are expected to master. Learning to read is actually the process by which a child identifies and associates the written code for spoken language. When he reads, he is actually "breaking" this code and, in so doing, deciphering the symbols.

The child who is not retarded, brain-damaged, or emotionally distressed and who cannot process sensory data efficiently most likely has some type of perceptual dysfunction. This dysfunction will usually affect his capacity to respond to information that he receives from his environment. The particular symptoms and causes of the dysfunction will vary from child to child. What does not vary is the fact that serious perceptual processing deficits invariably result in learning problems.

The inability to concentrate is one of the primary characteristics of a perceptual dysfunction. It is axiomatic that the student who cannot orient, focus, and maintain his attention will have difficulty decoding sensory data efficiently. His inability to concentrate will most likely affect his capacity to achieve in all subject areas. Parents who identify chronic inattentiveness (sometimes referred to by physicians, educators, and mental health professionals as attention deficit disorder or A.D.D.) should discuss their observations with the school psychologist and pediatrician, who may be able to recommend specific behavior modification, athletic, and/or medical protocols that might help the child to improve his attention span.

The following checklist is designed to help parents determine if their child is manifesting symptoms of a perceptual dysfunction. It is important to recognize that all children occasionally will be fidgety or inattentive. Parents should check the "yes" column only when a specific behavior or academic deficiency occurs with frequency.

The checklist is not intended to serve as a definitive indicator of a perceptual learning disability. Rather, its function is to help parents decide whether a diagnostic evaluation is advisable. In order to respond to certain questions, parents probably will require the input of the classroom teacher. In fact, it would be helpful to have the teacher complete the same checklist. Parents could then compare their own perceptions of their child with those of the teacher. Any discrepancies in perception should be discussed during a parent-teacher conference.

PERCEPTUAL DYSFUNCTION CHECKLIST

	YES	NO
BEHAVIOR		
Short attention span	☐	☐
Difficulty following directions	☐	☐
Overactive	☐	☐
Impulsive	☐	☐
Fidgety	☐	☐
Distractible	☐	☐
Accident-prone	☐	☐
Forgetful	☐	☐
Daydreams	☐	☐
Slow in completing tasks	☐	☐
Excitable	☐	☐
Unpredictable	☐	☐
MOTOR SKILLS		
Gross-motor coordination deficits (sports, etc.)	☐	☐
Fine-motor coordination deficits (drawing/handwriting, etc.)	☐	☐
Clumsiness	☐	☐
Awkwardness	☐	☐
Poor balance	☐	☐
Right/Left Confusion	☐	☐
ACADEMIC		
Poor reading comprehension	☐	☐
Difficulty with phonics	☐	☐
Letter and number reversals	☐	☐
Inaccurate reading	☐	☐
Poor handwriting	☐	☐
Inaccurate copying (from blackboard or at desk)	☐	☐
Difficulty with math computational skills (addition, etc.)	☐	☐
Difficulty understanding math concepts	☐	☐
Difficulty working independently	☐	☐
Sloppy work habits	☐	☐
Difficulty with spelling	☐	☐
Difficulties with language arts skills (essays/syntax, etc.)	☐	☐
Poor organizational skills	☐	☐
Poor planning skills	☐	☐
Incomplete projects	☐	☐

ACADEMIC
Difficulty following verbal and written instructions   ☐ ☐
Chronic procrastination   ☐ ☐
Disturbs other students   ☐ ☐

Interpreting the Checklist

A child need not have all or even most of the symptoms listed here in order to have a subtle, moderate, or severe perceptual dysfunction. It should be emphasized that some characteristics may also be symptomatic of other types of learning problems. A significant pattern of "yes" responses, however, should be interpreted as a red flag, and a diagnostic evaluation by a qualified professional is strongly recommended.

In addition to the symptoms listed in the checklist, parents should be alert to the following behaviors which may also be by-products of a perceptual dysfunction:

1. "Immature" behavior
2. A dislike for reading
3. A negative attitude toward school
4. Impatience
5. A low tolerance for frustration
6. An unwillingness to do homework
7. Difficulty accepting responsibility
8. Resistance to accepting help
9. Difficulty keeping up with the class
10. Little self-confidence
11. Excessive sensitivity to failure

As with any type of problem, the degree of a child's dysfunction can vary. Although a severe perceptual dysfunction can pose a formidable barrier to the mastery of academic skills, an even relatively subtle perceptual dysfunction can also seriously impede learning. Parents who identify perceptual processing deficits should not hesitate to discuss their concerns with the appropriate school authorities.

REMEDIATING PERCEPTUAL LEARNING PROBLEMS

Severe perceptually based learning problems generally require intensive learning assistance. Ideally, this assistance should consist of more than basic tutoring. Although tutoring is an excellent resource for helping a child "catch up," it may not adequately provide for the special needs of the learning disabled student. A child who has missed school because of illness, or a child who is having difficulty with Spanish can undoubtedly benefit from quality tutoring. Most learning disabled children, however, require specialized remedial methods to help them resolve their processing deficiencies. Remediation that does not address the *source* of the learning problem increases the probability that the learning problem will persist or recur.

A wide spectrum of learning assistance protocols have proven successful in treating perceptual dysfunction. The specific remediation protocol utilized by the resource specialist will be determined by such factors as the nature of the child's problem, the type of professional training the teacher has received, and the teaching philosophy of the school district, the tutor, or the private learning center.

Parents must recognize that their child's perceptual learning problems may not respond initially to the learning assistance program. This is especially true when the learning problems are severe or involve chronic distractibility and inattentiveness. Even moderate and subtle perceptual dysfunction may be difficult to resolve. Before making any decisions about the efficacy of the remediation strategy, parents must allow adequate time for the program to work. If no improvement is observed within eight months, parents should begin to explore alternative strategies. It must be emphasized, however, that significant learning problems are rarely resolved in eight months. Nevertheless, parents should be able to observe some positive response to the learning assistance program within this time frame. Any decision to discontinue a particular program, to seek another specialist or program, or to request a modification in the program should not be made unilaterally by the parents, but, rather, in consultation with those providing the learning assistance.

The ideal remediation program does more than simply teach children basic skills. It also trains children to develop and use their intellectual resources more effectively. Key factors that can directly affect how children respond to the assistance program include:

1. The quality of the remediation program
2. The nature and severity of the child's particular learning problem
3. The child's level of intelligence
4. The commitment of the child's parents
5. The commitment of the child's teachers
6. The child's effort

It is conceivable that a very bright child with a learning problem might ultimately go to Harvard Law School, assuming, of course, that his learning problems have been remediated. The prospects for the learning disabled child with average or below-average intelligence are more limited, even if his learning problems are corrected.

The remediation of a learning disability may require from twenty hours of intensive, individualized academic therapy to twelve years of ongoing learning assistance. Significant problems obviously require more time and effort. Although the objective of any sound remediation strategy is to eliminate the source of the learning problem, this may not be possible because of the severity of the child's problem. Certain perceptually based learning disabilities may never be totally remediated. In such instances, parents and teachers should establish realistic alternative goals that emphasize teaching the child how to compensate productively for his learning deficits.

In order to survive in school, the struggling child often develops compensatory mechanisms. These behaviors and attitudes can be productive or counterproductive. The student with poor reading skills, for example, who uses his index finger as he reads to help him "track" words is employing a productive compensatory mechanism. Realizing (or being told by his teacher) that his eyes are not moving efficiently from left to right as they scan the words in a line of print, the child has intuitively figured out (or has been instructed by his teacher) to use the fine-motor muscles of his finger to reinforce the deficient ocular muscles of his eyes. In contrast, the student with poor reading skills who avoids reading whenever possible is employing a counterproductive compensatory mechanism. Although he may reduce his pain and frustration in this way, he is simply postponing the inevitable. Unless corrected, his reading problems and his counterproductive compensatory behavior will pose a major barrier to academic and educational achievement.

The child who attempts to compensate for a visual tracking deficit (erratic movement of his eyes as he scans words horizontally across the page) is acting quite logically. The child's problems might be called a visual dysfunction or a tracking problem by some learning disabilities specialists. Others might describe the problem as dyslexia. The label is not important. What is important is that the child's visual dysfunction is causing inaccurate reading, mispronounced words, dropped syllables, transpositions, dropped word endings, and skipped lines. [Tracking deficits that cause children to reverse individual letters (*b/d*) are referred to as static tracking problems. Tracking deficits that cause children to reverse groups of letters (*saw* is perceived as *was*), or to substitute words (the word *introduction* may be substituted for the word *institution*), are referred to as kinetic tracking problems.]

The ideal remediation goal for the child who reads inaccurately is to correct the underlying tracking deficiencies. To achieve this objective, the child will require specialized assistance and sufficient time and patience. In the interim, the child must survive in school, and to complete his reading assignments, he may need to use a "crutch." His index finger or the eraser on a pencil can serve this function. By using his finger like a brake or a governor on a car, he can exert some control over his eye movements. The alternative to using this interim crutch is continued poor reading and demoralizing embarrassment.

Some classroom teachers discourage their students from using compensatory mechanisms of any type. They might, for instance, prohibit the poor reader from using his index finger or some other device to help him read. Their rationale is that the child may become dependent on his crutch. Unfortunately, these teachers fail to understand that the child's reading deficiency is physiologically and neurologically based. By using his fine-motor muscles to supplement his visual-motor muscles, the student is not only compensating productively for his deficiency, he is actually strengthening his visual-motor muscles. As the child's ocular pursuit muscles become stronger through practice and specialized learning assistance and his reading less labored, his need for a crutch will decrease. In time, he should be able to relinquish his compensatory system.

Teachers who are intransigent about permitting struggling children to use temporary, productive compensatory mechanisms are disserving their students. The child who concludes that he cannot read aloud without making a fool of himself will inevitably develop negative associations with reading. In time, these negative associations will evolve into an aversion to reading.

THE ORIGINS OF PERCEPTUAL DYSFUNCTION

The origins of perceptual dysfunction can be enigmatic. In some instances, genetic factors are responsible for the child's processing deficits, and several members of the same family may be affected by learning disabilities. Research has shown that learning problems can span many generations, and it is not uncommon for a grandfather, an aunt, a father, and/or a cousin to have experienced similar academic difficulties.

As has been previously stated, few children with subtle to moderate perceptual dysfunction have brain damage. Although they may have some of the "soft" signs of neurological dysfunction (e.g., poor balance and coordination), these children rarely manifest indications of organic brain damage. For this reason, the commonly used term "minimal brain dysfunction" (MBD), which is often used interchangeably with perceptual dysfunction, must be distinguished from the commonly misused term "minimal brain damage." The latter term should be used only when actual neurological damage can be detected. Unfortunately, these terms are often used synonymously, even by some professionals.

Once identified, perceptual dysfunction can usually be treated with a high degree of success. Even severe cases of perceptually based learning disabilities generally respond to appropriate treatment. In most instances, children can be trained either to overcome or to compensate successfully for their perceptual dysfunction.

The first step in the remediation process is to identify accurately the child's specific perceptual deficiencies. Once identified, resource specialists can then design a well-conceived remediation program that addresses the child's learning needs.

SHAW: OVERCOMING MINIMAL BRAIN DAMAGE

The little boy sat at the table struggling to sound out a two-letter word. I was struck by his intense effort and by the pain that was etched on his face.

Shaw had already attended our center for eighty hours of intense learning therapy, but he could still barely read. Despite the efforts of highly trained reading and learning disabilities specialists, the eight-year-old could not remember the sounds of the letters. We had utilized a phonics approach, a sight-word approach, neurological impress methods, kinesthetic techniques, and perceptual training. Our efforts were to no avail. It was clear that we were failing with this child.

Shaw's IQ was considerably above average. Although he was not hyperactive, or even overactive, he was highly distractible. His classroom teacher indicated that, with the exception of his chronic distractibility, he was well behaved. In addition to severe reading problems, she reported that Shaw had significant motor-coordination deficits. My tests had confirmed her observations.

I observed that Shaw had a unique habit of jerking his head slightly to the left when he was attempting to concentrate. The twitch increased as his anxiety level rose. Despite his anxiety, the second grader was always personable and cooperative at our center and in his regular class. He put forth total effort as he struggled with learning to read. It was heart-wrenching for us to acknowledge that, in spite of his efforts and our efforts, Shaw had made virtually no progress.

When I had first tested Shaw twelve months earlier, I asked the boy's parents if their pediatrician had ever recommended a neurological examination. They told me that he had never indicated concern about a possible neurological problem. Because I had detected motoric and behavior symptoms that suggested possible neurological damage, I recommended that they broach the subject again with the physician.

During the next eight months, nothing further was said about the matter of a neurological examination. As we worked with Shaw, I became more and more convinced that something neurological was impeding the child's progress. I once again advised a neurological exam, and I referred the parents to a medical center with an excellent pediatric department and department of neurology.

As I expected, the pediatrician recommended that Shaw be given a neurological exam. (In the state of California, neurologists will accept referrals only from other physicians.) The E.E.G. revealed minimal brain damage. The neurologist spent an entire hour helping Shaw's parents understand the nature of their son's problem. He explained that Shaw's intelligence was in the normal range and that he felt that Shaw would be able to learn to read if he were placed on medication. The medication would help him concentrate and remember.

The medication functioned like a magic potion. Within a few weeks, the eight-year-old had learned to read, and within six months he was consuming books. He progressed through the beginning readers like a whirlwind. His coordination improved, and he actually learned how to catch a baseball. He no longer jerked his head to the left when he was concentrating, and his self-confidence soared. For the first time in his life, Shaw had tangible evidence that he was intelligent and capable of learning.

Although Shaw still had specific learning deficits, he was now able to make progress. The improvement in his academic performance was an extraordinary moral booster, not only for Shaw but also for everyone involved in the remediation process. One evening as I was driving home, I actually saw the child leaving the public library with four books under his arm!

THE FACTS ABOUT NEUROLOGICAL DISORDERS

Any drug has the potential to be abused if it is prescribed indiscriminately. This is particularly true when medication (amphetamines) is used as a panacea for every type of learning problem. In Shaw's case, the medication served a vital therapeutic function. It spared the eight-year-old from remaining functionally illiterate and from developing serious emotional problems as a consequence of his inability to read.

Learning problems that are the result of organic neurological disorders usually manifest distinct symptoms. These symptoms include deficits in the areas of motor coordination, perceptual decoding skills (the auditory or visual processing of letters, sounds, and words), perceptual encoding skills (language expression), and behavior.

When neurological disorders involve damage to the brain or to the central nervous system, they are considered to be organic. Although such disorders can cause learning problems, they do not necessarily guarantee that a child will develop a learning problem. Some children may have very subtle neurological disorders and very serious learning problems. Other children may have more severe neurological disorders and very subtle learning problems, or in rare instances, no learning problems at all.

Children with severe neurological problems or brain damage often have significant motor-coordination deficits. They may have difficulty with such activities as skipping, balancing, handwriting, cutting with scissors, and orienting themselves. (Please note: It is normal for children under six to have some difficulty with these tasks. Children older than six may also have some difficulty with these tasks and may not necessarily have a neurological problem. Such children, however, should be closely monitored to see if the deficits persist.) A work-up by a physician is also standard procedure when a child exhibits significant motor-coordination deficits. Pediatricians suspecting an organic disorder should refer the child for more extensive neurological testing.

Neurological disorders may range from subtle, to moderate, to severe. Although brain damage may cause mental retardation, neurological problems and mental retardation are not synonymous. Many brilliant children have minimal brain damage. Again, it is important to emphasize that the acronym M.B.D. is sometimes used interchangeably to describe both minimal brain dysfunction and minimal brain damage. The conditions are *not* the same.

Effective educational and medical protocols have been developed to help children overcome or compensate for the learning deficits associated with neurological impairment. Certain perceptual training activities and sensory-motor integration activities have a documented track record for improving coordination and perceptual processing efficiency. Specific teaching techniques such as the Orton-Gillingham method, the Slinger-land method, and the neurological impress method have also proven highly effective in treating the specific learning disabilities that result from neurological impairment.

Medication is sometimes prescribed in cases in which children appear to be unable to learn because of extreme hyperactivity or distractibility. Special diets that eliminate artificial substances may also be effective with hyperactive and highly distractible students.

The following checklist describes some of the symptoms that might indicate the possibility of a neurological disorder. The child who manifests some of these characteristics does not necessarily have a neurological disorder. Parents who detect a pattern of "yes" answers to the questions are advised to consult their pediatrician or family physician. It is important to stress that relatively few learning disabled children have neurological impairment. (To complete this checklist, parents will probably need to consult with their child's teacher.)

NEUROLOGICAL CHECKLIST

	YES	NO

BEHAVIOR
Hyperactive (excessively overactive)   ☐ ☐
Short attention span   ☐ ☐
Perseverates (repeats the same mistake over and over)   ☐ ☐
Chronically distractible   ☐ ☐
Impulsive   ☐ ☐

MOTOR DEFICITS
Chronically awkward   ☐ ☐
Chronically clumsy   ☐ ☐
Pronounced physical immaturity   ☐ ☐
Delayed development   ☐ ☐
Reflex asymmetry (different reflex responses on each side of
   body)   ☐ ☐
Poor fine-motor skills (handwriting erratic, malformed, or
   spidery)   ☐ ☐
Poor and immature drawings   ☐ ☐

EMOTIONAL DISORDERS
Disinhibition (lacks socially appropriate control)   ☐ ☐
Lability (emotional instability)   ☐ ☐
Maturational lag (emotional behaviors are not appropriate to
   the child's age)   ☐ ☐

PERCEPTUAL SKILLS
Auditory memory deficits (forgets what is heard)   ☐ ☐
Auditory discrimination deficits (cannot hear the difference
   between sounds)   ☐ ☐
Visual memory deficits (forgets what is seen)   ☐ ☐
Visual discrimination deficits (cannot see the difference be-
   tween letters)   ☐ ☐
Letter reversals   ☐ ☐
Figure-ground deficits (cannot perceive spatial relationships)   ☐ ☐
Poor memory for designs   ☐ ☐

MEMORY & THINKING DISORDERS
Difficulty thinking abstractly (understanding ideas and concepts)   ☐ ☐

MEMORY & THINKING DISORDERS
Poor organization of ideas   ☐ ☐

VISUAL/HEARING/SPEECH IMPAIRMENTS
Tone deaf   ☐ ☐
Poor articulation (Inaccurate pronunciation of words/sounds)   ☐ ☐
Eye-control irregularities   ☐ ☐

LANGUAGE DISORDERS
Delayed development of language skills   ☐ ☐

ACADEMIC DEFICIENCIES
Pronounced reading deficits   ☐ ☐
Pronounced difficulty keeping up with class   ☐ ☐
Chronic disorganization   ☐ ☐

Interpreting the Checklist

As a general rule, neurological impairment will first be detected by the family physician or pediatrician. A pattern of "yes" answers should alert parents to a possible problem. Parents who suspect that their child may be manifesting symptoms of a neurological impairment should discuss their concerns with their child's physician. It must be reiterated that the symptoms of a perceptual dysfunction and a neurological impairment often overlap. Before drawing any premature conclusions, parents should seek professional advice.

THE ORIGINS OF PERCEPTUAL IMPAIRMENT

One of the most common sources of organic neurological impairment (minimal brain damage) involves trauma to the brain. This trauma may occur before, during, or after childbirth. A child, for example, may be born with the umbilical cord wrapped around his neck and may suffer organic damage as a result of oxygen deprivation. Neurological impairment may also result from prenatal injury, metabolic imbalances during gestation, genetic factors, and premature delivery.

Cerebral injury or severe illness during childhood represent other potential sources of neurological impairment. The brain of a child who falls into a swimming pool and nearly drowns may be damaged by oxygen deprivation. This deprivation may also result in other organic problems such as a hearing loss or heart damage. Childhood diseases such as spinal meningitis and Reye's syndrome may also cause organic brain damage.

A child with a severe organic problem such as cerebral palsy may actually be a superb student. With proper assistance, children with subtle to moderate neurological impairments can often be helped to prevail magnificently over their learning problems. Even those children with relatively severe organic brain damage can usually be taught how to learn more efficiently.

SENSORY RECEPTOR IMPAIRMENT

A child who has difficulty reading or copying from the blackboard may simply need glasses in order to overcome his learning problems. Another child who has problems following instructions or hearing the difference between sounds may be suffering from a hearing loss. He may spell poorly because he cannot discriminate between the *d* sound in *bed* and the *t* sound in *bet*.

Ruling out the possibility of an auditory or visual impairment should be the first step in the process of testing a child for a learning problem. A visual screening by the school nurse or a pediatrician can usually reveal if there are any visual acuity deficits. Those children manifesting visual acuity deficiencies should be comprehensively evaluated by an optometrist or ophthalmologist. If the reading disabled child does not have a visual impairment, the next step in the testing procedure would be to have him evaluated by either a school psychologist or a learning disabilities specialist to determine if he has a visual dysfunction.

The same process of elimination (sometimes referred to by professionals as differential diagnosis) should be applied to diagnosing children with learning problems of auditory origin. If testing by a pediatrician or audiologist reveals no hearing impairment, the child should be evaluated by the school psychologist to determine if his learning problems are attributable to an auditory processing dysfunction.

It is quite common for children to have ear infections when they are young. Although most of these infections can be treated with medication and/or surgical protocols, the infections may cause the child to experience temporary partial hearing loss. In severe cases, ear infections may result in permanent hearing impairment.

Many children with a sensory impairment do not develop learning problems. Even those children with relatively severe visual or auditory damage can learn to compensate successfully for their impairments. Corrective lenses, hearing aids, proper placement in the classroom, the support of learning therapists, parental encouragement, and the efforts of concerned teachers can often offset the effects of a sensory receptor damage.

Some children struggle in school because they have both a sensory impairment and a learning problem that is not directly related to the impairment. A child, for instance, who wears glasses to correct his near-sightedness may, despite his glasses, continue to suffer the effects of a visual discrimination problem (difficulty distinguishing the difference between letters such as *b* and *d*). Although corrective lenses will improve the child's vision, they will not correct his visual discrimination deficits if these deficits are the result of a nonorganic perceptual processing dysfunction. In addition to glasses, such a child requires learning therapy.

CHAPTER 4

Specific Learning Problems

BRENT: A BRIGHT CHILD WHO COULDN'T LEARN TO READ

When I said hello to Brent, the seven-year-old refused to respond or even acknowledge me. I could sense how angry and frustrated he was.

We had been attempting to teach this cherubic first grader to read for approximately four months. After more than twenty hours of intensive clinical learning and remedial reading assistance, the child was still unable to identify any of the basic letters or sounds with any consistency. Brent would seem to have mastered the sound produced by a particular letter and then one minute later he would be unable to remember either the sound or the letter. In desperation, my staff had employed several different teaching techniques. Initially, we had used a phonics approach. This had proven unsuccessful, and we then tried a "sight word" method. This system was equally ineffective. Brent made virtually no progress from week to week. He seemed incapable of recognizing letters and associating the sounds of the letters with their written symbols.

A Stanford-Binet intelligence test indicated that Brent's IQ was 141. It was clear from the results that the child's profound reading problems could not be attributed to intellectual deficiencies. Diagnostic tests and clinical experience working with Brent confirmed that he had a serious perceptual dysfunction. Because of visual and auditory memory deficits (remembering what is seen and heard), he could not associate sounds with letters and letters with words. Nor could he identify any of the basic words that most children master after one or two exposures.

I assigned the first grader to a teacher with extensive experience helping severely learning and reading disabled students. Despite her many talents and seemingly inexhaustible patience, I could sense her mounting exasperation as she struggled to help Brent learn to read.

Although I, too, had become very concerned about Brent's lack of progress, I was far more concerned about his growing unhappiness, frustration, and resistance. It was obvious that our teaching strategy was not working, and it was also obvious that our intense desire to teach Brent was doing more harm than good. The child sensed the teacher's frustration, and he was becoming increasingly resentful.

During a conference with Brent's mother, I recommended a work-up by a pediatrician who specialized in treating children with learning disabilities. If the physician uncovered symptoms of possible organic problems, she would refer Brent to a pediatric neurologist for a comprehensive neurological examination.

The next day's staff meeting was devoted to brainstorming new methods for helping Brent. We reviewed the techniques we had already used, and together we designed a new teaching strategy. A staff member who had not yet worked with Brent volunteered to implement the program, and the responsibility for teaching Brent was turned over to her.

The pediatrician who evaluated Brent at my recommendation reported no indications of a neurological disorder. He suggested that amphetamines might help the child concentrate and learn to read. Brent's parents had serious misgivings about the use of drugs and rejected this recommendation.

With infinite patience and perseverance, the newly assigned teacher began to make some inroads into Brent's reading problems. The progress was erratic, however, and periodically the seven-year-old would forget everything that he had seemingly mastered. Both Brent and his teacher learned to rebound from these periodic setbacks, and the child's anxiety and frustration level began to diminish. The setbacks became less frequent, and we all observed an improvement in Brent's self-concept.

It has now been one year since Brent began receiving help at our center. He can now read at a basic primer level. Although his gains are modest, they represent prodigious effort on everyone's part.

Brent is currently working with a highly talented reading specialist hired specifically to help him and several other of our most severely reading disabled students. She reports that the child's reading problems are among the most serious that she has encountered in her many years of teaching reading disabled students.

During our last conference, I recommended that Brent's parents discuss a recently developed, experimental drug protocol with their pediatrician.[1] Clinical experience with this drug, which is related to a commonly prescribed motion sickness medication, suggests that it can improve the academic performance of learning disabled and dyslexic children (symptoms: letter reversals and inaccurate reading). The theory behind this protocol is that these children suffer from a mild form of disequilibrium and that once the symptoms of the disequilibrium are eliminated, students can improve their reading and concentration.

The jury is still out as far as Brent is concerned. His parents are receptive to considering the experimental protocol with the approval of their physician. The next step is up to the parents and the physician. In the meantime, we are continuing to provide learning therapy.

READING PROBLEMS

Most children learn to read regardless of the reading system that is used to teach them. Two basic factors will influence the mastery of reading skills: the child's capacity to respond to the symbols that are used to communicate written language and the teacher's teaching skills.

Quality reading materials can, of course, facilitate the teaching of reading. Such materials, however, are not a panacea. Even the best materials cannot ensure that a student with a learning disability will learn to read with facility. Textbook publishing is a business, and planned obsolescence is as integral to this industry as it is to the automobile industry. To stimulate sales, publishing companies frequently change directions and continually develop new teaching systems. Just when a school district commits to a particular textbook or teaching approach, it is encouraged to switch to another supposedly "definite" system developed by a competing publisher.

A talented, intuitive, and motivated teacher can teach most children to

[1]See *A Solution to the Riddle of Dyslexia* by Harold N. Levinson (New York: Springer Verlog, 1980) for a comprehensive discussion of this protocol.

read using a 1920s primer. Publishers typically react to this statement by arguing that they have been forced to develop innovative, fail-safe reading systems because of inadequate teacher training. They also contend that their materials are designed to teach children to read regardless of the teacher's skill level.

These arguments notwithstanding, academic skills have been deteriorating throughout the United States for three decades. This has occurred in spite of the hundreds of millions of dollars spent each year on new textbooks. The explanations offered by educators for this phenomenon are varied and complex, and usually focus on sociological and environmental influences. Fault clearly cannot be attributed exclusively to teachers, teachers' colleges, school districts, the educational system, or educational publishers. Our society must share the responsibility.

Perhaps one of the most significant factors contributing to the deterioration of reading skills is the evolution of the cultural support systems which have historically encouraged reading, studying, and academic excellence. The often fragmented family of the 1980s is quite different from the more nuclear family of the 1940s. Single parent households, television, computer games, drugs, deteriorating standards of discipline, reduced parental involvement in (and support for) education, and lowered educational standards have replaced the traditional two-parent family, radio (which encouraged children to create their own fantasies rather than have them cast in Hollywood), the homework ethic, discipline, and rigorous educational standards.

Most children can learn to read using virtually any reading program. Whereas some teachers and school districts are committed to a phonics approach, others are equally committed to a sight word method. As a general rule most remedial reading teachers and resources specialists agree that some form of systematic phonetic approach is most effective with reading disabled students. If these specialists determine that a phonics method is not working, they will usually respond by experimenting with alternative methodologies which might include a combination of different teaching protocols.

Children who cannot learn to read are relatively uncommon. Usually, their perceptual processing system is unable to decode written symbols efficiently. To help such children, remediation specialists must identify the source of the perceptual dysfunction and then design a custom-tailored program that either corrects or works around the problem.

Some of the common sources of reading problems are included in the following checklist. Parents will note that the descriptions are quite precise and in many instances technical. To respond accurately to certain statements, parents will need to consult their child's classroom teacher. If they discover that the classroom teacher cannot provide the necessary information, they may need to consult the school's reading specialist.

SOURCES OF READING PROBLEMS CHECKLIST

YES NO

VISUAL IMPAIRMENT (Inability to see with acuity.) ☐ ☐

VISUAL TRACKING DEFICITS (Inability to see words, phrases, and sentences accurately because the eyes are not moving efficiently across the printed line. Typical symptoms: word substitutions, omitted syllables and words, word additions, word inversions, and loss of place when reading.) ☐ ☐

VISUAL DISCRIMINATION DEFICITS (Inability to distinguish certain letters from other letters.) ☐ ☐

VISUAL MEMORY DEFICITS (Inability to remember the visual shape of letters and words, and inability to associate these shapes with letters, sounds, and words.) ☐ ☐

VISUAL AND/OR AUDITORY ASSOCIATION DEFICITS (Inability to associate the sound or the visual configuration or the meaning of the word with what is seen or heard.) ☐ ☐

PHONICS AND/OR BLENDING DEFICITS (Inability to sound out words.) ☐ ☐

AUDITORY IMPAIRMENT (Inability to hear certain sounds, especially in the high-frequency range.) ☐ ☐

AUDITORY DISCRIMINATION DEFICITS (Inability to hear the difference between sounds such as the short *i* and the short *e*. The ability to distinguish the sounds letters make is the starting point in the process of teaching phonics to the primary school child. Discrimination skills are the key to decoding words.)   □ □

AUDITORY MEMORY DEFICITS (Inability to remember the sounds that letters make or to remember how groups of letters are pronounced.)   □ □

PART-WHOLE PERCEPTUAL DEFICITS (Inability to perceive relationships between individual sounds and whole words, or between words that are read and their meaning when used in sentences or paragraphs. Example: a child who can sound out a common word and yet not be able to tell you what the word means. Such part-whole difficulties usually manifest themselves in reading comprehension problems.)   □ □

RETRIEVAL DEFICITS (Inability to recall or associate information or skills that had been learned or mastered previously.)   □ □

VOCABULARY DEFICITS (Inability to recall the meaning of words or to associate the meaning of a word that had been mastered previously.)   □ □

CONCENTRATION DEFICITS (Inability to pay attention or to focus when reading.)   □ □

EMOTIONAL PROBLEMS (Distractibility or negative attitude that is the result of personal or family disharmony.)   □ □

Interpreting the Checklist

Parents who uncover a pattern of specific reading deficits should discuss the checklist with their child's classroom teacher. If the parents and teacher agree that the child has specific underlying reading deficits, they should then determine whether or not it is reasonable to expect these deficits to be corrected by the classroom teacher. If it is the consensus that the child's reading problems cannot be corrected in the regular classroom, specialized reading assistance should be sought.

The first step in procuring help for the reading disabled child is to have the child professionally evaluated by the school psychologist, resource specialist, or reading specialist. Many school districts provide a reading or resource specialist at each school. Others have itinerant specialists who visit different schools in the district.

Parents are faced with some difficult decisions if they determine that their child has a reading problem and are told that he fails to qualify for learning assistance. At this critical juncture they have three basic options: they can accept the district's pronouncement, they can insist that help be provided, or they can look for help outside of the district.

In the state of California, parents are not required to accept the conclusions of the local school authorities. They have the option of disputing the decision and can demand a review. In extreme cases, parents can request a hearing before an impartial state-appointed panel. At this hearing they can present their case and any data that documents the child's need for special help. They can also have a parent advocate represent them at the meeting. This procedure, however, is rarely necessary. Usually, disagreements about learning assistance can be resolved without having to create a confrontation between the parents and the school district.

THE DIFFERENT LEVELS OF READING COMPREHENSION

The major objective of the process of learning to read is to comprehend what is being communicated. Three ascending levels of comprehension are examined here.

Level 1: Literal (Recall of Facts)

> Example: Sarah went to the door, opened her umbrella, and walked
> down the path.

Literal Question: Can you name the things that Sarah did?

A child who is able to read the sentence but who cannot answer questions requiring the retention of factual information has literal reading comprehension difficulties. The child's difficulties may be attributable to the following factors:

1. Visual memory deficits
2. Part-whole perceptual deficits (can read words but does not associate the meaning with words)
3. Intelligence limitations
4. Concentration deficits

Level 2: Inferential (Perceiving Cause and Effect)

> Example: Sarah went to the door, opened her umbrella, and walked down the path.

Inferential Question: What kind of day was it?

A child who can read the sentence but who cannot draw conclusions based on the content of the sentence is manifesting difficulty with inferential reasoning ability. Such difficulty signals deficient comprehension and an inability to generalize about what has been read. Inferential questions are intended to probe a student's capacity to respond to information which is implied but not directly stated. Before the child can draw inferences, he must be able to relate to phenomena involving cause and effect. In the example, the child may not be able to associate the umbrella with the probability that it is raining or about to rain. Inferential understanding demands more than a simple literal regurgitation of facts.

Level 3: Applicative (Critical Processing of Information)

> Example: Sarah went to the door, opened her umbrella, and walked down the path.

Applicative Question: What would you have done if you were with Sarah as
she began to walk down the path?

To respond to the question, a child must be able to evaluate information and then apply this information to solving a problem. The ability to analyze, infer, and draw conclusions from data represents the highest level of comprehension. The quality of the child's responses will reflect such factors as educational training, cultural background, and intelligence.

The primary objective of education is to train children to think. With adequate instruction and sufficient practice, most children of normal intelligence can be taught how to comprehend, apply, and utilize information. As a general rule, extremely intelligent children have a greater natural facility to analyze, infer, comprehend, and apply data. Like natural athletes who can improve their skills with quality coaching, even these extremely intelligent children can also, with quality instruction, improve their thinking skills. Indeed, the goal of accelerated programs for gifted students is to teach such children how to develop and refine their genetically inherited abilities.

The first step in the development of higher level comprehension skills—whether the child be gifted or not—is the acquisition of basic reading skills. The ability to decode written symbols, however, does not guarantee comprehension. A child must be able to do more than simply read words. If he is to comprehend what he is reading, he must be able to relate to both the explicit and implicit meaning of the words.

The child's capacity to associate words with their meanings is the cornerstone of vocabulary and comprehension skills. For instance, the word *umbrella* or *path* used in the examples will elicit in most elementary school children an immediate mental image. These children will instantaneously pass those words through their mental computer. If they have had past exposure, experiences, or associations with the words, they will be able to relate to them.

Words such as *umbrella* or *path,* which represent concrete objects, comprise the basic building blocks of a child's vocabulary. Other words such as *allegiance* or *abolish* represent abstract ideas and understanding such words demands more developed memory and associative skills.

Abstract words can be particularly perplexing to children with comprehension and conceptualization deficits because the definitions of the words are themselves abstractions. For example, the synonym for the word *allegiance* is the word *loyalty*. Children who have difficulty operating on a conceptual level would probably be confused, not only by the word, but also by its abstract definition.

Most children of average or above intelligence have the capacity to deal with abstract ideas. Other potentially capable children can remember details but may struggle with abstractions. Fortunately, learning assistance specialists in most school districts have access to excellent teaching materials that have been specifically designed to help children learn how to comprehend nonconcrete words and concepts.

Parents and teachers should actively encourage children to use an elementary- or intermediate-level dictionary when they confront words they do not recognize or understand. Children who develop the habit of looking up unfamiliar words in elementary school will usually continue to do so throughout their lives.

The child with average or above intelligence may also have difficulty understanding or remembering concrete words and ideas. Such children tend to read quickly and are usually inattentive to details. They often skip over words which they do not recognize or cannot understand from context and make little effort to find out what the unfamiliar words mean, despite the fact that these words are essential to their comprehending the material. With sufficient parental encouragement and appropriate academic assistance, most students with counterproductive reading habits can be taught to read with greater comprehension. But first the child must be retrained and systematically taught how to read and study more efficiently.

PROVIDING HELP FOR
THE READING DISABLED STUDENT

In order to provide meaningful assistance, teachers and specialists must first pinpoint the specific reading deficits that are interfering with the child's ability to read. A test that simply provides the child's grade level or percentile score will be of limited use in designing a remediation strategy. Standardized reading tests are designed to indicate a child's grade level in reading comprehension and vocabulary. Although these tests will indicate if a child is functioning below grade level in a specific area, they are not designed to identify the source of the child's reading problem. Unless carefully analyzed, such tests offer little or no explanation of why the child is reading below grade level.

Children with reading problems can be given special diagnostic reading tests that are specifically designed to identify the child's deficit areas. Parents who are convinced that their child has reading deficiencies should not hesitate to request and, if necessary, insist that the appropriate diagnostic reading tests be administered.

If a tutor or resource specialist is to design a well-conceived remediation program, he must understand the underlying source of the child's reading deficiencies. The teacher must know if the child is struggling in reading because of perceptual decoding deficits or because of reading comprehension problems on the literal, inferential, or applicative level.

Standardized reading tests can be used to yield more than simply a child's relative grade level. A reading specialist can examine a child's errors on the test and identify specific reading deficiencies. This process is called item analysis. A teacher trained in this procedure can categorize the types of errors a child has made on the reading comprehension section of the test. If the pattern of errors indicates difficulty in the area of drawing inferences, these deficits can be addressed with specific materials designed to help children develop inferential skills. Difficulty in the area of literal recall can be addressed with other specially designed materials. Usually, only reading and resource specialists are trained in item analysis of reading tests. If parents become frustrated by a delay in having their child diagnostically evaluated by the school district, they may be able to request in the interim that someone trained in item analysis evaluate their child's standard reading test to determine his specific reading deficits.

Testing is only one means by which information about the child's deficits can be obtained. The subjective assessment of parents, classroom teachers, and qualified reading or learning disabilities specialists can provide invaluable insight into the child's deficits and educational needs.

Testing and subjective observations are prerequisites to designing an effective, individualized remediation strategy. A visual tracking problem (e.g., inaccurate reading in the form of letter reversals, transpositions, or omissions of letters or syllables) will require a specialized remediation protocol that emphasizes visual perception. The child who has deficits in the areas of information recall or inferential problem solving will require a different type of remediation strategy.

Ideally, children with reading comprehension problems must be taught how to identify key ideas. They must also be taught that they are responsible for thinking about what they read. Their teachers, resource specialists, and tutors must help them come to the realization that reading involves more than simply consuming words. If they are to comprehend and remember what they are reading, they must accept the fact that they have to work diligently. Bad study habits must be broken. Vocabulary-deficient students must be encouraged to use a dictionary when they are unable to understand key words from context, and vocabulary development must be emphasized as an integral part of their remedial instruction.

In theory, the exercises and questions that follow the units in most elementary reading textbooks and reading lab materials are designed to teach these critical thinking skills. Although these materials are helpful, they may not be enough, especially in the case of reading disabled children. Before such children can learn effectively, they must be taught how to become actively involved in reading, learning, and studying.

Most children can be taught how to decode efficiently, retain information, and perceive relationships. They can also be taught how to look for key words and ideas in paragraphs. Although extremely bright children tend to acquire these skills with little effort, those children lacking this natural facility can develop it in much the same way that a nonnatural athlete can become competent in a sport if he has sufficient desire and makes the necessary effort to practice.

The primary emphasis in the early stages of a child's elementary school education involves basic decoding skills ("word attack," blending, sight word recognition, phonics, and tracking) and information recall. Some children may perform well at this stage of learning to read but may begin to falter in fourth, fifth, or sixth grade when higher-level inferential and applicative skills are emphasized. Such children may need specialized remedial support until they can master the requisite comprehension skills. If the child's comprehension problem is due to limited intelligence, then he may require ongoing learning and emotional support.

SPELLING PROBLEMS

English is a particularly difficult language to spell, and spelling problems affect vast numbers of American school children (and American adults). The inherent difficulty in spelling English is largely attributable to the fact that there are glaring exceptions to the rules of spelling. Unfortunately for students, English pronunciation has evolved significantly, but the spelling of English words has not evolved commensurately. Three centuries ago, the words *though, thought, enough, through*, and *bought* were pronounced as they were spelled, and the spelling of the words corresponded to the pronunciation.

To spell proficiently, a child requires three essential perceptual processing skills: auditory discrimination, auditory memory, and visual memory. The child must first be able to distinguish the different sounds that letters make. This ability to discriminate sounds is especially critical when the word being spelled is phonetic (follows prescribed rules of pronunciation and spelling). A child who cannot hear the difference between such words as *pen* and *pin* and between *pup* and *pop* will have difficulty spelling many of the words that make up the English language.

The second component in spelling proficiency is the ability to remember auditorily. The sound *ou* in the word *round* can be made only by two letter combinations: *ow* and *ou*. A child who is asked to spell this word would have to remember the two combinations of letters that produce the sound, and then he would have to remember that the *ow* combination is seldom found in the middle of a word (exception: *crowd*).

Good spellers may not be consciously aware of phonetic rules and exceptions, but they have the ability to retrieve instantaneously the correct letter combination that produces the word *round*. For these children this process of discriminating, remembering, retrieving, and associating sounds and the written symbols which represent those sounds occurs with relatively little effort. Children who lack spelling facility typically find the process a monumental challenge.

Visual memory is another requisite to spelling proficiency. The ability to remember what is seen plays an especially important role when words are nonphonetic. English is replete with nonphonetic words, and the exceptions to the general rules of spelling make good visual memory skills an invaluable resource for a student. For example, the word *respondent* might be spelled with an *ant* or an *ent* in the last syllable. In theory, the endings *ant* and *ent* should be pronounced differently. In practice, these endings are often pronounced in the United States in the same way. Because there is no pronunciation differentiation, there is no guide for correctly spelling the word. Nor is there a spelling rule that dictates how the word should be spelled. The student must simply memorize the correct spelling. If a child has visual memory facility and can remember that the correct ending is *ent*, he will have a distinct advantage over his classmates with less natural spelling facility.

Sloppy pronunciation is a significant source of spelling errors. For example, the word *prerogative* is often misspelled because most people pronounce it *perogative*. Parents of poor spellers who recognize that their child is mispronouncing and misspelling words might attempt—selectively and diplomatically—to correct their child's pronunciation. Parents, however, must exercise caution and restraint. Excessive corrections of pronunciation can elicit resentment and work at cross-purposes with helping the child.

Other factors that can affect a person's spelling ability include attention to detail, concentration, desire, and practice. Attention to detail is the benchmark of good spellers. Only one letter need be incorrect for a teacher to circle the word in red ink. Teachers do not give credit on spelling tests for words that are "almost correct."

Desire is another key factor in the acquisition of good spelling skills. Students who intend not to make spelling mistakes generally spell better than students who are less concerned about making mistakes. Good spellers will take the time to look up words in a dictionary if they have doubts about the proper spelling. They will also edit and reedit their essays and reports more carefully.

With practice, effort, and desire, even those students with poor visual memory skills can learn how to compensate for their lack of natural facility. They may need several exposures to a particularly difficult word before they can master it, but they can usually become better spellers if they are willing to work.

Some students who study diligently and discipline themselves to do well on a weekly spelling test may, nevertheless, spell poorly in essays and reports. To spell words correctly in context, a student must force himself to look very critically at what he is writing. He must be sufficiently motivated to find and correct his mistakes, and he must discipline himself to look up words when he senses that the words do not "look right."

Despite the fact that spelling skills can be developed and children can be taught phonetic rules and spelling rules, some children remain poor spellers. If these students are ultimately to improve their skills, they will need to develop or be taught practical methods for memorizing and associating words with their correct spelling. They will also have to develop their own self-editing system. There are no magic pills that can transform a poor speller into a good speller, improvements will come only through practice and effort.

Resource specialists should be able to incorporate techniques that are specifically designed to help children with spelling problems. Parents can also orchestrate opportunities for a child to improve his spelling skills. For example, there are enjoyable spelling-oriented games that families can play together. The staff at a good teacher supply store should be able to suggest specific games. Parents can also avail themselves of the suggestions of the resource specialist at their child's school.

MATH PROBLEMS

Like his counterpart with reading problems, the child who is struggling with math also may have a perceptual dysfunction. Efficient auditory and visual memory skills and visual discrimination and tracking skills are as essential to the development of math skills as they are to the development of reading skills.

The poor math student with a perceptual processing dysfunction may have deficits in the areas of concentration, attention to detail, or visual decoding. A student, for instance, who chronically disregards operators and adds when he should subtract is not going to do well on math tests. Nor is the child who reverses number sequences (79 is perceived or written as 97) or who confuses the number 6 with the number 9 (a manifestation of dyslexia).

Not all math problems can be attributed to perceptual problems. Many students who do poorly in math do not have difficulty processing sensory data, but rather, have difficulty with conceptual skills (understanding how numbers function) or with computational skills (performing specific mathematical operations such as multiplication). Some children with severe math problems have both conceptual *and* computational deficiencies.

The successful resolution of math problems requires that the student's specific deficit areas be accurately identified. To assign a confused child additional practice problems or to have him recite multiplication tables seldom serves a positive function. The starting point in any remediation process is to figure out *where* the child is stuck and *why* he is stuck. Drilling number facts may help the child remember that $5 \times 5 = 25$.

Knowing this fact, of course, is important, but mastering this "splinter" skill without understanding the process will ultimately interfere with the mastery of division.

A child who has difficulty adding numbers with decimals may simply not be adding accurately. If the child understands how to add and understands the concept of decimals but has difficulty performing the math operations, he is probably struggling with basic computational deficiencies. If, however, the child does not understand how to add whole numbers or does not understand decimals, he has a conceptual deficit. Before the teacher can help the student, he or she must determine the nature of the child's problems. If the student is confused, he must be helped to understand the concepts. If he makes "silly" mistakes when he adds or forgets to insert the decimal point, then he needs more practice. Extra homework sheets may be all that is required. Were the teacher to determine that the child's problems are due to inattentiveness or sloppiness, then he may need to design a creative incentive program that rewards the child for neatness and accuracy.

Most children of average intelligence are capable of grasping basic arithmetic. When shown how to add or subtract, they will generally catch on quickly to the operations involved. Most children can also master more complicated operations such as multiplication and division with relative ease. Although these operations do involve rote memory, they can best be performed by children who understand how numbers "work." The child who understands math concepts will be far better prepared to handle higher-level math functions than the child who does not understand these concepts.

Diagnostic math tests can quickly reveal whether the origins of a child's math difficulties are conceptual or computational. These tests can pinpoint the child's specific deficits. For example, a child may be confused about fractions because he doesn't understand the part-whole concepts. Once the teacher identifies this conceptual difficulty, specific remedial methods can be employed to help the child master the necessary concepts. For example, manipulatives (units such as pennies, cubes, or popsicle sticks) can be used to represent the ways in which numbers interact. Fraction tiles can used to explain part-whole relationships. These tactile and visual props can be an invaluable resource for helping a child who is "stuck" and who does not understand basic math concepts.

Behavior modification systems can be quite effective in helping the student whose computational deficits are due to inattentiveness. The child's parents and/or teacher could set up a system in which the child receives points for each problem he does accurately and legibly. A prize, an award, or even money could serve as the incentive. If appropriate, negative reinforcement might also be integrated into the system. The parents or teachers of a child who does chronically sloppy and illegible work might simply say: "These problems need to be recopied so that they are more legible." (See "Monitoring Your Child's Performance," in Chapter 7, for a discussion of the use of rewards as incentives for children.)

HANDWRITING PROBLEMS

To write legibly and accurately, a child must be able to control the fine-motor muscles of his hand. The ability to control these muscles is acquired in stages during the course of the child's development.

Most three-year-olds naturally gravitate to crayons and chalk. Their first attempts to grasp and control the crayon are invariably awkward. With practice, their ability to control their fingers improves, but their drawings are initially disjointed and incomplete and bear little resemblance to reality.

As the child matures and has more practice using his fingers to manipulate objects, his fine-motor proficiency increases. In preschool, he learns how to cut with scissors and in kindergarten he develops the ability to draw pictures of objects that can be identified by others. Later, the child is taught how to form letters and numbers. Reproducing these symbols at first requires great effort, but as the child's hand and fingers learn how to obey the commands of his brain, the effort becomes less onerous.

The kindergartner's ability to control the fine-motor muscles of his fingers usually improves with practice and maturity. Through a process of trial and error, the child begins to perceive spatial relationships more accurately. He recognizes that the house is bigger than the chimney and that objects in the foreground are bigger than objects in the background. As his fine-motor control improves, he acquires the ability to scale down his letters and numbers so that can they fit into the prescribed space on his paper.

While most children naturally learn how to form their letters and numbers, others have difficulty developing the requisite spatial judgment and fine-motor proficiency. Their letters continue to be misshapen, disproportionate, and illegible. Despite having as much practice as the other children in the class, their small-motor control improves only marginally.

Potential handwriting problems usually begin to manifest themselves in kindergarten or first grade. Parents and teachers are likely to recognize more blatant fine-motor problems and to overlook the more subtle problems. In some cases, handwriting deficits do not become a source of concern until third or fourth grade.

Poor handwriting is often associated by parents and teachers with inattentiveness, impulsiveness, irresponsibility, or sloppy work habits. Although these behavioral characteristics can contribute to poor handwriting, they are not necessarily the source of the problem. Usually illegible handwriting is directly attributable to fine-motor or spatial deficiencies (difficulty distinguishing size, shape, and relative positioning) which were not accurately identified in kindergarten or first grade. The child's lack of attention to detail is most likely a symptom of the underlying motor-coordination and perceptual dysfunction, and not the cause of the problem.

Poor handwriting usually can be corrected by means of a well-conceived remediation program. Resource teachers can assign fine-motor activities and exercises specifically designed to improve the child's ability to control his fingers. Spatial perception deficits can also be treated with other materials specifically designed to help children perceive relative size and proportions.[2] Chronic sloppiness can be corrected by means of a behavior modification program and extensive practice, guidance, and feedback.

Older students with handwriting problems tend to be quite defensive about their illegible writing. This defensiveness is the result of having been nagged and lectured for years about how impossible it is to read what they have written. Counterproductive habits tend to become entrenched, and teenagers can be as resistant to giving up their bad habits as their adult counterparts are. Parents who recognize that they and their child have become locked into counterproductive scripts might consider creating incentives for the teenager to improve his handwriting. Although rewards might be construed as bribes, they can be highly effective motivators. Parents, for instance, might offer a reward in return for their teenager making a genuine effort to write more legibly for a month. Hope-

[2]Spatial deficits are identified by a test called the Bender-Gestalt. See Glossary of Educational Terms and Testing Appendix for a description of this test.

fully, as the student's handwriting improves, he will be willing to exert the extra effort requisite to writing neatly and legibly.

Helping a student improve his handwriting is akin to helping a person improve his tennis game. If someone sincerely desires to become a better tennis player, he probably would seek out a competent tennis coach. The coach would analyze the person's tennis game and identify its weaknesses. He would then recommend a specific set of exercises designed to correct the identified deficits. The exercises would focus on specific skills such as the serve, the backhand, the forehand, or timing. With competent coaching and sufficient practice, the individual's tennis game should improve.

The principles of identifying deficits and providing coaching also apply to improving a child's handwriting. There are no "magic bullets" that can help a child write more legibly. The retraining process requires effort, practice, instruction, and encouragement.

SELBY: A STAR IN A FAMILY OF SUPERSTARS

I needed only a few minutes to recognize that Selby was exceptionally bright and perceptive. He had been referred to our center by the principal of his private school. Despite an IQ of 142 and a very academically oriented family, the sixth grader was in danger of flunking out of the school.

Selby's mother was an artist; his father was a surgeon who also had the distinction of having won an Olympic gold medal in swimming. Although the parents had recently divorced, they remained good friends. Both parents felt that their sons had handled the divorce relatively well. Selby and his brother saw their father regularly. During the early stages of the separation, the entire family had seen a family therapist for several sessions. The therapist had advised that the children did not require ongoing therapy.

The parents were convinced that Selby was "stuck" academically, and they felt that he was becoming increasingly demoralized. His reading comprehension scores had not improved during the last two years, and he was now testing approximately six months above grade level. Because of the highly accelerated curriculum at his school, the ten-year-old was no longer able to keep up with his class.

Selby did not begin talking until he was four years old. At first, his parents suspected that he might have a hearing impairment, but a diagnostic hearing test confirmed that there was nothing organically wrong with his hearing. Dysphasia (difficulty using spoken language to communicate) was also considered as a possible explanation for his slow language development, and Selby was provided with private language therapy. He responded to the therapy so quickly that his language therapist became convinced that the child was not truly dysphasic. Within eight months of beginning treatment, Selby was talking normally. Neither the pediatrician nor the speech therapist was able to pinpoint the source of the child's language problem.

During the first three years of elementary school, Selby was an excellent student. He was one of the best readers and math students in his class. Quick and eager to learn, Selby enjoyed school and was proud of his academic accomplishments.

In fourth grade, Selby's parents began to perceive a significant deterioration in their child's performance and attitude. Academic work was no longer easy for the boy. He complained of being confused by the material, and getting him to finish his homework had become a monumental struggle. Selby was completely dependent on his mother to help him complete his assignments.

Selby's older brother, Jeff, was an exceptionally accomplished student with an IQ of 170. His straight A average underscored the disparity between the two children. In addition to his academic talents, Jeff was an excellent competitive diver and appeared destined to make the U.S. Olympic Diving Team. Although Selby was also a good athlete, his brother was a superb athlete.

On the surface, Selby did not appear to be envious or resentful of his very exceptional brother. In fact, he gave the impression of being quite proud of his brother's many academic and athletic accomplishments.

Despite the assurance of Selby's parents that they did not compare their children, it was clear that they were especially proud of their older son's achievements and disappointed by Selby's lack of achievement. Surrounded by a family of superstars, Selby realized that he was not measuring up to the standards of his exceptional family.

My diagnostic tests found no conclusive evidence of a significant learning disability. Although Selby had not improved in reading during the last two years, he was still reading slightly above grade level. The diagnostic assessment, however, did reveal subtle auditory processing deficits and visual memory deficits. An item analysis of his reading test revealed that the sixth grader was having some difficulty with inferential and applicative reading comprehension skills. The symptoms were poorly defined, and if I had relied exclusively on the standard diagnostic criteria, I would have been hard-pressed to attribute the child's academic difficulties to a learning disability.

I suspected that emotional factors were contributing to Selby's learning problems, despite the therapist's assessment (which I had received secondhand). The ten-year-old was experiencing intense pressure at school and at home. I was also convinced that the divorce had taken an emotional toll on Selby, and I inferred from certain statements made by the parents that there was more competition between Selby and his brother than the parents acknowledged.

Selby realized that his brother was excelling in school while he was not. He could not help but be aware of his parents' value system with its strong emphasis on achievement. The realization that he was not fulfilling his parents' expectations intensified his stress and anxiety. Anger, frustration, envy, and disappointment were inevitable. Although he attempted to repress the feelings they could not help but affect him.

By most traditional diagnostic standards, Selby was not learning disabled. Nevertheless, the intellectually gifted boy was an underachiever and a candidate for learning assistance. To correct his subtle perceptual processing deficits and improve his reading comprehension skills, I recommended a three-hour weekly learning assistance program. Rebuilding Selby's confidence in his own abilities was a key objective of the remediation strategy.

I urged Selby's parents to be patient for six months. Because of their son's fragile self-esteem, I strongly recommended that they resist any conscious or unconscious inclination to compare the accomplishments of their two sons. I explained that although Selby might continue to struggle for several months, he did not have serious learning problems, and he would probably respond quickly to learning assistance. I was confident that once Selby began to experience success, his self-confidence would soar.

My prognosis proved accurate. Selby is now in high school and is an A student. His goal is to become a physicist.

ATYPICAL LEARNING PROBLEMS

A bright child with an IQ of 142 from a highly achievement-oriented family would normally be found at the top of his class. Upon graduation from high school, such a child would be expected to go to a first-rate university and, ultimately, to enter a profession where he could capitalize on superior intellectual gifts.

Selby, however, was not a typical child. He attended an excellent school. He was loved and encouraged by his parents. He did not have significant learning problems or blatant emotional problems. Why then was he struggling? The answer to this question involves a complex mix of family, learning, and emotional factors. These factors, operating in tandem, had undermined the child's ability to cope with an accelerated academic curriculum and a family of superachievers. Selby's parents had unintentionally communicated their lowered level of expectations, and the boy had become resigned to his "second-team" status in the family.

The child with nonspecific learning deficiencies frequently confounds parents, teachers, school psychologists, and learning disabilities specialists. Identifying the source of an atypical learning problem can be one of the most challenging assignments an educator or a therapist faces. Although everyone may recognize that the child is not learning efficiently, no one is quite sure why he is stuck. Because the child's learning deficits are subtle, unusual, intermittent, or enigmatic, they do not conform to the classic patterns and diagnostic criteria. As a consequence, these problems may never be properly identified. In the absence of a precise identification of the source of the child's underlying problems, his marginal performance in school may be erroneously attributed to laziness, irresponsibility, poor attitude, or delinquent behavior.

The younger child with nonspecific learning disabilities often defies the standard criteria used by educators to assess learning deficiencies and remediation needs. The child may do excellent work in some subjects and terrible work in others. In second grade, he may do well in math and poorly in reading. The following year he may do just the opposite.

The high school student with atypical learning problems may pay attention in history class and be totally distracted in math class. He may be inspired by an art teacher and completely unresponsive to an English teacher. Or he may work conscientiously during the first semester and then give up for no apparent reason and do nothing during the second semester.

Because of the complex mix of subtle factors that can contribute to atypical learning problems, it may be difficult to pinpoint the precise source of a child's academic difficulty. In fact, many atypical learners are never properly identified, diagnosed, or treated. Even if testing does occur, the tests may not supply the necessary evidence of an underlying learning disability that the schools require to provide assistance. In many school districts, there are little or no resources for helping the atypical learner. The parents of such children either must resign themselves to the fact that their child will not be provided with assistance or they must resign themselves to procuring private help.

One of the unfortunate consequences of an atypical or nonspecific learning problem is that the child's parents, teachers, and the child himself often arrive at erroneous conclusions about his ability and potential. Marginal school performance can convince everyone that the student is capable only of marginal achievement. Negative expectations have a disturbing tendency to become self-fulfilling. Although some children with atypical learning patterns discover ways to resolve their own learning problems, many continue to perform marginally throughout school and throughout their lives.

Parents who conclude that their child is an atypical learner will need to do some soul-searching. They must examine their values and their attitudes about achievement. They must realistically assess their child's abilities and personality. If they conclude that their child's enigmatic learning patterns may ultimately deprive him of the opportunity to attain his goals in life, they must then do everything in their power to help him overcome the underlying deficits that are preventing him from achieving.

There is nothing intrinsically wrong with doing C work if that is the best that a child is capable of doing. There is also nothing intrinsically wrong with a young adult deciding that school is not particularly important to him and that his priority is to train himself to succeed in a trade or other career. Parents must decide, however, if they are willing to accept C work from their child if he is potentially capable of doing better. If they are not willing to accept marginal performance, then they must logically and systematically identify why their child is struggling and then insist that appropriate assistance be provided. The identification process will usually require the efforts of a trained professional.

Parents should resist judging their child until they understand why he is struggling. Before they label their child as lazy or irresponsible, they must understand the source of the behaviors. The child's underlying problems may be quite subtle, but he may not be able to overcome or compensate for these problems without assistance or counseling. The laziness and irresponsibility may simply be symptomatic of the academic struggle, and not the source of the struggle.

Identifying a nonspecific learning disability inevitably involves a degree of subjectivity. The school psychologist who is locked into relying exclusively on objective standardized tests may overlook or disregard a child's atypical learning problem because the profile of deficits does not conform to the standard diagnostic criteria. A child need not deviate significantly from the standardized norms in order to have learning problems or to be an underachiever.

Understanding why a child is functioning poorly in school requires more than simply administering a test and grading it. The child's home and school environment, learning strengths and deficits, perceptual skills, and emotional responses are factors that must be carefully examined and considered.

A child's school performance must be assessed not only in relationship to national norms but also in relationship to his potential, to his family's values, and to the academic standards of the school he is attending. The expectations of the child's parents and teachers and of the child himself must also be factored into the assessment.

Parents who feel that their child is an atypical learner who is not performing commensurate with his ability should request that he be diagnostically evaluated. If they are told that he does not qualify for testing, they must decide if they want to have the child privately tested.

The child with atypical learning problems may need to be taught how to concentrate, how to organize his ideas and time, how to prepare for exams, and how to write a report. These objectives can be achieved by means of a wide spectrum of specific teaching techniques and incentives.

Because of economic considerations, most school districts have had to prioritize the needs of children with specific, identifiable learning disabilities. These children, and not the less disabled underachievers, are the ones targeted for help. Although excellent arguments can be made for giving top priority to the needs of the moderately and severely learning disabled children, an equally compelling argument can be made for providing learning assistance for children with nonspecific, atypical learning disabilities. The atypically learning disabled child who is unable to achieve represents a loss of potential that is no less significant than the lost potential of the child with a severe, identifiable learning problem. Any waste of human potential is tragic, whatever the reasons. Parents and teachers are charged with the compelling responsibility to do everything in their power to prevent this tragedy.

CHAPTER 5

Language, Intellectual, and Cultural Factors

ANDREW: TWO YEARS OF SILENCE

As the eight-year-old stared at me with his big brown eyes, I could sense immediately that there was something profoundly wrong. When he spoke, his speech was slow and had the unique tonal quality of someone who is deaf and has never heard the sound of his own voice. The child, however, was not deaf.

Andrew's mother explained that until two years of age, her son appeared to be developing normally. He crawled and walked at the age-appropriate times, and he began to babble at the age children are expected to begin babbling. Suddenly, Andrew stopped making any noise whatsoever. He became cranky and had a continuous low-grade infection. Despite extensive tests, the pediatrician could not find an explanation for his symptoms or behavior.

At first, Andrew's mother was only mildly concerned about her son's delayed language development. As the months passed, her concern turned to alarm. Andrew became lethargic, and his silence was eerie. His mother took him to several different doctors, but none of the specialists could identify the problem. Although unable to talk, Andrew's hearing was normal. Finally, one doctor suggested that Andrew be comprehensively tested by an allergist. This evaluation indicated that he was severely allergic to milk.

Once all dairy products were removed from Andrew's diet, he slowly regained his ability to produce sounds. However, an E.E.G. revealed that the allergic reaction had been so severe that it had caused organic brain damage.[1] Although the long-range educational implications of this damage were not clear, it was obvious that Andrew's learning skills had been impaired. His mother had brought the child to our center in the hope that we might be able to help him.

Andrew attended a school for aphasic children.[2] The school, which was funded by the state and the local county, dealt exclusively with seriously language disabled children and offered language therapy and highly specialized learning assistance as an integral part of the curriculum.

Andrew had made significant language gains at his school, but his mother was concerned about his lack of academic improvement. The eight-year-old was barely able to recognize the letters of the alphabet. He also had difficulty paying attention and following instructions.

My diagnostic evaluation confirmed that Andrew had both encoding problems (deficient expressive language) and decoding problems (deficient perceptual processing). After completing the testing procedure, I knew that the child's severe language problems demanded priority treatment and that he required a full-time program that emphasized extensive speech, language, learning, and occupational therapy.[3] I explained to his mother that our clinical program focused on decoding skills and writing skills and that we did not offer language therapy. Inasmuch as Andrew's school provided all of the services he required, I recommended that he remain there. To assuage the mother's concerns about her son's lack of academic progress, I gave her the names of several private schools that also worked with language disabled children, and I suggested that she evaluate and compare each school's program with Andrew's current program. This comparison convinced her to keep Andrew at the county school.

---

[1]It is rare for an allergic reaction to dairy products to cause organic brain damage.

[2]Aphasia is an inability to communicate with spoken language. The condition may involve deficits in the areas of receptive, expressive, or written language, reading, and/or mathematics. The term is often used synonymously (and erroneously) with dysphasia, which is a less severe language disorder. Relatively few children are actually aphasic. Most children with language deficiencies are dysphasic. See Glossary of Educational Terms.

[3]Occupational therapists will frequently employ a method called sensory integration to help brain-damaged patients organize their central nervous system functions. See "sensory integration therapy" in Glossary of Educational Terms.

THE FACTS ABOUT
LANGUAGE DISORDERS

The capacity to affect others with our words is a gift that is often taken for granted. Most of us simply open our mouths and out spill the words that communicate our needs and our ideas.

Language is a response to either external stimuli (e.g., a question) or internal stimuli (e.g., an idea or emotion).

External stimuli:	"When are you leaving on your trip?"
Language:	"After Christmas."
Internal stimuli:	How can I convince her that I'm really not upset?
Language:	"Honey, you know it really doesn't matter."

The brain's processing of sensory information in the form of external stimuli (spoken words or visual symbols) is called decoding. The subsequent process of producing responses (spoken or written language) is called encoding. Although encoding is distinct from decoding, the two processes overlap. When a person is asked a question, or when he wants to describe a beautiful sunset, his brain must first sort out the external sensory stimuli. In the case of a question, the stimuli consist of the words addressed to the person. In the case of the sunset, the stimuli consist of visual images. The sensory data must be perceptually processed before the person can express his responses to the data.

The interrelationship between decoding and encoding is most evident when children are attempting to learn. A student is constantly being bombarded with sensory information to which he is expected to respond. If the child's brain has properly decoded the sensory input, it can then encode the appropriate output. For example:

Question:	"What is the capital of California?"
Decoding:	Receive input.
	Decipher sensory signals (words).
	Associate information with stored data in memory.
Encoding:	Retrieve appropriate expressive language.
	Respond with written or spoken words.
Answer:	"Sacramento."

To respond to the question cited in the example, the child must run the sensory input through his mental computer. Visual symbols must be processed if the question is written. Auditory symbols must be processed if the question is spoken. The child's brain instantaneously connects the meaning of the symbols with information that has already been programmed into the computer. This assumes, of course, that the child knows the answer and that his brain is functioning efficiently.

Discrimination, memory, and association skills are essential components in the decoding/encoding process. Once the brain has deciphered the information, it can then retrieve other spoken or written words to express a response to the question. Sometimes, however, the "computer" does not function properly:

> Teacher: "What is the capital of California?"
> Child: "Buffalo."
> Teacher: "No, that's incorrect."
> Child: "Sacramento."
> Teacher: "That's correct."

In the example, the child is forced to repeat the decoding/encoding process. He makes a mistake and must order his brain to search once again for the proper response. If his memory fails him, or if he has never learned the information, he will not be able to encode the answer. If, however, the student knows the answer to a question but cannot express it, he probably has deficient expressive language skills.

Certain people have a greater facility than others for expressing themselves. This facility may indicate a particularly efficient decoding/encoding system, language aptitude, superior intelligence, good educational background, or great motivation to develop effective communication skills.

To express a complicated idea or to respond to a complex question (e.g., "What are your thoughts about God?") requires highly sophisticated language skills. A person who struggles to answer such a question does not necessarily have a language disability. The enormity of the issues involved may simply overtax the person's analytical thinking and/or communication skills.

The struggle to express complex or abstract thoughts is quite distinct from the struggle experienced by the person with a significant language problem who has difficulty communicating in virtually all situations. The combined effects of poor verbal skills, anxiety, and frustration may cause him to talk haltingly or stammer whenever he attempts to express his thoughts or feelings. Such a person would benefit from the assistance of a speech specialist. To reduce the stress and anxiety, counseling may also be appropriate.

Some people with poorly developed communication skills telegraph their verbal deficiencies and insecurities by repeatedly interspersing the phrase "you know" throughout their conversations. Unfortunately, this speech habit has become pandemic in America. The words serve two functions: They act as transitions between thoughts, and they represent an awkward attempt on the part of the speaker to convince himself and others that he is indeed being understood.

It is important to differentiate speech deficiencies from language disorders. The child who has difficulty communicating has a language disorder. The child who has difficulty pronouncing words properly or articulating has a speech disorder. (Speech disorders will be examined in the following section.)

The child with an expressive language disorder may struggle to respond to even a simple question (e.g., "What time is it?"). His encoding dysfunction prevents him from expressing what he knows. Such a deficiency can pose a formidable barrier to communication and can impede the child's ability to respond to stimuli, to express feelings and ideas, and to make his needs known. The child who is unable to use language as a bridge between the internal world and the external world is at risk emotionally. His language deficiencies may cause him to become isolated. The psychological implications of this isolation can be calamitous.

In most instances, children with speech or language disorders can be helped by means of specialized therapy. To reduce the potential for psychological damage, this therapy should begin as early as possible.

Delayed language acquisition is a primary symptom of a possible language disorder. The typical progression from cooing, to babbling, to speaking isolated words may not occur, or, as in the case of Andrew, the progression may be interrupted. In kindergarten, the child with a language disability may not be able to say the names of the colors, the days of the week, or the months of the year. He also may not be able to count verbally or sing the words to the songs in class.

A wide spectrum of specific symptoms may signal a language disability. The child may manifest some or all of these characteristics, and the symptoms may range from subtle to severe. The following checklist is intended to help parents determine whether or not their child should be evaluated by a qualified speech and language therapist. The list includes both decoding and encoding deficits. To complete the list, parents probably will need to consult their child's classroom teacher.

LANGUAGE DISORDERS CHECKLIST

	YES	NO
AUDITORY PROCESSING DEFICITS		
Difficulty paying attention to auditory stimuli	☐	☐
Difficulty discriminating sound versus no sound	☐	☐
Difficulty locating where sound is coming from	☐	☐
Difficulty discriminating different sounds	☐	☐
Difficulty distinguishing primary sounds from background sounds	☐	☐
Difficulty associating sounds with the source of the sounds	☐	☐
Difficulty filtering out extraneous sounds	☐	☐
Difficulty sequencing ideas	☐	☐
Oral reversals (e.g., *emeny* instead of *enemy*)	☐	☐
Circumlocutions (imprecise, roundabout communication. For example: "that place down there where they sell the thing-amajig")	☐	☐
LINGUISTIC PROCESSING DEFICITS		
Poor grammar	☐	☐
Wrong verb tenses	☐	☐
Use of only broad meanings for words	☐	☐
Lack of understanding of subtle meanings or differences between words	☐	☐
Difficulty understanding spatial prepositions *(beneath/beside)*	☐	☐
Difficulty understanding words denoting time and space *(before/here)*	☐	☐
Difficulty understanding comparatives and superlatives *(bigger/biggest, far/near, rough/smooth, fast/slow)*	☐	☐
COGNITIVE (THINKING) PROCESSING DEFICITS		
Difficulty following oral directions	☐	☐
Difficulty expressing thoughts and information	☐	☐
Difficulty classifying	☐	☐
Difficulty putting events in sequence or order	☐	☐
Difficulty making comparisons	☐	☐
Difficulty understanding or expressing the moral of a story	☐	☐

COGNITIVE (THINKING) PROCESSING DEFICITS
Difficulty predicting the outcome of a story or event   ☐ ☐
Difficulty differentiating between fact and fiction   ☐ ☐
Difficulty remembering and expressing facts   ☐ ☐

EVALUATION DEFICITS
Difficulty drawing conclusions ("Why did she need her mit-
    tens?")   ☐ ☐
Difficulty relating to cause and effect (Hot fudge is made
    from a. ice cream b. chocolate c. dessert)   ☐ ☐

SOCIAL PROBLEMS
Difficulty understanding subtle verbal and nonverbal
    cues   ☐ ☐
Excessive talking   ☐ ☐
Talking at inappropriate times   ☐ ☐

WRITTEN LANGUAGE PROBLEMS[4]
Difficulty expressing in written words what is known (dys-
    graphia)   ☐ ☐
Difficulty copying letters, numbers, or words   ☐ ☐
Difficulty writing spontaneously or from dictation   ☐ ☐
Difficulty drawing (but no problems copying)   ☐ ☐
Difficulty organizing thoughts for writing   ☐ ☐
Difficulty writing with good syntax (but no difficulty with
    spoken grammar)   ☐ ☐

APHASIA/DYSPHASIA[5]
Difficulty making facial motor movements to produce sound[6]   ☐ ☐
Difficulty imitating sounds   ☐ ☐
Difficulty remembering words (but can repeat them)   ☐ ☐
Difficulty formulating sentences (but can use single words)   ☐ ☐
Difficulty naming common objects   ☐ ☐
Difficulty recalling a specific word   ☐ ☐
Substitutions (*rattle* for *beetle*)   ☐ ☐

[4]See subsequent section in this chapter, "Written Language Arts Problems."
[5]See note on page 95 for a discussion of the differences between aphasia (complete loss of language) and dysphasia (partial language deficiency). Note that motoric symptoms that are characteristic of aphasic and dysphasic children are similar to those that are characteristic of minimal brain damage.
[6]This condition is called dyspraxia (see Glossary of Educational Terms).

APHASIA/DYSPHASIA

Distorted body image (as reflected in drawings)   □ □
Difficulty copying designs   □ □
Difficulty with directional concepts (right/left/up/beside) □ □
Poor attention span   □ □
Poor coordination   □ □
Clumsiness   □ □
Hyperactivity   □ □
Emotional disturbances   □ □
Difficulty recognizing common objects by touch   □ □

Interpreting the Checklist

Parents who see a pattern of "yes" answers should contact a qualified speech and language therapist. The therapist will be able to evaluate the information, provide diagnostic testing, and design an effective treatment protocol. The earlier a child's language problems are diagnosed, the sooner remedial therapy can begin. With early intervention, the risk of demoralizing frustration and possible emotional damage is significantly reduced. Even subtle problems such as common articulation deficits (e.g., difficulty pronouncing a particular sound or immature speech patterns) can cause painful embarrassment and should be professionally assessed.

Fortunately, highly effective techniques have been developed to help children with language disabilities. Parents who feel that their child may have a language or speech disability should request that their child be evaluated at school. If language therapy is not available, or if their child fails to qualify for help, parents should consult their pediatrician. He should be able to refer them to a qualified speech therapist for an independent diagnostic language assessment.

SPEECH DISORDERS

Speech patterns that interfere with communication and detract from what is being said and speech patterns that cause self-consciousness or apprehension are primary symptoms of a speech disorder. Although such disorders are often classified under the general category of language problems and the symptoms may appear to overlap, the two problems are actually separate phenomena with distinct characteristics and causes.

Language disorders usually occur when the brain has difficulty associating thoughts with the words that can express those thoughts. Such disorders are primarily of neurological origin, and may range from subtle to severe.

In contrast, many speech disorders are caused by physiological factors that interfere with the production of sound. In severe cases, these deficits may result in an inability to use the muscles or organs that produce sound.

Although most children with speech disorders appear to be physically normal, some manifest motor-coordination deficits, developmental delay, and behavior problems. (It should be noted that this latter characteristic is the result of the speech disorder, not the cause.) Approximately 15 percent of the children with speech disorders actually have measurable physical or neurological abnormalities. Specific genetic and organic factors which can cause serious speech problems include:

1. Cleft palate
2. Physiological defects in the mouth or jaw
3. Muscular paralysis of the larynx
4. Loss of the larynx
5. Brain damage
6. Nasal obstruction
7. Hearing loss

At the subtle end of the spectrum of speech disorders can be found the relatively common articulation problems which affect many young children. The child with articulation deficits has difficulty enunciating or pronouncing words properly. In severe cases, these deficits can render the child's communication all but incomprehensible. In less severe cases, the child may omit sounds (e.g., *at* for *cat*) and/or substitute one sound for another (e.g., *pag* for *bag*).[7] Children with articulation problems frequently distort words (e.g., *furog* for *frog*) or distort sounds such as *r* and *l*. (This symptom is sometimes referred to as lalling, a somewhat outdated term.) Other symptoms of a speech disorder include lisping,

---

[7]Word substitution, as opposed to sound substitution, is considered to be a language disorder, not a speech disorder.

stuttering, stammering, and cluttering. These deficits are the result of disturbances in speech rhythm and may be caused or exacerbated by genetic, physiological, or emotional factors.

There are many theories about the source of speech disorders. Research suggests that children who stutter have a higher incidence of central nervous system disorders. Children born prematurely and those born of multiple births also appear to be more predisposed to these types of speech problems. Attributing specific causes to stuttering is, however, controversial, and some authorities contend that there are no clearly defined causes.

The ability to articulate is acquired sequentially. A three-year-old might say *wawa* instead of *water* because he has not yet acquired the ability to pronounce *t*. His parents should not be alarmed by this. As the child matures, his articulation skills should improve.

Minor articulation problems often disappear of their own accord by age eight or nine. The child whose articulation skills do not improve as he matures may require speech therapy. The following chart indicates the approximate developmental stages at which children acquire specific articulation skills.

ARTICULATION SKILLS

Age	Sounds
3 years and 5 months	b,p,m,w,h
4 years and 5 months	t,d,g,k,ng,y
5 years and 5 months	f,u,s,z,
6 years and 5 months	sh,l,th

Parents should not be concerned if their four-year-old has difficulty pronouncing *l* because a four-year-old normally would not have acquired the developmental maturity to pronounce this sound properly. A six-year-old child, however, who cannot pronounce *b* may be manifesting a potential speech disorder.

Delayed speech may be the result of any of the following factors:

1. Deafness
2. Developmental aphasia
3. Mental deficiencies
4. Cerebral palsy

5. Mental illness
6. Personality disorders
7. Lack of motivation

Parents and teachers suspecting an articulation problem should insist that the child be evaluated by a speech therapist.

Other speech problems involve deficient voice production. Such disorders are characterized by deviations in loudness, pitch, duration, flexibility, and quality of sounds. Specific symptoms include harshness, hoarseness, nasality, and "breathiness."

Speech disorders can be a serious source of embarrassment for a child. Because the ability to communicate is one of the primary criteria by which children and adults are judged, the proper acquisition of language skills is of vital importance. Untreated language and speech disorders can warp a child's perceptions of himself and his world and can destroy his self-confidence. Common sense dictates that providing appropriate assistance is one of the wisest investments parents can make. The challenge of rebuilding a defeated child's self-image is invariably more heart-wrenching, time-consuming, problematical, and costly than the early diagnosis and treatment of a correctable speech disorder.

WRITTEN LANGUAGE ARTS PROBLEMS

The words that a person chooses to express his feelings, ideas, and perceptions can range from magical and awe-inspiring to mundane and incomprehensible. That one's words can so profoundly affect another person's thoughts and emotions underscores the importance of teaching children the craft of expressive language.

The capacity to write effectively is the product of a complex neurological and educational process. Although genetically based language aptitude can affect the efficiency with which a child is able to perceive, process, and express sensory data, inherited aptitude does not guarantee that a child will acquire superior language arts skills. The ability to communicate effectively must be developed and refined. Children lacking natural aptitude can be taught to communicate more effectively, and those possessing natural aptitude can be taught how to refine and perfect their inherent facility. The responsibility for providing the feedback, practice, and quality instruction requisite to the development of these skills falls squarely on the shoulders of teachers.

In order to encode (express) thoughts and emotions in writing, a child must first learn how to decode (decipher) the objects, events, and symbols in his environment. The foundation for this encoding/decoding process is established in infancy, and by the time the child enters school, he should have acquired his basic oral language skills. At the age of five, the primary arena for the subsequent development of communication skills shifts to the classroom. By means of carefully prescribed, sequential training, the elementary school student learns how to use written words to express his thoughts and feelings. If this sequential process is interrupted or impeded because of learning problems or inadequate instruction, the interference can undermine the development of higher-level language arts skills.

A child's eyes, ears, and sensory receptors are the conduits from the world of external experiences and symbols to the world of internal reactions, emotions, and thoughts. These conduits carry the sensory data from the environment to the central nervous system and the brain where it is filtered through the labyrinth of chemical and electrical circuitry. The brain decodes this data (accurately or inaccurately) and, if a verbal or written response is required, it then encodes the response (effectively or ineffectively) in the form of language. Under most circumstances, the brain has the capacity to process sensory data instantaneously. Within a microsecond, it can discriminate, associate, analyze, integrate, organize, and interpret a continuous barrage of stimuli in the form of words, symbols, and sensations. Within another microsecond, it can produce words and symbols which express its response to this data.

Communication is impeded when a child is unable to decode sensory data or link it with expressive words and symbols. Imagine a poet who is unable to describe the petals, stem, color, and shape of a rose. Without the capacity to perceive, discriminate, and associate impressions, the poet could not communicate his vision.

If a child is to find the words to express his perceptions, he, too, must be able to process sensory stimuli. These perceptual processing skills can not be developed without practice, feedback, and competent instruction. Each new writing assignment provides the child with an opportunity to perfect his ability to observe, think, analyze, and communicate his ideas and responses. As he progresses through school, he slowly develops the capacity to transform simple declarative sentences that communicate isolated ideas, facts, or feelings (e.g., "Yesterday we played football in the park") into more complex sentences. With practise, the child learns how to link these sentences to form paragraphs which express more intricate information, thoughts, and feelings. Ultimately, the child acquires the skills requisite to molding these paragraphs into cogent essays and reports that testify to his ever-expanding intellectual and educational development.

Certain children, of course, possess natural language aptitude. The origins of this aptitude are undoubtedly genetic. Researchers have actually pinpointed specific areas of the brain responsible for language output, and the research strongly suggests that the organic and neurological composition of these encoding areas of the brain affect expressive language aptitude.

Children with a natural facility for language generally master the mechanics of written expression with greater ease than those having less language aptitude. They quickly acquire self-editing skills. As a consequence, their essays and reports are more accurate, and their syntax (sentence structure) is more precise and aesthetically pleasing.

Even natural writing talent must be developed. Children with good language aptitude require instruction and guidance during the formative years of their language development. Like gifted ballerinas or basketball players, they, too, must be encouraged, coached, and critiqued.

Children lacking natural aptitude for language expression especially require coaching. Unfortunately, far too many American schools are providing less and less opportunity for children to practice written expression and receive meaningful criticism. The tradition of the weekly essay has been largely abandoned by some teachers who simply do not want to be burdened with the responsibility of grading essays and book reports. Because many younger teachers are themselves the products of an educational system which has de-emphasized written expression, they themselves often lack good writing skills.

As a consequence of the de-emphasis of language arts in school districts throughout the United States, many fifth- and sixth-grade students are not being required to write weekly book reports and essays. The consequences of abandoning this time-tested tradition have been calamitous. To improve their language arts skills, students must have their spelling, syntax, and grammatical mistakes corrected and critiqued. Practice and feedback are essential to this process.

A child with writing talent usually recognizes his natural facility at an early age. He derives pleasure from expressing himself and thrives on the praise that his writing elicits. A reinforcement, motivation loop is created. Knowing that he has the ability to write well, the good writer willingly takes the extra time and makes the extra effort to do a first-rate job.

Despite the fact that relatively few of the students in our school have natural writing talent, the vast majority can be taught to write intelligibly and effectively. When exposed to well-conceived teaching methods, even language-deficient, culturally disadvantaged, or intellectually handi-capped students can be taught to write grammatically correct sentences that clearly communicate their ideas and feelings. Those unable to master language arts skills generally have severe intellectual or neurological handicaps and represent a relatively small percentage of the student population.

The ingredients that produce effective language arts skills are quite basic:

1. Quality instruction and a well-conceived language arts program
2. An emphasis on writing skills in the curriculum
3. Adequate practice (regularly assigned essays, book reports, and term papers)
4. Meaningful criticism with an emphasis on training children to develop self-editing skills
5. Parental support for the student and the teacher (this means making sure the writing assignments are completed, handed in, and corrected)

Relatively few of the hundreds of thousands of American students with poor language arts skills have severe underlying language disabilities. In most instances, the language arts deficiencies of these students can be directly attributed to a lack of adequate exposure to one or more of the five factors listed here.

The child with poor language arts should be identified as early as possible. Usually, the first indications of a potential problem begin to manifest themselves in second, third, or fourth grade. Chronically poor grammar and punctuation, fragments and run-ons, and incomprehensible sentences are the primary danger signals. If untreated, these deficits can create serious impediments for the child in fifth, sixth, and seventh grade.

The following checklist has been designed to help parents determine if their child has a language arts problem. It is intended to be used to evaluate students in fourth grade and above; hence, most of the statements are not applicable to children in lower grades. Parents should ask their child's teacher to help them complete the checklist. The teacher will know which specific skills the child is expected to have mastered at a particular grade level.

LANGUAGE ARTS CHECKLIST

	YES	NO
Uses capital letters when appropriate	☐	☐
Uses correct punctuation	☐	☐
Sentence formation		
Avoids sentence fragments (sentences which do not contain subject and verb)	☐	☐
Avoids run-on sentences (too many ideas included in sentences)	☐	☐
Uses proper subject/verb agreement (e.g., ''the boy goes,'' not ''the boy go'')	☐	☐
Topic sentences express main idea of paragraph or essay	☐	☐
Paragraphs are well organized	☐	☐
Knows when to start new paragraph	☐	☐
Ideas are presented sequentially	☐	☐
Can summarize in writing what has been read	☐	☐
Spelling is essentially correct	☐	☐
Can identify parts of speech	☐	☐
Can express ideas within a reasonable time frame	☐	☐
Can edit own work and find most grammatical and syntactical errors	☐	☐
Essays and reports are written neatly and legibly	☐	☐

Interpreting the Checklist

A pattern of ''yes'' answers indicates that a child does not have a language arts problem. Conversely, a pattern of ''no'' answers suggests language arts deficiencies. Parents perceiving such a pattern should discuss their responses with their child's teacher, who may be able to make specific suggestions about how the child might improve language arts skills.

Specialized developmental language arts materials and workbooks that can help a child acquire greater writing proficiency are available in teacher supply stores. If the child's writing deficits are chronic, he may qualify for special assistance from the school's resource specialist. Parents who discover that their child does not qualify for learning assistance should consider engaging a qualified tutor who has taught writing skills or enrolling their child in a private language arts program.

TEACHING STUDENTS TO BE RETARDED

The high school classroom looked like a clubhouse. The room contained a comfortable sofa, a stereo, big pillows on the floor, and posters on the walls. While the teacher sat at her desk reading a magazine, her students listened to music or chatted with their friends. The teacher later explained that this "socializing time" was vital to developing social awareness.

All of the junior and senior students in the class, who ranged in age from sixteen to eighteen, had been identified as EMR (educably mentally retarded). The curriculum was designed to prepare the students for the "outside world" and focused on teaching basic survival skills. The ultimate goal of the program was to help the students find employment when they graduated.

From what I could observe, the occupational and vocational training consisted of the teacher helping the students fill out sample application forms for jobs and driver's licenses. Occasionally, students would wander back to their desks and practice filling out one of these forms. If they had questions, they would go to the teacher, and she would help them. Most of the time, however, was spent talking, listening to music, or flirting.

The students in the class ate their lunch at eleven o'clock. After the "regular" students finished their lunch, the boys served as part-time school janitors. They cleaned up the lunch area and emptied the trash cans. For performing this service, they were paid a minimum hourly wage.

The teacher informed me that most of her students were functionally illiterate. Only five of the fourteen students in the room spoke English as their native language. Eighty percent represented minorities.

As I chatted with several of the teenagers, I was surprised to discover that the Spanish-speaking students were quite articulate when talking to me or their friends in their native language. Each, however, had accepted the fact that he or she was mentally deficient. Having acquiesced to this, they had also accepted that they were being groomed for their rightful roles in life—to do menial work. Although I had not seen their IQ scores, nor had observed how the IQ tests were administered, I intuitively sensed that some of these students were far more capable than the school psychologist, the teacher, or the students themselves believed. If I were correct in my perceptions, I had observed a tragic waste of human potential.

LANGUAGE AND CULTURAL FACTORS

The child who does not speak English fluently can easily be victimized by the American educational system. Significant language deficits and divergent cultural values can so seriously distort the student's classroom and test performance that a potentially capable child with severe language or culturally based learning problems may be erroneously identified as retarded. The results of standardized academic tests are particularly suspect. IQ test results may also be spurious when the student being tested is not a native speaker.

Our educational system and its testing protocols are oriented toward students who are able to understand and communicate in spoken and written English. Those who are unable to do so may become so overwhelmed by the seemingly impossible challenge of trying to survive in a middle-class, English-oriented curriculum that they simply give up.

Unintentionally, our educational system frequently disserves the non-English speaker. Although special programs, such as bilingual and ESL (English as a second language) classes, have been developed specifically for language deficient students, they have often proven inadequate.

The challenge of providing a quality education for language-deficient children from other cultures is complex and does not lend itself to a facile solution. Thousands of highly dedicated teachers and educators have devoted their energies to providing for the needs of these students. Nevertheless, despite the professed goal of ultimately integrating children from other cultures into the mainstream of American education, seriously language-deficient and/or culturally deprived children are far too often shunted into programs for the learning disabled or the retarded. Others are simply allowed to vegetate for twelve years and emerge from the educational production line functionally illiterate. As the previous anecdote clearly underscores, the implications of misdiagnosing language-deficient students can be disastrous.

It should be noted that the child with language problems may also have specific learning disabilities. Because of underlying perceptual processing deficits, he may be unable to process sensory information in the form of spoken or written language, and his language skills development may be impeded.

The overlap of language and learning problems can complicate the accurate identification of the needs of the language-deficient student. Ironically, many children with language deficiencies in English are also deficient in their native language. This is especially true when children speak a dialect with their family or friends, or when they speak their native language only in limited contexts.

Subcultures that de-emphasize education, or that place little value on academic achievement, tend to produce children with academic problems. This reality may obscure the true source of the learning problems experienced by children living in ghettos. The chronically inattentive child who reads poorly has difficulty learning because of a misdiagnosed learning disability. Cultural influences may be only tangentially responsible for the problem. Before an appropriate, individualized remediation strategy can be designed, it must be determined if the child's deficits are the result of learning problems, disinterest, poor teaching, cultural factors, or lack of parental support. If the diagnostic testing of the language-deficient or culturally disadvantaged child is to have validity, the assessment must take into consideration the child's home and social environment.

Culturally biased tests penalize the child who has not been exposed to experiences that reinforce the values and objectives of the American educational system. The child's lack of facility with English must also be factored into the assessment equation. Disregarding the underlying factors responsible for poor academic performance significantly increases the risk of an inadequate diagnosis and a subsequently inadequate education.

MENTAL RETARDATION

In most school districts in the United States, two primary criteria are used to identify the mentally retarded child (some school districts are now using the term "mentally delayed" instead of mentally retarded):

1. The child's level of intellectual functioning is determined to be below 70 on an IQ scale.
2. The child's behavior is determined to be nonadaptive.

Mental retardation generally affects a child in four overlapping areas: education, health, emotions, and social interaction. Usually, mental retardation is associated with a pattern of specific deficiencies. Although these deficiencies vary, depending on the degree of retardation, they typically affect the ability to concentrate, organize, remember, use language, and develop socially acceptable behavior.

In some instances, the characteristics that signal possible mental retardation can be identified during infancy and early childhood. The symptoms include:

1. Difficulty applying academic skills to daily life situations (e.g., figuring out proper change in a store)
2. Difficulty applying appropriate reasoning and judgment to solving problems (e.g., "What do we have to do to get there on time?")
3. Difficulty acquiring acceptable social skills

The retarded child's awareness of the fact that he is "different" may cause him to experience more anxiety than other children.[8] Because the child has greater difficulty acquiring academic skills and grasping concepts, he often begins to anticipate failure, especially when he is confronted with challenging tasks and projects. To protect himself emotionally, he may acquire a rigid set of behaviors that mimic or imitate the behaviors of others who are not retarded. For instance, a retarded child may look to other children for cues as to what is right or wrong because he does not trust himself to make certain types of social decisions.

[8]These general characteristics do not apply to all retarded children. See the discussion of Down's syndrome and PKU on page 115.

Articulation deficits, limited vocabulary, poor auditory and visual processing skills, and poor grammar create serious language and communication obstacles for retarded children. These language deficiencies can make social adjustment all the more difficult.

As a general rule, retarded children respond positively to rewards and many work hard to achieve praise, money, or comfort. These rewards can be used as effective incentives and reinforcements for achievement.

IQ scores are the primary criterion used by educators to classify retarded children. In most states, three common educational classifications are used to distinguish the different levels of retardation: EMR (educably mentally retarded), TMR (trainably mentally retarded), and PMR (profoundly mentally retarded).

Children are classified as EMR when their IQ range is 55 to 70 (in some states 50 to 75). EMR students are capable of mastering basic academic skills such as reading, writing, and math. In most cases, children classified as EMR can become economically self-sufficient. When EMR students graduate or leave school, few appear to be blatantly retarded. Those who complete their education and master basic survival, academic, and vocational skills are generally able to hold jobs, marry, and become responsible parents and citizens.

Children classified as TMR have IQ scores that are in the 25 to 55 range. The TMR student can usually read very basic words and can master elementary number concepts. Few TMR adults, however, become totally self-sufficient. Most require varying degrees of supervision and financial support.

Children classified as PMR have IQ scores under 25. From an educational standpoint, the primary objective is to help these children acquire basic self-help skills. Some of the more severely retarded, however, do not achieve this objective. Those classified as PMR will need continued care and supervision as adults and will not be able to function without supervision and financial support.

The point at which a definitive diagnosis of mental retardation can be made varies and depends on the nature of the child's retardation. Children ultimately diagnosed as EMR are seldom identified until they enter school. Because their appearance and social behaviors are usually normal, these children are referred for testing to the school psychologist only when it becomes apparent that they are having serious difficulty mastering academic material.

Marginally retarded children who are not properly identified are sometimes retained (i.e., repeat a grade level) while in elementary school. This "solution" is at best a stop-gap measure that is used most frequently in school districts which do not have adequate testing and learning assistance programs. Most school districts, however, do provide special programs with less demanding curricula for EMR students. School districts without special programs are required by federal law to make alternative arrangements for the education of EMR children.

Diagnosis of TMR and PMR children typically occurs at an earlier age than diagnosis of EMR children because the symptoms are more profound. Usually, the pediatrician will be the first to recognize and identify the physical and developmental deficits.

Certain medical conditions and genetic factors normally alert physicians to the possibility of retardation. These include gross developmental delays involving atypical patterns of sitting, crawling, walking, speech, toilet training, socialization skills, and common sense. Severely deficient gross-motor and fine-motor skills may also indicate possible retardation. Although these motoric deficits may be symptomatic of retardation, such deficits could be symptomatic of a perceptual dysfunction or neurological damage. The entire spectrum of symptoms must be examined before an accurate diagnosis can be made. Other characteristics of retardation include facial disproportions, abnormalities of the eyes, ears, and fingers, and certain skin conditions.

Mental retardation may result from many factors including complications during pregnancy, a family history of retardation, exposure to disease, accidents, or infections. Genetic factors can also play a significant role. Down's syndrome, which affects approximately 10 percent of the moderately to severely retarded children, is the result of a chromosomal defect. The condition occurs more commonly when women conceive after the age of thirty-five; recent research suggests that the father's age may also be a factor. The overall incidence of Down's syndrome is 1 child per 600 live births.

Distinctive physical and personality traits are associated with specific types of retardation. The physical characteristics of Down's syndrome include flattened facial features, a small nose with a low bridge, upward slanting eyes (the result of epicanthic folds of skin), colored spots in the iris of the eyes, flattened back skull, small ears, small mouth, furrowed tongue surface, and fine, thin, straight hair. In general, those affected by Down's syndrome are basically happy and good-natured and appear to have less severe emotional disturbances than TMR and PMR children.

PKU (phenylketonuria) is another genetically based condition which causes an enzyme deficiency. The physical and personality characteristics of children with PKU are quite distinct from those with Down's syndrome. PKU characteristics include fair skin, blond hair, blue eyes, eczema, undeveloped tooth enamel, and seizures. Fifty percent of the children affected with PKU have microcephaly (abnormal smallness of the head). Unlike children with Down's syndrome, those affected by PKU tend to be unhappy and unfriendly. The behavioral symptoms include emotional instability, aggressiveness, temper tantrums, and schizophrenic outbursts.

A large percentage of mentally retarded children can be educated and can learn to become self-sufficient and productive members of society. Even the more severely retarded children can be trained to contribute to their own welfare and to function with varying degrees of independence. With extra love, parental support, and good teaching, many retarded children can learn to maximize their potential and enjoy many of life's rewards.

CHAPTER 6

Emotional Problems and Learning Disabilities

STEVE: NO ONE WAS LISTENING

It was Friday morning, and the buzzer had just sounded. As the ninth graders left the classroom, they placed their quizzes on my desk. A student who had been in my class for approximately six weeks handed in his test, picked up his books, and left the room.

The student's name was Steve, and later when I was grading the quizzes, I noticed that he had drawn a chain of little circles through all his answers. Although I could still read the answers with some effort, I was annoyed that he had chosen to cross them out.

At the time, I was working on a graduate degree and teaching two periods a day at a local high school. Being a new teacher, I felt that it was essential that I establish and clearly define my standards and requirements for my students. I decided to give Steve an F on the quiz. On the top of his paper I wrote: "Why did you cross out your answers?" When I returned his quiz the following Monday morning, I asked Steve the same question. He smiled, shrugged, and responded, "I don't know."

After leaving my class that Monday, Steve went to his English class, where he received an F on a report he had handed in the previous week. After English class, he went to the gym and informed the freshman basketball coach that he had decided to quit the team. From there he returned home, went to his father's dresser, took out a revolver, pressed the barrel

116

to his temple and, while his three-year-old sister watched, pulled the trigger.

When I learned of Steve's suicide the next day, I was devastated. I had hardly known the boy, and frankly, he had not been one of my favorite students. He seldom contributed in class, and he hadn't seemed particularly interested in what I was teaching. Shocked and profoundly saddened by the tragedy, I began to examine my own role in what had happened.

Three days prior to Steve's suicide, I had attended a lecture in an educational psychology course which had dealt with behavior modification. The essence of this methodology is to reward children when they meet or surpass the established standards and to alert and/or punish them if they do not fulfill the requirements. The reward is called a positive reinforcement and the punishment is called a negative reinforcement. I felt that I had followed these precepts exactly. What had gone wrong?

The next day I approached the professor after his lecture. "What would you have done if one of your high school students had drawn a chain of circles through all of his answers on a quiz?" I asked. He responded, "I would have recognized that there was something troubling the student, and would have talked with him to find out what it was." I was crushed. I wanted him to tell me that I had handled things properly and that I shouldn't feel bad. But obviously I had not handled things properly, and Steve was dead.

The reasons for Steve's suicide became apparent as I pieced the story together. Steve's father was a physician who had the highest expectations for his son. He wanted his son to be like him—the best at everything he did. He expected Steve to make the basketball team and to be an A student. At some point, Steve must have realized that he couldn't fulfill—or didn't want to fulfill—his father's expectations, and he began to sabotage himself in school. His decision to fail expressed not only his rejection of his father's values, but also his own sense of hopelessness and worthlessness. When he finally realized that failing would not permit him to escape the stress and depression, he must have seized on suicide as the only recourse for resolving his inner turmoil. With this anguished and senseless act of self-destruction, Steve freed himself from the pain, futility, and anger that overwhelmed him.

Although it was possible that Steve had a learning disability, it is unlikely that a specific learning disability was the exclusive or even the primary source of his academic problems. There had been no prior evidence that the fourteen-year-old had any specific, identifiable learning deficits. The more I delved into his background, the more convinced I became that his poor school performance was caused by imploding, conflicting emotions that he could not placate.

Like so many profoundly unhappy children, Steve wore a mask. He affected indifference and unconsciously used this facade to camouflage his anguish from others and from himself. Offended by his lack of enthusiasm in my class and preoccupied by my own needs to be competent and appreciated, I had failed to look beneath the mask. The consequences of this failure had been tragic.

RECOGNIZING THE ANGUISHED CHILD

The child who affects smugness, toughness, resistance, or indifference is invariably unhappy, insecure, and frightened. Unconsciously deluding himself that his mask deflects attention from his disowned feelings, the child fails to realize that his behavior is actually a red flag that signals his emotional distress.

Unfortunately, parents and teachers do not always see the flag. Sometimes, the anguished child's behaviors are so distressing that parents and teachers become fixated on the behavior and do not recognize that the behavior is a complex and often desperate defense mechanism. These parents and teachers may become so intent on disciplining the child that they neglect to delve beneath the surface and identify the underlying source of the child's negative behavior.

Parents who do recognize that a child is struggling to cope with emotional discord have two basic choices: They can do nothing in the hope that the behaviors and the discord will disappear of their own accord, or they can provide the means by which the child can begin to resolve his unhappiness. Those who choose the first option must recognize that deep-seated emotional disharmony seldom disappears of its own accord. Although the manner in which a child manifests his emotions may change as he becomes older, the underlying feelings will continue to affect and control him in one way or another. As an adult, the chronically angry child may manifest his unhappiness through abusiveness, alcoholism, or criminality. The chronically depressed child may ultimately become a recluse, a prostitute, a junkie, or a mental patient.

Although an unhappy child can, of course, "turn his life around," he can seldom do so without help.

Children learn at a very early age to hide their negative feelings. Explosive anger, jealousy, fearfulness, and resentment are behaviors whose expression is discouraged at home and in school. Children may attempt to disown their feelings because they have unconsciously concluded that these feelings are unnatural or "bad." Society, of course, reinforces the repression of negative feelings. Children are taught that only *bad* children hate or hurt others and that *good* children are always loving, responsible, and respectful. When a child concludes that his innermost feelings are "bad," he may then quite logically conclude that he, too, is bad. To cope with his badness, he may pretend that his feelings do not exist, or he may decide to punish himself by sabotaging himself. Some children may act out their negative emotions by pressing their parents' and teachers' "hot buttons," knowing that in so doing they will probably be punished. By orchestrating their own punishment, they may be attempting to atone for their "badness." Although these self-defeating acts may be quite willful, the children are rarely consciously aware of the underlying motives for their actions.

Suicide is the ultimate expression of a child's disowned emotions. The child overwhelmed by pain, frustration, futility, anger, and feelings of worthlessness may become convinced that self-destruction is the only solution to his problems. Tragically, American children are now destroying themselves at the rate of one suicide every fourteen minutes. Suicide is now one of the primary sources of death among teenagers and has become epidemic in some communities. The antidote to this epidemic is the early identification and treatment of the potentially suicidal child. This early identification and treatment is possible if parents and teachers train themselves to recognize the behaviors and symptoms that signal a child's dispair.

IDENTIFYING EMOTIONAL PROBLEMS

Emotional problems can academically immobilize a child. Whereas a child with specific learning disabilities usually can be identified and treated in school, the child with subtle to moderate emotional problems usually requires services that most school districts do not provide. (In fact, in some high schools, school counselors have actually been eliminated because of budgetary restraints.)

The quality of programs for emotionally disturbed children varies from state to state. Despite this variance, all states are mandated by federal law to provide for the educational needs of children who cannot function in a regular classroom. Some states, counties, and school districts fund special schools. Others find it more cost-effective to pay the tuition charges for private programs.

Like their adult counterparts, insecure children learn to repress their feelings and to hide their weaknesses and insecurities from others and from themselves. They may attempt to camouflage their fear with toughness or their self-doubt with aggressiveness. They may pretend to be happy when they are really unhappy. They may feign indifference when their feelings are actually very intense.

Because a child may try to repress unwanted or unmanageable feelings, his emotional problems may not become apparent to parents and teachers until after much emotional damage has been done. To protect himself from pain, the child often develops an elaborate system of coping and defense mechanisms that may be all but impenetrable. If the child is confused and frightened by his feelings, he may deny their existence, hoping somehow that they will go away. The denial is, of course, unconscious. A smiling, seemingly happy-go-lucky child may actually be a seething cauldron inside. Another child may give vent to his anger by means of sarcasm, manipulative behavior, or indifference. The facade the child presents to the world may be so effective that his parents and teachers may fail to recognize the conflicting emotions which are torturing the child and causing the behavior.

A child may also be deceived by his own facade. He may be convinced that he is ok and have no idea how unhappy and angry he is inside. Telltale signs, however, often signal the underlying feelings. When a seemingly well-adjusted child teases his little sister unmercifully or a seemingly confident child is compelled to control others, he is broadcasting his inner turmoil.

The child with emotional problems may manifest many of the same learning deficits as does the child with a learning disability. This overlapping of symptoms may result in misdiagnosis and improper treatment. A learning problem may be inaccurately identified as an emotional problem, and an emotional problem may be inaccurately identified as a learning problem.

The identification process is further complicated by the fact that there is frequently a reciprocal relationship between learning and emotional problems. Although a learning problem can cause emotional problems, the converse is also true. The child who is intent on sabotaging himself or the child who is indifferent, chronically angry, or withdrawn rarely achieves academically. His internal discord makes it all but impossible for him to work at a level commensurate with his potential.

The internal disharmony experienced by children with emotional problems invariably spills over into the external environment. These children are often caught up in a complex and desperate struggle not only with themselves, but also with their parents. Sometimes this struggle is obvious, and other times not. The child who purposefully chooses to fail is making a statement about how he feels about himself.

Had Steve, the teenager described in the introductory anecdote, been evaluated by a school psychologist, he most likely would have been diagnosed as an underachiever. The school psychologist's tests might have identified specific learning deficits and perhaps even the boy's underlying emotional turmoil.

A clinical psychologist or psychiatrist would have undoubtedly diagnosed Steve as being alienated, troubled and desperately in need of therapy. A family therapist or social worker probably would have identified serious disharmony within the family system and would have recommended family therapy. Unfortunately, Steve had never been evaluated by a mental health professional. Undiagnosed and untreated, he was left to his own devices, with tragic consequences.

The learning problems of an emotionally disturbed child can rarely be remediated exclusively by a tutor or learning disabilities specialist. Before he can make academic gains, the anguished child must be helped to confront and resolve the emotions responsible for his unhappiness. Unless he is provided with counseling or psychotherapy, he is destined to continue struggling and ultimately will become overwhelmed by his psychological disharmony.

DOUG: THE VICTIM OF
A MESSY DIVORCE

A cute little boy of seven with a mischievous smile and sparkling eyes entered my office with his parents. His name was Doug, and he was in second grade. Doug had been referred to me by the headmaster of his private school because the child was fighting a valiant but losing battle to keep up with his class.[1]

My diagnostic evaluation revealed a classic textbook profile of specific learning deficits. The symptoms included poor fine-motor coordination (sloppy and illegible penmanship), poor concentration (inattentiveness and daydreaming), poor visual tracking (inaccurate oral reading), and poor reading comprehension.

Despite his learning problems, Doug appeared to be well adjusted and happy. His parents, however, were quite concerned about his lack of progress in school, and they were anxious to have us work with him. This concern was shared by the headmaster and Doug's teacher. Both expressed serious reservations about the seven-year-old's ability to handle the school's accelerated curriculum.

Doug's parents reported no significant family or medical problems. The testing and the background information provided by his teacher and parents indicated that the child had a moderate learning disability. Although not severe, his learning problems required immediate attention, especially in view of the fact that Doug was attending a demanding private school with a highly accelerated curriculum.

Having identified Doug's learning deficits, I proposed a learning assistance strategy to his parents. The program would provide intensive training activities designed to correct the child's perceptual processing dysfunction and his fine-motor and visual-motor deficits. Phonics and reading comprehension would also be emphasized.

After twelve hours of remediation, the staff observed a noticeable improvement in Doug's academic skills. The child seemed quite pleased

[1] It may appear from many of the anecdotes in this book that most of the students at our center attend private schools. This is not the case. Approximately 25 percent of the children we work with at our clinic are enrolled in private schools. In many instances, these schools do not offer specialized learning assistance and consequently refer struggling students to outside agencies.

with his progress, and his classroom teacher reported that his school work had improved significantly.

Suddenly, Doug's classroom performance deteriorated. He forgot basic skills that he had mastered. He seemed incapable of paying attention or following directions. His handwriting became sloppy again. Whenever he encountered the slightest frustration, he would become resistant or cry.

It was clear that Doug was experiencing serious emotional turmoil. Although I had worked with many learning disabled children who had temporarily regressed during the remedial process, I sensed that there was something more profoundly amiss.

When I conferred with Doug's father, I discovered that he and his wife had decided to divorce. The divorce proceedings were bitter, and the parents were very angry at each other. In a misguided attempt to be "fair," they had given Doug the option of deciding with which parent he was going to live. Under the circumstances, it would have been impossible for the child not to have been distracted in school. He was being asked to make a monumental decision, that he was not emotionally equipped to make. The child had been placed in a double bind. Loving both parents, he could not help but feel overwhelming guilt when forced to choose between them.

A basic learning disability was now compounded by a serious family problem. It was clear that the child's emotional needs took precedence over his academic needs. Either his parents or the court would have to take responsibility for working out the details of his custody before any further academic gains would be possible. I strongly urged family counseling, not to save the marriage, but to save the child.

DIFFERENTIATING EMOTIONAL PROBLEMS FROM LEARNING PROBLEMS

The line delineating an emotionally based learning problem from a perceptually based one is not always clear. The behavioral characteristics common to both types of problems include disruptive behavior, indifference, resistance, sloppy work, daydreaming, incomplete assignments, difficulty paying attention, and difficulty following instructions. Few parents are trained to distinguish between a "simple" and a more complex emotionally based problem, and most will have to rely on professionals to provide an assessment.

The advice from professionals can sometimes be confusing and conflicting. The family pediatrician may recommend medication to calm the child. The classroom teacher may recommend retention. The psychologist or psychiatrist may recommend individual or group therapy. The family therapist may recommend family therapy. And the private learning disabilities specialist may recommend perceptual training. When faced with a myriad of sometimes conflicting recommendations and diagnoses, parents have no choice but to rely on their intuition. They must trust the advice that "feels" right and be guided accordingly. In the end, parents must follow the advice of the professional who has the most credibility. Before making the final decision, parents may need to consult several professionals. This process of seeking a confirmation of the diagnosis can be both expensive and time-consuming. Dealing with the consequences of doing nothing or making the wrong decision, however, ultimately can be far more costly.

A child who has a poor self-concept because he is not succeeding academically generally does not require psychotherapy or long-term counseling. If the child's poor self-image is directly attributable to school failure and frustration, his self-image should improve as his learning problems are remediated. Once he becomes convinced that he can succeed in school, his feelings about himself and his abilities usually will become more positive. However, the longer the child is forced to suffer with his learning disability, the more difficult it becomes to repair the associated emotional damage. Without help, the child's self-concept will probably continue to deteriorate. Fortunately, learning assistance implemented during the first critical years of elementary school can significantly reduce the risk of self-concept damage.

Parents and teachers have a compelling responsibility to help the learning disabled child acquire the emotional resources that can sustain him during the difficult times. They must recognize that the child's self-esteem is the resource most threatened by a learning disability, and that this most precious resource must be protected and nurtured.

Parents and teachers must intentionally create a context in which a child can experience success and learn to enjoy and appreciate his uniqueness as a human being. The success need not be monumental, at least at first, but the child must ultimately become convinced that success is within the realm of possibility. Those parents and teachers who orchestrate opportunities for a struggling child to "win" are practicing affirmative parenting and teaching. Providing this experience of winning is the most effective means that parents have for building and rebuilding the self-esteem and self-confidence of the demoralized child.

It is sometimes possible to coordinate counseling and learning assistance for the academically struggling child with emotional problems. As a general rule, however, the child will probably need to make inroads into his emotional problems before he can make substantive progress in resolving his learning problems.

By attempting to repress his negative feelings and by forcing his feelings into compartments within his mind and locking the door to the compartments, the unhappy or distraught child may give the appearance of being ok. This appearance, however, is an illusion. Before the child can begin to function effectively in school and in life, he must be helped to unlock the doors to the rooms that contain his disowned emotions.

SCOTT: TERRIFIED BY ANYTHING NEW

The woman on the phone sounded very distressed. She requested that I test her eight-year-old son as soon as possible for a learning disability.

On the day scheduled for our appointment, the mother came into my office and informed me that her son refused to get out of the car. She explained that the boy, Scott, was always frightened by new situations, and his reaction to coming into my office was very typical.

I went out to the car to talk to the child. When he saw me coming, he jumped out of the car, picked up a big rock, and climbed onto the roof of the car. I could see the terror reflected in his eyes, and I realized that talking with him now would be fruitless. The child's mother and I went back into my office. I suggested that she observe one of our classes and pay no attention to her son. We left the door to the observation room open.

After about twenty-five minutes, Scott got down from the top of the car. From a vantage point far from the door, he could see his mother in the observation room. Slowly he began to move closer and closer to the door. He seemed curious about what his mother was doing in there. Finally, Scott came right up to the doorway and asked her what she was doing. She replied that she was watching some children in a class who were being helped with their reading and spelling. Scott also began watching. After about ten minutes, I asked him if he would be willing to come into my office with his mother so that I could test him and find out if he needed help in reading, too. He agreed.

When I tested Scott, I discovered that he had significant learning problems. It was also very clear that he had serious emotional problems.

Scott urgently needed psychotherapy. When I discussed this need with his mother, she refused to accept my recommendation. She would only consider learning therapy for her son.

I agreed to work with Scott in the hope that ultimately I would be able to establish enough credibility with the mother to convince her of the absolute necessity of taking her child to a psychiatrist or clinical psychologist. I had no illusions about being able to correct Scott's emotional problems at our learning center. His problems were profound, and we were educational therapists, not psychotherapists. I knew that the child's learning problems could not be resolved without psychotherapy. His mother, however, was not yet willing to admit the seriousness of her son's emotional problems. She would need to be convinced.

I designed an interim academic support system for Scott. As I suspected, we only were able to make modest gains. Scott's profound inner turmoil defeated our efforts. After several months, I finally succeeded in persuading Scott's mother to have her son evaluated by a child psychiatrist. The therapist concurred that Scott had serious emotional problems, and she convinced the mother to enroll Scott in a private school for children that provided the services of a psychiatrist, a clinical psychologist, and a social worker.

COMMON SYMPTOMS OF AN EMOTIONAL PROBLEM

There is a reciprocal relationship between a child's emotions and his academic performance. Each can affect the other. Because of overlapping symptoms, delineating the learning disabled child from one who has emotional problems, and identifying the child who has learning problems and emotional problems, can pose a difficult challenge, not only to parents, but also to teachers, pediatricians, even psychologists and psychiatrists.

A child's behavior is a barometer of his emotions. The spectrum of behavioral symptoms which signal an emotional problem is quite broad. The danger signals may be blatant or subtle. One child may act out his anger in the form of hostility or sarcasm. He may become a bully or prankster. Another may express his anger by attempting to control or manipulate others, or he may cope with his underlying feelings by repressing them and becoming shy or withdrawn. He may be unable to relate to other children and may have no friends. Another child may telegraph his internal conflict by means of bizarre or inappropriate behavior. He may act silly and immature, or he may be fascinated by fire or violence.

Although most parents can recognize chronically inappropriate behavior, many do not know how to respond to such behavior. At this juncture, they have two basic options: They can seek professional help, or they may allow the situation to persist in the hope that the problem will correct itself. The reluctance to seek assistance for the emotionally troubled child can have dire consequences. Emotional problems rarely disappear of their own accord. When left untreated, these problems tend to become more pronounced and entrenched.

The following checklist is intended to help parents recognize the blatant symptoms of potential emotional problems. The checklist is not intended to be definitive. Its function is to help parents decide if a psychological evaluation is advisable.

PROFILE OF EMOTIONAL PROBLEMS

	YES	NO
DISORGANIZED THINKING		
Lack of orientation (time, place, people)	☐	☐
Delusions (persecution, grandeur)	☐	☐
Sensory distortion (auditory and/or visual hallucinations)	☐	☐
NONADAPTIVE BEHAVIORS		
Withdrawal (seclusiveness, detachment, excessive sensitivity, inability to form friendships)	☐	☐
Tantrums	☐	☐
Superstitious activity (motor rituals which must be performed before doing a task)	☐	☐
Extreme mood changes	☐	☐

NONADAPTIVE BEHAVIORS
Excessive fantasizing   □ □
Phobic reactions (fear of people or germs)   □ □
Fixations (excessive and exclusive interest in something)   □ □
Suicidal tendencies   □ □

PHYSICAL DYSFUNCTIONS
Bed-wetting (in older children)   □ □
Incontinence (in older children)   □ □
Repeated stomachaches (also possibly a symptom of a phys-
   ical problem)   □ □
Sleep disturbances   □ □

Interpreting the Checklist

As parents complete the checklist, they should differentiate between occasional episodes of sleep disturbances, for example, and more chronic occurrences. A child may at times fantasize or have an occasional temper tantrum without being emotionally disturbed. Recurring symptoms warrant concern.

There are other behavioral characteristics which may also signal that a child is in conflict with himself, his family, or his environment. Although these symptoms do not necessarily indicate that a child has an emotional problem, recurring and/or excessive symptoms should alert parents to a possible problem which should be monitored closely. The characteristics include:

1. Explosive anger or hostility
2. Excessive fearfulness
3. Chronic bullying
4. Chronic lying
5. Depression
6. Excessive anxiety
7. Attempts to control self and others
8. Chronic manipulative behavior
9. Unwillingness to communicate

10. Chronic stealing
11. Fixations
12. Self-sabotaging behavior

The behavior of the child with emotional problems is a consequence of powerful psychological forces. These forces are often intertwined with fear, guilt, and confusion. To protect himself, the child may attempt to lock his emotions within compartments in his mind. The child's unconscious need to compartmentalize the underlying negative forces can be particularly compelling if he senses that his innermost emotions are tainted by anger and hostility. Of course, the child does not realize that his attempt at containment is doomed to failure. The underlying emotions will continue to exert control over his life.

As has been stated previously, parents can fall into the trap of becoming fixated on their child's negative behaviors and fail to perceive that the behaviors are symptoms of the problem, not the source. Although some behavioral psychologists feel strongly that it is possible to treat and correct the symptoms of the problem without addressing the source, others are equally convinced that a child must be helped to examine his underlying unhappiness, pain, and guilt before his behavior can change. In the case of the child with both emotional and learning problems, perhaps the ideal treatment strategy is to deal with both the symptoms and the source of the overlapping problems by combining behavior modification with traditional introspective therapy.

The child with emotional problems has limited options for coping with the underlying psychological forces that are controlling his behavior and emotions. If he expresses his feelings and permits his emotions to explode, he will act out. If he represses his feelings and forces his emotions to implode, he will become withdrawn, socially isolated, and depressed. The child who chronically lies, steals, bullies, resists, or acts irresponsibly is signaling his emotional pain. His parents or teachers must be able to identify and respond to these signals if he is to be helped.

Behavior is a window into the child. This window, however, is often covered by thick curtains. Although parents may not be able to push the curtains aside, they can sensitize themselves to the symptoms of their child's emotional discord and take the necessary steps to provide the help.

SELECTING A THERAPIST
OR COUNSELOR

Parents who conclude that their child would benefit from a diagnostic psychological evaluation must confront a difficult challenge: How do they select the best person to diagnose the problems and treat their child or their family?

Given the many different types of therapies, the selection process can produce much anxiety. One treatment method may prove more effective than another with a particular child or family. Despite the spectrum of treatment methodologies, the ultimate success of any technique hinges primarily on the skills, perceptiveness, and training of the therapist and on the trust, support, and respect that the therapist is able to engender.

Parents of children with psychological problems are often emotionally vulnerable and may feel ill-equipped to evaluate objectively the relative merits of different therapeutic techniques. Trusting one's intuition in this assessment process, however, is essential. A therapist may be highly trained and impressively educated, but if there is poor rapport between the therapist and patient, the efficacy of the treatment will be undermined.

Perhaps the safest way to select a therapist is to rely on the recommendation of someone respected by the parents. Primary sources of referrals include the child's pediatrician, the family physician, and trusted friends. Other sources include the school psychologist, the child's teacher, the school resource specialist, the family minister, or the local mental health association.[2]

The entire family must be willing to make a commitment to the therapy process if it is to be effective. Patience is also essential. Parents must recognize that emotional problems usually develop over the course of many years. It is unrealistic to expect that an emotional problem can be resolved in one or two sessions.

---

[2]The local mental health association can provide information about therapists in the community. When calling for an appointment, parents should not hesitate to ask about fees. The association may be able to recommend alternative counseling resources for families with limited finances.

CONFRONTING AN EMOTIONAL PROBLEM

The child who has acquired a distorted sense of himself and his world almost inevitably will develop emotional problems. Although the specific symptoms of a child's emotional problems vary, these problems usually share a common denominator: fear.

Many different factors can produce fear in a child. The most blatant sources usually involve some form of psychological and/or physical abuse of a child by his parents. There are, of course, many other less blatant causal factors. Parents, for instance, may have difficulty expressing their love, and their child may conclude that he doesn't deserve to be loved. He may become frightened by the resentment and anger he feels toward his parents. Unconsciously sensing hostile emotions within himself, the child may feel a profound sense of guilt which can in turn taint and distort all of the child's other emotions.

Understanding why a child has developed distortions in his perception of himself and his world is more difficult when a child's environment does not appear to be responsible for his emotional distress. The child's parents may do everything in their power to love and support him. They may be demonstrative in expressing their affection and may actively encourage family communication. They may be scrupulously fair in showing their love to each of their children. They may acknowledge each child's unique qualities and encourage each to express and develop these qualities. In short, they may be doing everything that ideal parents should do in raising their children. Despite this seemingly near-perfect job of parenting, one of their children may develop emotional problems. For reasons that seem to defy explanation, the child who appears to have excellent parents can sometimes become troubled and insecure, while the child with less than ideal parents can sometimes emerge relatively unscathed.

At one time or another, every parent loses patience or overreacts to a stressful situation. No parent is perfect, and there isn't a parent alive who hasn't regretted a misguided statement or action. Despite the inevitable mistakes that all parents occasionally make, minor errors in judgment generally do not cause emotional problems.

A single traumatic event, of course, can cause serious emotional damage, especially if the event triggers profound guilt, fear, or shame. Usually, however, children develop emotional problems as a result of an ongoing pattern of negative environmental conditions. For example, a child who is exposed to continual deprecation or explosive anger can not help but suffer emotional damage.

A child's emotional problems invariably affect the entire family's emotional health. Emotional problems tend to become enmeshed in a cyclical, counterproductive family system. The child's emotional turmoil causes him to act out. This behavior creates family stress, which in turn fuels additional turmoil and inappropriate behavior. Logic clearly dictates that the family dynamics must be realigned if this counter productive cycle is to be broken.

The objective of individual therapy is to help the child examine and resolve his underlying emotional disharmony, *not* to affix blame. The objective of family therapy is to help all the members of the family to examine their roles in the family dynamics, *not* to make one person responsible for the disharmony.

It may be advisable for the child with emotional problems to participate exclusively in individual therapy or for the entire family to become involved in the therapy process. The therapist should be able to assess the situation objectively and recommend the most appropriate therapy.

The prospect of counseling or psychotherapy can be very threatening to a child. If the child is frightened by feelings he has suppressed, he may resist the prospect of therapy because he realizes that he will have to deal with emotions he would prefer to disown. Confronting one's fears requires great courage. The natural instinct is to run away, and the child will need an extra measure of support, patience, and understanding from his family during the therapy process.

Children receiving therapy or counseling may attempt to extricate themselves by insisting that everything is fine and that they no longer need to continue in the program. Before deciding unilaterally to discontinue, it is essential that parents consult with the therapist. To allow the child to stop before he has worked through his problems could be a terrible mistake. The child who manipulates his parents into permitting him to discontinue therapy is unconsciously engineering another failure for himself.

Although parents undoubtedly will be curious about what is being discussed during their child's therapy sessions, they must accept that these sessions are subject to the same rules of confidentiality that safeguard an adult's therapy session. The therapist may be willing to discuss a child's progress with parents, but he would not be willing to reveal information that the child provided in confidence. To do so would damage the patient-therapist relationship, which must be built on trust. An exception to the rules of confidentiality would be made if the child's life or someone else's safety were in jeopardy.

Parents may have misgivings about seeking counseling or therapy for their child, themselves, or their family because they fear that the therapist will hold them responsible for their child's emotional problems. Like their child, they, too, may be reluctant to explore their innermost feelings and their family relationships. This reluctance can be particularly compelling when parents have unacknowledged marital problems or repressed feelings of anger, guilt, or hostility.

Therapy encourages people to look at what is going on in their personal lives and in their collective family life. Its purpose is to reveal alternative strategies for dealing with problems and to unlock psychological doors which may have slammed closed because of fear or misunderstanding. As repressed feelings are expressed and examined, there may be intermittent pain and joy. A commitment to the therapy process, however, can ultimately lead to a liberation from the fears, anger, and guilt that can distort the emotions of every member of the family.

The child who has emotional and learning problems is aware that he is different from his siblings and classmates. This sense of being different can cause profound feelings of isolation. If the child's coping and defense mechanisms involve socially nonadaptive behaviors, they will accentuate the fact that the child is different and intensify his sense of isolation. (See Chapter 8 for a more comprehensive discussion of defense mechanisms.)

The atypical child has atypical needs. He requires more patience, more assurance, and, usually, more firmness than the less troubled child. To identify the child's special emotional and academic needs and to respond appropriately to these needs demand exceptional sensitivity and parenting skills.

Parents are fallible, and even the best of parents occasionally may be oblivious or unresponsive to their child's needs. Even if parents are aware and responsive, they may recognize that they cannot handle their child's expressed or imploding anger, hostility, or depression. For such parents to admit their limitations and seek outside professional help is not a sign of weakness, but rather an indication of love, wisdom, and strength.

CHAPTER 7

Communicating with Your Child's Teacher

CHRISTINE: LEARNING THE RULES OF THE GAME

I could sense Christine's anger and resistance the moment she walked into my office. I could also sense her mother's anxiety. During the diagnostic assessment, the woman intently monitored everything her daughter did. At first, I attributed her concern to the fact that she herself was a teacher. Later, I realized that her anxiety was a major contributing factor to her daughter's academic problems.

The diagnostic tests confirmed the classroom teacher's assessment that the ten-year-old's academic skills were at or above grade level. The child's reactions to certain questions and tasks on the tests signaled a profound lack of self-esteem and self-confidence. Whenever she made a mistake, she would become either sullen and withdrawn, or she would berate herself for being stupid.

Christine's teacher reported that the fourth grader was having difficulty paying attention in class. She noted, however, that when Christine was working on an art project or something else that interested her, she could concentrate for an hour without looking up. Her selective capacity to concentrate suggested either an attention deficit disorder or underlying psychological stress.

As a teacher, Christine's mother was particularly sensitive to the notes she was receiving each week from her daughter's teacher that complained about the child's chronic distractibility and misbehavior in class. Despite above-grade-level test scores on standardized reading and math tests, the ten-year-old was unable to keep up with her class.

Christine was now refusing to do her homework and was expressing an intense dislike for her teacher and for school. Alarmed by the deterioration in her daughter's attitude and schoolwork, the mother had initiated several parent-teacher conferences. To the mother's dismay, these conferences had consisted mainly of the teacher's chronicling all of Christine's many shortcomings. Exasperated and frustrated by her inability to motivate the child or to get her to behave in class, the teacher pointed out that she was responsible for thirty other children who were eager to learn. She felt that it would be unfair to devote 30 percent of her time to supervising Christine.

Christine's mother had sat on "the other side of the table" during countless parent-teacher conferences. On these occasions, parents were soliciting information from her about their children. Now, she was the concerned parent desperately trying to find a solution to her own child's learning problems. She was perplexed and frustrated by the fact that the teacher seemingly had given up on Christine.

The teacher evaluation form completed by the classroom teacher indicated that Christine's primary deficits were in the areas of behavior, attitude, and work habits (facsimile of this form can be found on page 144). Her assignments were seldom completed on time and were invariably sloppy and illegible. The teacher also reported that Christine continually disturbed the other children in the class and was impulsive, hard to discipline, and resistant to help.

The strained relationship that had developed between the teacher and Christine concerned me. Suggesting that the child be transferred to another class was a potential solution to the personality conflict, but I had misgivings about such a strategy. If the child were rescued, she might conclude that her mom would save her every time she experienced difficulty. Helping Christine resolve her learning problems and her personality conflict with the teacher was a far preferable alternative. I sensed that if the child could succeed in school, her self-concept and her behavior would improve. Christine was at a critical academic and emotional juncture. She needed to learn a vital lesson: In certain situations she would have to accommodate herself to someone she might not particularly like.

In spite of my misgivings about transferring Christine to another class, I realized that this might prove necessary if the relationship between the child and her teacher could not be salvaged. Six months remained in the school year, and six additional months of negative feedback and conflict could result in serious self-concept damage. Unless there was intervention, I feared that Christine would develop a profound aversion to school.

Helping Christine acquire the capacity to concentrate more effectively was the immediate priority. To accomplish this, I recommended an individualized perceptual training program that would focus on developing her attention span. The academic component of the program would be practical and would address the immediate school crisis. It would stress attention to detail, handwriting, and organizational skills. A behavior modification system would be implemented at home to reinforce the clinical program. It was agreed that when appropriate, the clinic staff would assist Christine with her schoolwork. The learning therapy program would be structured to permit Christine to experience repeated opportunities for success and, in so doing, would provide her with lots of praise, support, and encouragement.

I proposed an incentive system to encourage Christine to do her assignments accurately and legibly and to complete them on time.[1] Realizing that the system would require the active cooperation and participation of the classroom teacher, I suggested that a conference be held at Christine's school so that we could involve the teacher in the proposed strategy. Visiting the school would also afford me an opportunity to observe Christine in class.

Given the child's sensitivity and her mother's anxiety, I strongly recommended that our staff take over the responsibility for monitoring the fourth grader's schoolwork. If we saw no improvement in her attitude and performance within three months, we agreed that she would be referred for a psychological evaluation.

At first, the classroom teacher was cautious about supporting the learning assistance/behavior modification strategy. Her initial caution, however, quickly dissipated when she began to see a dramatic improvement in Christine's attitude and work. She soon became highly supportive and enthusiastic. Each day the teacher completed a simple progress report that required approximately one minute of her time (a facsimile of this report can be found on page 158). This form was sent home with Christine each day to be initialed by Christine's mother. In this way, both the

---

[1] This system of incentives and consequences is discussed later in the section entitled "Monitoring Your Child's Performance" (see page 157).

child and her mother were provided with important information about the child's daily performance and effort.

It proved unnecessary to refer Christine for a psychological evaluation. Within four months of beginning the program, her schoolwork improved dramatically. As she realized that she was capable of succeeding, Christine became very enthusiastic about her progress. She discovered that she had choices. She could *choose* to concentrate, or not to concentrate. She could also *choose* to do good work, or to do poor work.

Christine's self-confidence and self-esteem soared, and her attitude about school underwent a remarkable transformation. She thrived on the acknowledgment and praise she received at our center, at home, and in school. As she became less resistant, her mother became less intense. By the end of the school year, Christine was one of the best students in her class. She and her teacher not only resolved their conflict, they actually became very fond of each other!

THE VITAL ROLE OF THE CLASSROOM TEACHER

A child does some of his most important learning during the first four years of his life. During these critical years, he acquires a sense of his own power to influence the world around him. He can smile, cry, pout, be good, or be bad. He soon discovers that his actions will usually elicit a reaction. When he is crabby, he will cause people to be upset. When he is happy, he will make others happy.

During the first four years of life, a child also discovers the limits of his power. He learns that there are standards of behavior to which he is expected to conform. He cannot bite or hit other children indiscriminately without being reprimanded. He learns that he must obey his parents, whether he wants to or not. As he gets older, more and more rules are imposed on him. He realizes that when he breaks the rules, he probably will be punished. If he fails to accept that there are consequences for misbehavior, he most likely will have difficulty throughout his life conforming to the codes and strictures of society.

During the early stages of his development, a child's sense of self is in flux. Sometimes the child is omnipotent. As a two-year-old, he only needs to say *daddy* for his parents and grandparents to go into ecstacy. Despite this capacity to elicit acknowledgment and praise, the child also confronts the fact that he is dependent on his parents and subject to their wishes. At bedtime, he has little choice but to go to bed. Although he may cry and make a fuss, he is required to acquiesce to his parents' rules.

The five-year-old who is deposited in his kindergarten classroom on the first day of school quickly realizes that his teacher's authority is an extension of his parents' authority. The teacher now has the power to give and rescind permission, to praise, and to punish. For five hours each day, the teacher will inculcate the social and academic skills that are intended to prepare him to succeed in a competitive world where he will be increasingly acknowledged and rewarded on the basis of his skills, intelligence, attitude, responsibleness, competence, and ambition.

School is the primary arena where the child's resources are put to the test. If he is socially and academically successful in this arena, his self-confidence and self-esteem will grow. If unsuccessful, his self-confidence and self-esteem will falter.

Although the foundation of a child's self-concept is created before he enters school, this foundation can be reinforced, extended, or dismantled as a consequence of his school experiences. As he matures, the child's appraisal of his own capabilities and potential can change in response to his environment. If the child's early school experiences are positive, they can produce mortar which is strong and resilient. If negative, the experiences can produce mortar which is fragile and brittle. By the age of seven, many children already have determined unconsciously whether they will be leaders, followers, or iconoclasts. Many also already have decided whether they will be achievers, underachievers, or nonachievers. Some even have determined by seven if they are to be winners or losers in life.

Children and adults can, of course, alter their self-concept, but they do not make such changes easily. In obvious and subtle ways, a child's life experiences influence the development of his self-image, which in turn reciprocally influences the nature of his life experiences. The child who feels good about himself will tend to seek positive experiences that reinforce his positive sense of self. Conversely, the child who doesn't feel good about himself tends to do things that reinforce his negative perceptions of himself. He may do so by continually getting into trouble or by repeatedly failing at everything he undertakes.

The influence of a child's teachers on the development of a child's self-esteem and self-image cannot be overemphasized. By reinforcing the rules, ethics, and values of society, teachers play a monumental role in shaping a child's attitudes and self-concept. While the teacher's ostensible role is to inculcate skills, he or she is also charged with the awesome responsibility of providing the child with continual feedback about his abilities and performance. The manner in which this feedback is communicated can either nurture or undermine the child's confidence and self-esteem. In the same way the teacher's praise and criticism can either stimulate or undermine effort, responsibility, and achievement. If the teacher's assessment of a student is off target, or if the teacher is indifferent, insensitive, prejudiced, incompetent, or simply burned-out, the child can be severely and permanently damaged.

HELEN: HER STUDENTS' PARENTS SERVED NOTICE

To fulfill a requirement of my graduate school program, I taught two periods a day in a local high school. A close friend in the same program taught two periods each day at a local junior high school. Helen's school was located near the Stanford campus, and many of her students' parents were in some way associated with the university. During September, several of these parents made a special point of visiting her class to introduce themselves.

The high school where I was teaching was located twelve miles from the university. The majority of my students came from working-class backgrounds. Their parents never visited my class, and unless I initiated a conference, I had no interaction with them.

In October both of our schools scheduled the traditional open school night. All of the parents of Helen's students attended her presentation. In contrast, only fifteen percent of my students attended my presentation.

Among the parents visiting Helen's class were many Stanford professors and two Nobel Prize winners. The parents listened respectfully as she carefully defined her educational objectives, explained her teaching methodology, and presented the criteria she would use to evaluate the students' progress. After the presentation was completed, the parents began to ask questions. Their questions were incisive and raised some issues that Helen had not considered. The parents were very interested in what their children were being taught and how she proposed to achieve her stated objectives. Although none expressed criticism, they served notice that they would be monitoring her teaching performance very closely. They clearly communicated that they would not lower their expectations simply because she was an intern teacher. They expected their children to master the skills specified in the curriculum. Although supportive, they made it clear that they would hold her accountable for achieving her stated objectives.

None of the parents attending my open house expressed any concerns about my educational objectives, nor did they raise any questions about my teaching methods. They appeared to trust me implicitly and to be somewhat in awe of my position as a teacher and my status as a graduate student at a prestigious university. Their primary concern seemed to be getting home as early as possible.

That evening, Helen and I compared our impressions of our first open school night. She was excited and, at the same time, apprehensive. I, on the other hand, felt somewhat complacent. That year Helen worked much harder preparing for her classes than I did. She also did a much better job of teacher.

PARENTAL INVOLVEMENT

The issue of parental involvement in education is controversial. Although some school districts and teachers welcome parental participation in the educational process, others do not.

The participation of parents in such organizations as the local PTA traditionally has been encouraged, but this involvement is often limited to sponsoring paper drives, helping out on the playground, or chaperoning field trips. Were a PTA member to attempt to become involved in formulating teaching philosophy or methodology, establishing academic priorities, or determining teachers' qualifications, they undoubtedly would encounter stiff opposition.

Most teachers resent parents "meddling" in their affairs for much the same reasons that physicians might resent nonprofessionals meddling in the affairs of the local community hospital. Professionals tend to establish territoriality, especially when they are convinced that laypersons can not understand fully the issues involved in their work. Unfortunately, some professionals may develop an inflated sense of their expertise, autonomy, and prerogatives. Teachers are no exception. Most would react quite negatively to suggestions from parents about how they should teach, grade papers, or run the classroom.

The right of parents to become involved in their child's education is not a license to interfere in the operation of the classroom or the school. Many educators would argue, with justification, that relatively few parents possess the professional expertise to formulate educational philosophy, develop curriculum, or critique a teacher's methodology. Although it is true that relatively few parents have the background to evaluate a teacher—unless the teacher's methodology is so blatantly flawed that the children are clearly suffering educationally—this lack of professional expertise does not negate the value of the parents' perceptions and insights. A parent, for instance, who sees a lack of structure or discipline in the classroom may be on target when he discusses this issue with the teacher and suggests more clearly defined guidelines for behavior and performance.

Parents do not have to be educators or Nobel Prize winners to sense intuitively that the teacher or a school is not meeting their child's academic needs. Those who are concerned, reasonable, and, when appropriate, persistent deserve the right to express their concerns. They have the right to expect that the school and teachers will carefully and objectively consider and examine the issues they raise, even if the parents' perceptions should ultimately prove inaccurate, excessive, or unwarranted. Parents, however, who are unreasonable, accusatory, hostile, or arrogant should anticipate justifiable resistance from both teachers and administrators.

When parents become actively involved in their children's education, they serve notice on schools and teachers that not only are their children being held accountable for their performance, but so, too, are the teachers and the administrators. Teachers, parents, and administrators share the same basic objectives—to help students become productive, self-sufficient, competent, and confident. In view of these mutually shared goals, they must recognize the value of working in tandem.

TEACHER FEEDBACK

The parents of children with learning problems have a critical need for information about how their child is functioning in the classroom. Without this data, it is impossible for parents to participate intelligently in the process of helping their child overcome learning problems.

General descriptions of a child's classroom performance provide little insight for designing a meaningful learning assistance strategy or an effective behavior modification program. Examples of nebulous descriptions include:

> "He's immature."
> "She's not keeping up."
> "She's reading below grade level."
> "He's creating a disturbance in class."
> "She's having trouble with math."

Although all of these statements may be accurate, they are not very precise. A specialist in the field of learning disabilities would probably respond this way:

> "In what way is he immature?"
> "How is she not keeping up with the class?"
> "What specific reading deficits does she have?"
> "What does he do that creates a disturbance in the class?"
> "Is she having difficulty with math concepts or math computations?"

The more precise and specific the teacher's input, the more prescriptive value the input has. To design a focused and effective remediation strategy, a resource specialist needs data. Without highly precise information, the efficacy of the remediation strategy can be jeopardized.

As has been emphasized repeatedly, parents also have a compelling need to know as much as possible about their child's academic deficiencies if they are to evaluate their options intelligently. A child who has a minor reading problem simply may require competent tutoring. However, if the child has an underlying perceptual dysfunction, he will need a more comprehensive learning assistance program. To provide the wrong type of assistance could have dire educational and psychological consequences. A seriously dysfunctional child may benefit most from placement in a full-time EH (educationally handicapped) class. A child with a less severe sensory processing problem may require only a daily session of thirty to sixty minutes with the resource specialist. The optimal learning assistance strategy clearly hinges on the nature and severity of the child's problem.

Parents who are presented with a range of remediation options, or even one specific recommendation, may find themselves caught up in a dilemma that they fell ill-equipped to resolve. Without clear, comprehensible, and precise input from the classroom teacher, they cannot evaluate properly the recommendations or their options. Those who lack data and who have reservations or concerns are at a severe disadvantage and risk making a possibly flawed decision. Adequate information is a requisite to making informed decisions.

Although a little knowledge can sometimes be dangerous, no knowledge can be disastrous. The more parents know about their child's learning problem, the more they can contribute to the remediation process in the form of support and, perhaps, even direction.

A copy of the teacher evaluation form that is used by our staff to get precise information about the nature of a child's learning disability follows. This form is sent to the regular classroom teacher of each child who is to be evaluated. If the child is in a special program, a second form is sent to his resource specialist. The form provides very specific information about how a child is functioning in the classroom. During the diagnostic evaluation, parents are also asked to record their perceptions about their child's academic performance, behavior, and attitude. Test results, the clinical impressions of the diagnostician, input from the teacher, and input from the parents are all integral and vital components in the assessment process.

The teacher evaluation form serves many important functions at our center. It provides information that helps the diagnostician make an accurate assessment. At the same time, it helps the clinic staff understand a child's academic strengths and weaknesses so that they can design the most effective remediation strategy.

The form can also be a valuable resource for the classroom teacher. It permits the teacher, who might otherwise describe a child's learning difficulties in nebulous terms, to identify the specific deficits more precisely. Once these deficits are identified, the teacher can then ideally assign appropriate remedial materials that will provide in-class support. These materials can supplement and reinforce the work of the resource specialist and/or the outside agency that is working with the child. Finally, the identification process also facilitates the establishment of definitive goals and the creation of specific teaching strategies.

TEACHER EVALUATION FORM

Code: 0 = Never   1 = Rarely   2 = Sometimes   3 = Often   4 = Always

BEHAVIOR

Easily frustrated .... _____
Short attention span .... _____
Social problems .... _____
Sensitive .... _____
Appears immature .... _____
Disturbs other students .... _____
Resistant to help .... _____
Difficulty concentrating ... _____
Overactive .... _____
Impulsive .... _____
Fidgety .... _____
Distractible .... _____
Poor self-concept .... _____
Impatient .... _____
Hard to discipline .... _____
Unhappy .... _____
Accident prone .... _____
Forgetful .... _____
Daydreams .... _____
Slow in completing tasks .. _____
Excitable .... _____
Unpredictable .... _____
Procrastinates .... _____
Difficulty accepting
    responsibility .... _____

MOTOR SKILLS

Gross-motor deficits .... _____
Fine-motor deficits .... _____
Clumsy .... _____
Awkward .... _____

Poor balance .... _____
Right/left confusion .... _____

ACADEMIC

Poor reading
    comprehension .... _____
Difficulty with sight word
    recognition .... _____
Difficulty with phonics .... _____
Difficulty with word-attack
    skills .... _____
Difficulty with blending
    skills .... _____
Omits syllables and word
    endings .... _____
Reverses letters and
    numbers .... _____
Inaccurate reading .... _____
Difficulty with
    handwriting .... _____
Inaccurate copying from
    blackboard .... _____
Inaccurate copying from
    desk .... _____
Difficulty with math
    computational skills ..... _____
Difficulty understanding
    math concepts .... _____
Difficulty working
    independently .... _____
Difficulty keeping up
    with class .... _____

ACADEMIC	and planning projects ... ____
Sloppy work habits .... ____	Leaves projects
Difficulty with spelling .... ____	incomplete .... ____
Difficulty verbalizing ...... ____	Difficulty following oral
Difficulty with language	directions .... ____
arts skills .... ____	Difficulty following
Difficulty organizing	written directions .... ____

Interpreting the Checklist

A pattern of 3s and 4s suggests that a child is manifesting the classic symptoms of a learning disability. Parents desiring to have their child diagnostically evaluated by the school psychologist may be able to use the form to support their request. Teachers responding to the statements on the form with "oftens" and "always" are clearly signaling that a child desperately needs to be tested and helped.

The teacher evaluation form can also be used to orient and focus the remediation efforts of the person providing learning assistance. Once the child's deficits have been identified, specific remedial methods can be used to correct the deficits. For example, a behavior modification strategy might be designed to help the highly distractible child, and an incentive program might be created for the child who does not complete his assignments on time. Were the form to reveal significant difficulty with motor coordination, the child might be enrolled in an adaptive physical education program. More subtle coordination deficits might be corrected by enrolling the child in a karate or gymnastics class.

Were the form to indicate that a child is having difficulty copying from the blackboard, an evaluation by an ophthalmologist or optometrist is clearly advisable. Glasses may be required, or the child may need to be placed closer to the blackboard. On the other hand, if the child does not have a visual impairment, he should then be tested for a visual dysfunction by the school psychologist or a learning disabilities specialist.

As they attempt to interpret the teacher's responses on the checklist, parents should focus primarily on the 3s or 4s. Although virtually every child daydreams, a child who chronically daydreams in class is at risk academically. This concentration problem should be considered a primary symptom of a learning problem. Unless the attention deficit disorder is treated, it will probably cause continued academic problems.

The teacher evaluation form is a diagnostic tool. It serves the same function as a questionnaire that a physician might ask a patient to complete before a physical exam. It is designed to alert the professional and the parent to a potential problem. The sooner the problem is accurately identified, the sooner appropriate treatment can begin.

Parents who are convinced that their child needs to be diagnostically evaluated and who encounter resistance from the school authorities may need to become assertive. Those who are thwarted in their effort to procure testing and remediation through the school district may need to seek help privately.

PARENT-TEACHER CONFERENCES

Quality communication between parents and classroom teachers is especially important in the case of the learning disabled child. Parents need to be apprised periodically of their child's academic status.

Parents who know which questions to ask can participate more actively, effectively, and intelligently in the remediation process. Penetrating questions serve notice on the school personnel that penetrating answers are required. By defining the child's problem, the teacher evaluation form can provide focus to parent-teacher conferences. Substantive issues can be examined, and substantive ideas for remediating the child's learning problems can be explored. The form can also be used to gauge progress. By periodically resubmitting the checklist to the teacher, parents can monitor their child's improvement.

Parents who suspect that their child has a learning problem will find it useful to request that the classroom teacher complete the checklist prior to their scheduled conference. They are advised to review the teacher's responses before the meeting. During the conference, the child's specific deficit areas can be examined and remediation options and strategies can be explored.

It would be helpful for the parents of a struggling child to ask the classroom teacher to complete a teacher evaluation form before each parent-teacher conference. In this way, initial and subsequent evaluations can be compared to determine if the child's work is improving. If parents conclude that there has been little or no improvement, they can use the information contained on the forms to document the need for a diagnostic work-up or a reevaluation by the school psychologist.

Parents should be realistic about their expectations of the classroom teacher. The child with a significant learning deficit usually requires specialized assistance from a trained resource specialist. The classroom teacher cannot be expected to provide this assistance.

Teachers tend to become defensive when parents become offensive or inappropriately aggressive during parent-teacher conferences. Adversarial situations invariably undermine successful communication. The needs of the child tend to become obscured when parents and teachers are intent on defending themselves. Most teachers are far more cooperative when treated with respect.

It is the prerogative of parents to communicate their concerns about their child's lack of academic progress. To blame the teacher for this lack of progress, however, not only would be a tactical mistake, it might also be unfair. The purpose of parent-teacher conferences is to address the needs and evaluate the progress of the child. Parents who express their concerns in a nonaccusatory, nonderogatory way will generally elicit cooperation. They might ask the teacher: "What can we do to help our child solve these problems?" Parents using such a strategy are far more likely to gain the teacher's active support than parents who are critical or demeaning.

JARGON

Parents who become involved in their child's education must communicate with educators, which frequently means dealing with educational jargon. When used to enhance communication, jargon, and specifically learning disabilities jargon, can serve a positive function. It permits professionals to convey with precision the technical information that identifies and describes the symptoms of a child's learning deficits.

At the same time, jargon can also impede communication. This is especially true when professionals employ highly specialized words with someone not familiar with this language. Because jargon tends to exclude "outsiders" from understanding what is being said, it can become a barrier between the professional and the layperson. This phenomenon is as true in the field of education as it is in the field of medicine or electronics.

When jargon is employed as a smokescreen, it undermines effective communication and excludes parents from understanding vital information about their children. Those who use jargon to create an aura of professionalism are typically insecure about their credibility, authority, or competence. Threatened by what they consider to be "interference," they realize on either a conscious or unconscious level that it is more difficult for the nonprofessional to question or challenge someone whose vocabulary they find incomprehensible.

A child's learning disability can be explained to parents without having to resort to jargon. Although the educator, psychologist, or physician may find it useful to employ technical words to describe a complex process, a competent professional should be able to explain the problem in terms that parents can understand. For example, a school psychologist may report that a child has a perceptual dysfunction involving deficits in auditory and visual discrimination. Parents who are embarrassed to reveal their "ignorance" might be reluctant to ask for clarification. Were they willing to risk appearing "dumb" and were they to ask for an explanation, they would learn that their child is having difficulty processing the information he receives through his ears and/or eyes. He may not be able to hear the difference between the *i* in the word *pin* and the *e* in *pen*. When reading, he may confuse *b* and *d*.

Parents may also discover that they are confused about the meaning of the scores that their child has received on standardized or specialized tests. For instance, parents may be told that their child did poorly on the ITPA in the area of grammatic closure. To eliminate this confusion, they need only ask what the letters ITPA stand for and what the test is designed to measure. The psychologist could then explain that the Illinois Test of Psycholinguistic Abilities is a specialized test that measures the degree of perceptual processing efficiency a child has achieved (see Testing Appendix for a description of this test). Ideally, the psychologist would then provide several examples of correct and incorrect grammatic closure.

Examples: The boy and his father go/goes to the store.
She likes the girl what/who sings.

Test scores should be presented to parents with a clear, written explanation of what the tests measure and what the scores mean. Unfortunately, this is not always done.

If parents find themselves confused by terminology or test scores, they should not hesitate to request clarification. If, at a later point, they feel that they need further clarification, they should feel justified in requesting it. Admitting that one is not familiar with technical jargon, or that one does not understand a test score, is not an admission of ignorance. Parents have the right to see any educational information that pertains to their child, and they also have the right to insist that this information be explained to them in terms they can understand.

EVALUATING PROFESSIONAL RECOMMENDATIONS

The results of a diagnostic test must be analyzed, interpreted, and correlated with the subjective impressions of the classroom teacher. The child's performance in class and his attitude and effort during the testing procedure are critical components in the diagnostic process. Once properly assessed, this data permits the development of an individual educational plan or IEP.

In California, parents are encouraged to attend and participate in the IEP meeting.[2] Typically, the school psychologist, the classroom teacher, the principal, the school nurse, the learning disabilities specialist or resource specialist, and the child's parents attend this conference. Parents also have the option of inviting a professional from outside the school district to represent them. During this meeting, the results of previously administered standardized and diagnostic testing are examined, the child's learning needs are delineated, a remedial strategy is designed, and specific academic goals are established.

[2]The term that is used to describe this evaluation conference may vary from state to state, and the format of the meeting also may differ. The meeting described here represents the standard procedure in California.

Several different remediation options may be explored. For example, a child may qualify for a self-contained special class. The specialist, however, may recommend that the child spend only one or two periods in this class and be "mainstreamed" into the general population for certain classes. Or it may be recommended that the child be "mainstreamed" for all classes and spend a specific amount of time each day working with a resource specialist who would help him with his assignments and provide remedial assistance. The parents of the child being evaluated may accept or reject the proposed strategy and objectives. This decision-making process can be traumatic, especially if the parents feel that they do not fully understand the issues or do not possess the knowledge and/or experience to evaluate adequately the recommendations and options.

Parents who are confused about the issues being examined during the conference may be hesitant to express their concerns or ask questions. They may feel that it would be presumptuous to question or challenge the recommendations of highly trained professionals and specialists. It is, however, precisely at this point that parents should express any concerns or confusion that they might have. The purpose of the meeting is to serve the child. Professionals *can* make mistakes. If the proposals appear inappropriate, inadequate, or poorly conceived, parents have a right and a responsibility to express their reservations. A whole academic year can be wasted before the parents and the school personnel will have another opportunity to design a more suitable learning assistance strategy. Losing an entire year can have tragic implications for a child who is struggling to survive in school.

The following checklist is intended to help parents participate with greater confidence in the evaluation process. The checklist has been designed specifically to identify those areas which should be explored during the IEP conference.

EDUCATIONAL PLAN CHECKLIST

	YES	NO
Has the teacher evaluation form been completed?	☐	☐
I agree with the teacher's assessment of my child's classroom work.	☐	☐
I need to discuss certain areas of disagreement or confusion.	☐	☐

I have seen the results of the diagnostic tests which my child
has taken.   □ □

I understand what the tests measure.   □ □

I understand the scores that my child achieved on the diagnostic tests.   □ □

I feel the scores are valid.   □ □

I have a clear understanding of the available remedial programs.   □ □

I concur with the conclusions that have been drawn in this
meeting.   □ □

I feel that I must consult an outside authority before I agree
to the recommendations that have been made today.   □ □

Interpreting the Checklist

Areas of confusion or disagreement should be discussed during the IEP
meeting. Parents who conclude that the recommendations or explanations provided by the professionals participating in the conference do
not make sense, or are in conflict with their own impressions, have the
right—indeed, the obligation—to request that the professionals clarify
the issues to their satisfaction. Once parents decide to follow the school's
recommendations, they should allow the school personnel a reasonable
amount of time to demonstrate the efficacy of the learning assistance
program.

The academic deficits of a child tested by a competent school psychologist or resource specialist usually can be identified with a high degree of
accuracy. Most testing protocols are reliable, and the majority of school
psychologists are well trained. Because of this competence, the prescrip-
tions that result from IEP conferences are usually on target. Once parents
concur with the assessment and recommendations, it is essential that they
then commit themselves to supporting the school personnel charged with
implementing the agreed-upon remediation program.

Parents have the right to expect that their child's learning problems will
be properly assessed, competently treated, and efficiently remediated.
Parents also have the right to express misgivings without fear of ridicule

or negative repercussions. In the event that the local school district cannot or will not provide the requisite assistance, parents may need to seek the services of an independent learning therapist or tutor.

DEVELOPING REALISTIC EDUCATIONAL GOALS

Learning problems are rarely resolved in a week or a month. Although some specific deficiencies (e.g., difficulty understanding fractions) may be resolved quickly, other learning deficiencies are like the links of a twisted chain. These links are comprised of psychological factors, intelligence, environment, and family dynamics, and they must be carefully and often laboriously disentangled. The amount of time required varies. Factors influencing the timetable include the severity of the problem, the age of the child, the skills of the teachers, the amount of support provided by parents, and the child's desire to overcome his problems.

Because there are so many factors involved, it may be difficult to predict how long it will take to remediate a child's learning problem. Remedial learning curves generally assume four distinct patterns.

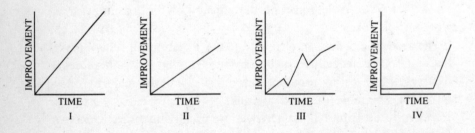

Learning Curve #1 is, of course, the most gratifying for everyone concerned. The learning assistance strategy seems to function like a magic potion, and the student begins to make immediate dramatic improvement. At our center, perhaps 15 percent to 20 percent of the students respond this way.

Learning Curve #2 is more typical of the improvement made by most learning disabled children once they begin to receive remedial assistance. As the child responds to this assistance and his deficiencies become less incapacitating, his enthusiasm for learning and self-concept improve commensurately. The improvement may be slow, but it is steady. The regularity of this learning curve makes it somewhat easier to predict when the child's learning problems can be expected to be resolved. At our center, 50 percent of the children respond in this way.

Learning Curve #3 represents a more erratic improvement in learning skills. Children whose progress is characterized by this learning curve tend to manifest spurts of improvement followed by periodic regression or plateauing. A child with letter-reversal problems, for instance, may eliminate reversals for a period of time then revert to writing or reading words with the *b*s and *d*s reversed. Or a child may be less distractible for a month or two and then begin to manifest concentration problems once again. Our experience at the clinic with over 7,000 learning disabled children has demonstrated that most children described by this learning curve ultimately do resolve their learning problems. Their periodic plateaus and regression, however, can be very frustrating. During these periods, parents, teachers, and children simply have to grit their teeth and await the subsequent upturn. At some point in the remediation process, the gains usually solidify and classroom performance becomes less erratic. Learning curve #3 describes approximately 20 percent of the children at the clinic.

Learning Curve #4 is characteristic of approximately 10 percent of the children at our center. This learning curve is by far the most frustrating of all for parents, teachers, clinic staff, and children. Typically, a child in this category will show no improvement for many months. Because of this lack of progress, everyone tends to become quite demoralized. It is not uncommon or unreasonable for the child's parents to begin to question the efficacy of the learning assistance strategy. Before abandoning any remedial program, however, parents should be prepared to allow a reasonable period of time for the program to demonstrate its effectiveness. Although perseverance can ultimately lead to a breakthrough, it alone cannot transform an inadequate or inappropriate program into an effective one. Knowing when to persevere and when to "bail out" can be very difficult. Parents must be guided by—and must trust—their intuition.

Resistant learning problems such as those described by this curve are examined during staff meetings, and alternative remedial methods are explored. Teachers who have not worked with the child are encouraged to suggest ideas and share their insights. This brainstorming process not only can infuse new and creative energy into the remediation program, it can also lead to new and more effective strategies. In some instances, it may be decided that the child should be assigned to another learning therapist who possesses specific skills or expertise in treating a particular problem.

Parents must accept that their child may not respond in accordance with their preferred remediation timetable. Several different methods may need to be tried before the learning therapist finds the most effective protocol.

It is impossible to predict with absolute certainty a child's remedial learning curve. Some children with severe problems respond very quickly and positively to learning therapy. Others with relatively moderate or subtle problems may respond more slowly.

Educational goals for the learning disabled child must be reasonable and must also take into consideration the range of potential response patterns. These goals must be reviewed periodically. If the educational strategy appears to be bogging down, alternative approaches should be considered.

Despite initially poor gains, children described by Learning Curve #4 often make miraculous breakthroughs just when their parents and teachers are despairing most. The reasons for this sudden and dramatic improvement are difficult to explain, and predicting when the breakthrough will occur is at best problematic.

Parents and teachers have no choice but to trust their intuition while wrestling with the decision to persist with a particular learning assistance strategy or to change course and implement a new strategy.

EVAN: FINDING AN ANTIDOTE FOR CHRONIC DISTRACTIBILITY

It was clear from the test results that Evan did not have reading or math deficits. Yet despite good academic skills, his report card indicated that the fifth grader was doing terribly in school. The teacher evaluation form indicated that his work was disorganized and inaccurate and that his hand-writing was sloppy and illegible. Evan's assignments were seldom completed and were rarely handed in on time. The classroom teacher was clearly concerned, and so was Evan's mother.

Tutoring, counseling, and punishment had been to no avail. Despite the fact that Evan was testing more than a year above grade level in all academic areas, his school was recommending that he be retained.

Evan seemed incapable of concentrating on anything that did not interest him for more than a minute at a time. He would gaze out the window during class and invariably lose his place when it was his turn to read aloud. A constant distraction to the other students, he would make faces and strange noises whenever the teacher turned her back. Alternating between daydreaming and disruptiveness, he had become a major behavior problem in class.

Given the nine-year-old's profound attention deficit disorder, it was clear that any effective remediation program would have to focus on teaching him how to concentrate. Traditional tutoring would not achieve this objective. The child required a program that stressed self-discipline and a behavior modification system that would provide him with daily feedback about how he was functioning in class and that would also provide incentives that would motivate him to become more conscientious and meticulous. In addition to these programs, I also recommended an experimental yoga meditation program that had been designed specifically for chronically hyperactive and distractible children.

The situation was critical. Unless Evan gained control over his mind and body, he would be unable to function at a level commensurate with his intelligence. He would probably become increasingly demoralized by his lack of success and by the negative attention he was continually receiving. A gifted child stood a good chance of ultimately becoming a school dropout.

During the evaluation session, Evan told me that he enjoyed creative writing, and I decided to capitalize on this. To increase his awareness of himself and his behavior, I suggested that Evan's instructor at the clinic encourage him to keep a diary in which he could record his experiences and impressions of what had happened that day in school and at home.

After observing Evan in his regular classroom, I concluded that he required more supervision and structure in school. He needed immediate feedback from his teacher when he was misbehaving or becoming distracted. Unfortunately, his teacher had a sedentary teaching style and seldom got up from her desk, which she had placed at the back of the class.

When I conferred with the teacher, I suggested a system that would provide both feedback and acknowledgment for Evan. I recommended that she put a wide piece of masking tape on the upper righthand corner of Evan's desk. The masking tape would contain two columns. At the top of one column would be a happy face and at the top of the other, a sad face. Each time Evan misbehaved or was distracted, the teacher would signal him to place a check in the sad face column. When he was attending to his work or simply behaving appropriately, the teacher would signal him to place a check in the happy face column.

When I proposed the system, I wasn't certain if the teacher would agree to implement it. Much to my pleasure, she readily accepted my suggestion.

We discussed rewarding Evan for the number of checks he received in the happy face column and taking away privileges if he collected more than a certain number of checks in the sad face column, but we decided against this approach. I sensed that simply acknowledging Evan's good behavior would be preferable. The child had already experienced three years of almost constant negative feedback from his teachers and parents. He did not need any more. I was certain that positive recognition would be a far more effective means of changing his behavior.

The teacher agreed to whisper an agreed-upon cue or to signal Evan unobtrusively when he was becoming distracted or misbehaving. The goal of the behavior modification system was to help the child internalize the teacher-imposed external control and to help him recognize when he was not focused and attending to the task. The system was also designed to provide Evan with immediate acknowledgment when he was focused and paying attention.

As I suspected, Evan began to enjoy the positive recognition he was receiving. The in-class system worked in tandem with his program at our center. Within a month, Evan's attention span and behavior had improved dramatically. In fact, the other children in his class requested that they too have masking tape on their desks! The strategy worked, and Evan began to participate actively in his own education.

MONITORING YOUR CHILD'S PERFORMANCE

Some children with learning problems compensate for their deficits by becoming very conscientious. Despite their academic struggle, they give 100 percent and spend long hours doing their homework and studying. In some instances, this determination is sufficient to permit them to overcome or, at least, to compensate for their learning deficiencies. Such children may require little or no learning assistance.

As a general rule, highly motivated, conscientious learning disabled students are anomalies. The majority of the learning disabled children in our school do not know how to control, motivate, and monitor themselves. Their lack of self-regulation often manifests itself in distractibility, sloppiness, inattentiveness, and irresponsibility. For many learning disabled students, school is a battlefield. It should come as no surprise that these children are tempted to give up.

Children capitulate in different ways. One child may drift off into daydreams or may fail to complete his assignments. Another may seek attention through misbehavior, and thus unconsciously attempt to divert attention from his academic deficits. Children locked into elaborate defense mechanisms frequently fail to perceive that their behavior calls attention to the very inadequacies that they are attempting to camouflage.

Children who have developed counterproductive or self-sabotaging behaviors require careful monitoring by their parents. Those who exhibit chronic misbehavior or irresponsibility are broadcasting their inner turmoil. Before their parents can respond appropriately to the symptoms, they must attempt to determine the source of the behavior. Once identified, this source can then be treated by a wide range of options that might include learning therapy, counseling, or a redefinition of standards and guidelines. Although chronic irresponsibility or manipulative behavior usually requires professional intervention, less severe patterns of counterproductive behavior may respond to extra love, encouragement, and/ or firm, consistent parental discipline.

Before they can intervene effectively, parents need accurate and current information about how their child is functioning in school. Because children often perceive their school situation inaccurately and report facts selectively, parents cannot rely exclusively on their child's perceptions. Parents suspecting a problem cannot risk waiting until a quarterly report

DAILY PERFORMANCE CHECKLIST
(First and Second Grades)

1 = Poor   2 = Fair   3 = Good   4 = Excellent

	Mon.	Tues.	Wed.	Thurs.	Fri.
Reading work					
Math work					
Handwriting					
Listening in class					
Keeping up with class					
Effort					
Behavior					
Comments					
Parents' initials					

DAILY PERFORMANCE CHECKLIST
(Third Grade and Above)

1 = Poor   2 = Fair   3 = Good   4 = Excellent

	Mon.	Tues.	Wed.	Thurs.	Fri.
Completes assignments					
On time					
Neatly					
Completes homework					
On time					
Neatly					
Independence					
Effort					
Attention					
Attitude					
Behavior					
Comments					
Parents' initials					

card comes home. They need daily information about a child's behavior and academic performance.

Two daily performance checklists are included here. These checklists are designed specifically to help parents acquire vital information about their child's performance in school. The forms are particularly helpful in monitoring the effort and performance of children who are unaware that they are functioning irresponsibly in class.

The first checklist is intended for children in grades one and two. The second checklist is intended for children in grades three through eight. A third type of checklist is sometimes also used by our staff. This form is blank and allows parents and teachers to fill in behavioral and performance criteria that are appropriate for a particular child.

The irresponsible, unmotivated, or distractible child is a prime candidate for the checklist. It is our practice at the clinic to send a cover letter explaining the rationale for the behavior modification strategy and the daily performance checklist to the child's teacher. The teacher is asked to evaluate the child's performance every day. The procedure requires only one or two minutes of the teacher's time, and it is the child's responsibility to hand it to the teacher at the end of each class day. Although some teachers may resent this "extra" work, it has been our experience that most teachers recognize the value of the system and are very cooperative about completing the form.

The teacher, of course, has the option of eliminating any behavior or attitude that he or she feels is not relevant to the child. The teacher can also add categories that are more relevant. The child is responsible for showing the completed form to his parents. The parents initial the checklist and send the form with their child to class the following day.

Interpreting the Checklist

The daily performance checklist is not intended for all children, but, rather, is oriented primarily toward the child who is not able to regulate himself and who is oblivious of his own behavior. The checklist will quickly reveal if a child is misbehaving, falling behind, not completing assignments, or functioning irresponsibly in class. In the event that retention is recommended at the end of the year, parents would have been alerted well in advance.

The information provided by the checklist can also help parents and teachers gauge the efficacy of the learning assistance strategy and can suggest if additional remedial assistance is required. The child's scores in particular categories should indicate if the child requires academic therapy, more discipline, more structure at home and in school, and/or more acknowledgment.

The checklist can also be used as an component of an incentive program designed to modify the child's counterproductive behaviors. Parents may want to link the checklist with a point/reward system that encourages the child to improve his classroom performance.

The maximum possible points that can be achieved on the older student's checklist is 220 per week. Parents establishing an incentive program are advised to begin with a reasonable minimum requirement. A good starting point might be 135 points per week. This minimum requirement permits the child initially to have quite a few scores of 2 (fair) on the checklist. Were the child's score to slip below 135 for the week, certain privileges such as watching TV might be withdrawn. On the other hand, if the child achieves a score exceeding 150, he might be given a special reward or prize such as a movie, a trip to the skating rink, a model airplane, a T-shirt, or a doll. Some parents may elect to use only positive incentives. They may give their child a penny for each point he receives. This money might be saved in a jar for special occasions such as Christmas or a day at an amusement park.

An incentive system may be offensive to certain parents because they feel that offering a child a reward for behaving or acting responsibly is the equivalent of a bribe. While an incentive for working hard might be considered a bribe, this same logic could also be applied to a paycheck or a bonus. Most people work for incentives. It is wonderful when children are motivated by pride and the intrinsic satisfaction of doing a good job. Years of defeat and frustration, however, tend to undermine the motivation and positive expectations of the typical learning disabled child. An incentive may serve as the catalyst that propels the unmotivated child to become actively involved in his own education. Success is, of course, the ultimate catalyst and motivation. Success creates the desire for more success. From these achievements evolve self-esteem, self-confidence, and pride.

As parents review the checklist with their child, they should be able to identify specific problem areas. They will want to discuss these areas with both the classroom teacher and the child. Parents should not hesitate to ask the child what he thinks can be done to bring up his scores in a particular area. Children like to be involved in the process of solving their own problems. Brainstorming solutions to problems can be a pleasurable and bonding experience for parents and children. By acknowledging the value of their child's insights, parents are encouraging him to participate actively in the resolution of his learning problem. This active participation is a powerful and positive force in the remediation process.

WORKING AS A TEAM

The effectiveness of any diagnostic procedure or learning assistance program hinges on the expertise and commitment of the people charged with the responsibility of implementing the program. Their skill, enthusiasm, and support significantly improve the prognosis for resolving a child's learning problems.

The more insightful and knowledgeable the parents are, the more capable they will be of discovering and utilizing the resources that exist within their community. Their ability to evaluate professional recommendations, to select appropriate programs, to monitor a child's progress, and to support the child and his teachers are pivotal factors in determining whether or not their child's learning problems are ultimately remediated.

Parental involvement may be perceived by the school district and school personnel as a nuisance, a threat, or a valued contribution. Parental attitudes can profoundly influence how the school authorities react to their participation.

Most learning disabled children require a great deal of emotional support during the remediation process. Parents must accept the fact that even the best remediation programs can bog down occasionally. Should this occur, they must be prepared to offer extra encouragement and support to the child. A child who learns to rebound from an occasional setback is acquiring an essential survival skill.

Parents and teachers also may need encouragement and support from time to time, for they, too, can periodically become demoralized. This is especially true when a child's learning problems prove resistant to remediation.

The impact of teachers on parents who are concerned, confused, and discouraged cannot be overemphasized. Those who sensitize themselves to parents' anxieties significantly improve the chances of successfully resolving their students' learning problems.

Parents and teachers play a vital role in creating the proper alignment of educational and emotional resources that support the learning disabled child. Ultimately, the child's ability to conquer his learning problems will directly reflect the attitude, expectations, and encouragement of his teachers and parents. When the support systems are firm and parents and teachers are committed, the probability of success increases dramatically.

CHAPTER 8

Parenting the Learning Disabled Child

LISA: FIGHTING A LOSING BATTLE

Lisa's parents were adamant. As long as their daughter could continue to fulfill the requirements of the private school she was attending, they would not consider another school for her.

The report from Lisa's teacher indicated that the fourth grader was battling desperately to keep up with her class. The struggle was taking a terrible toll, and the teacher was concerned about the child's increasing demoralization. Despite three hours spent on homework each evening, the ten-year-old was falling further and further behind. A recently acquired nervous tic evidenced the effects of the stress she was experiencing.

Refusing to acknowledge their daughter's increasing anxiety, Lisa's parents were certain that she would be able to fulfill the school's requirements if she received medication "to get her to concentrate" and learning assistance at our center. When I attempted to examine the issues of their daughter's stress and the appropriateness of her school placement, I observed that the parents became quite agitated. Convinced that Lisa could not possibly acquire as good an education at another school, they refused to consider any alternatives. They also refused to consider counseling.

My tests confirmed that Lisa had a relatively severe learning disability. Her learning deficits appeared all the more significant when her school performance was compared to that of her academically gifted classmates.

163

Lisa manifested a classic profile of learning deficits. She had difficulty following verbal and written instructions, and her reading, handwriting, and language arts skills were poor. Her teacher reported that Lisa required continual supervision and did not seem capable of working independently. Although the ten-year-old tested only slightly below grade level on standarized reading and math tests, she was competing with students who were testing three and four years above grade level on the same tests.

I had serious misgivings about Lisa attending an academically accelerated school. Despite her school's highly dedicated staff and excellent curriculum, no on-site specialized remedial assistance was available for children with academic deficiencies. Students either "made the grade" or were asked to leave the school. Without learning assistance, a child such as Lisa with average intelligence and a relatively severe learning disability had virtually no chance of succeeding.

During a subsequent conference with the parents, the classroom teacher, and the principal, Lisa's parents requested that any decision about their daughter's status at the school be deferred until the end of the academic year. At that time, they proposed that her performance be objectively evaluated. If she did not fulfill the school's requirements, they agreed to withdraw her. If, however, she did succeed in fulfilling the school's requirements, they insisted that she be permitted to return the following year. In the interim, they wanted Lisa to continue to receive intensive learning assistance at our center.

During the conference, background information was revealed that helped me understand the parents' intransigence. I learned that Lisa's learning problems were enmeshed in a complex family drama involving her twelve-year-old sister, Karen. This child, who had also once attended the same private school, had become increasingly incapacitated by a degenerative disease. Because the school was not equipped to handle the needs of students with serious physical handicaps, the headmaster had asked that Karen be withdrawn from the school. Although the parents were quite distressed, they reluctantly agreed to enroll her in a special county-sponsored program for the orthopedically handicapped.

Lisa's parents had reacted to our suggestion that their daughter could not handle the school's academic demands as tantamount to taking away their "only hope." To the parents, Lisa's difficulties seemed negligible in comparison to Karen's.

By virtue of superhuman effort, Lisa somehow succeeded by the end of the school year in meeting the school's minimum grade point average requirement and qualified for promotion to the next grade. Nevertheless, the school administration still had grave reservations about the appropriateness of her continuing at the school. I concurred with their assessment. The child was at the bottom of her class and faced a continual struggle, with little chance of succeeding. Her parents, however, were convinced that the struggle was "character building." They would not consider that the battle was seriously jeopardizing Lisa's self-esteem.

Lisa's parents had allowed their own emotional needs to take precedence over their daughter's needs, and in the process they had placed their child in a no-win situation. Lisa's only payoff for her effort was to be permitted to struggle for another year. Her attendance at the private school had assumed symbolic importance for her parents, and this symbolism could easily destroy the child's self-esteem. Forced to become the family flagship, Lisa was listing dangerously. Unless the course was changed, she was in danger of sinking.

During the next ten months, we continued to provide learning assistance, and Lisa made slow, steady academic progress. Despite these gains, she was unable to keep up in fifth grade.

At the end of the school year, Lisa's parents consented to withdraw her from the school. They finally acknowledged that they needed help in dealing with the emotional implications of Karen's illness and Lisa's learning problem, and agreed to see a family therapist. Lisa began attending her local public school where she received daily learning assistance from the school's resource specialist. Within a year she was functioning above grade level. Currently a sophomore in high school, Lisa is maintaining a B average. Her goal is to become a learning disabilities specialist.

REASONABLE VS. UNREASONABLE EXPECTATIONS

Encouraging a child to struggle when success is possible is quite distinct from encouraging a child to beat his head against a wall. Children who are asked to face unrealistic challenges are being set up to fail or to struggle unrelentingly. If unchecked, the cumulative effect of the failures and the struggle can lead to the destruction of a child's self-esteem and self-confidence.

Under the proper conditions, urging a child to confront and prevail over something difficult can serve as a catalyst for growth. When challenges are realistic and fair, they provide an important opportunity for the child to test himself and his resources. Few experiences in life are more exhilarating, confidence-building, and character-building for a child than prevailing over a difficult challenge.

Parental expectations are a fulcrum on which a child's self-concept balances precariously. If reasonable and positive, these expectations can stimulate the development of a strong and resilient self-concept. If unreasonable and negative, such expectations can cause the child's self-concept to become fragile and vulnerable.

Unrealistic expectations can trigger devastating emotional stress. Some parents become fixated on their children achieving in life what they have achieved, or what they have failed to achieve, and they disregard their child's own emotional needs. A father may want his daughter to become a physician because he is a physician. Or he may want his child to become a physician because he had never realized his ambition to become one. Impelled by his own psychological needs, he assigns his daughter a role in a script that he has written. The part may or may not be congruent with the child's abilities or desires. If the role does fit, and she accepts it, it may provide inspiration. Diligently applying herself to her studies, the child may ultimately become the physician her father hoped she would become. On the other hand, if the role does not fit, the fear of disappointing her father may cause the child despair. Having been coerced into a role for which she is not suited, she may react by becoming depressed or by becoming frustrated, angry, and resentful.

A child's aptitude, interests, temperament, and desire must be factored into the parental expectation equation. A child whose father wants her to become an engineer may lack scientific or mechanical aptitude. Although intelligent, her intelligence may manifest itself in other areas. She may enjoy art and theater and may be better suited to become an actor or a singer.

Parental expectations can have an impact on all areas of a child's life. There are dangers at both ends of the expectation spectrum. Having too few expectations for a child can be as emotionally damaging as having too many. Whereas the autocratic parent with highly defined expectations may elicit anxiety, resistance, and rebellion in their children, the permissive parent with poorly defined expectations and standards may encourage laziness and irresponsibility. For most children, achievement requires focused effort. Few children are willing to make this effort when they feel that their parents do not expect it from them.

Communicating to a child that he is expected to try his best is very different from insisting that he become an attorney. Parents who attempt to orient their child toward establishing personal goals and focusing energies on attaining these goals are preparing the child to survive in a highly competitive world where diligence, responsibility, and attention to detail are recognized and rewarded. Encouraging a child to develop these qualities is not the same as insisting that he receive As. For some children a B, a C, or even a D may represent a major achievement. Parents who fail to acknowledge the efforts and accomplishments of their struggling child because of their own unrealistic expectations should not be surprised when their child fails to develop self-confidence. Their lack of acknowledgment defeats the development of motivation, self-acceptance, and self-appreciation. Without parental affirmation, support, and encouragement, most struggling children simply give up.

Parents who impose unfair and self-serving demands on their child obscure the line that delineates the child's ego from their own. A student may feel that he must achieve an A in a course or make the varsity basketball team to please his parents and to gain their love and approval. He dedicates himself to achieving these objectives. If he is successful, he may suffer no psychological stress. In fact, he may attribute his success to his parents' influence. If he is unsuccessful, he may suffer a serious erosion of self-esteem.

There is another danger when a child strives to achieve goals exclusively to please his parents. The child may become so other-directed that he fails to develop a well-formulated sense of his own identity. Such a child is at risk of becoming disillusioned as an adult. One day, he may discover that the goals he had always assumed were his own are someone else's goals. The realization may be devastating.

Despite the risks inherent in orienting children toward establishing goals, parents must communicate certain vital expectations and guidelines. Parents who expect and insist that their child bathe regularly are clearly imposing a reasonable and appropriate standard. Those who expect and insist that their child call home if he is going to be late for dinner are also acting rationally, as are those who expect and insist that their child not cheat or lie.[1] Such clearly conveyed standards create a sense of order and encourage children to develop social awareness. These standards must be differentiated from those of parents who require that their child take piano lessons for five years, despite the fact that their child demonstrates no interest in piano and little musical aptitude.

Parents who fail to examine objectively their motives and their expectations risk entangling their own emotional needs with those of their children. These entanglements at best cause confusion, and, at worst, psychological damage.

DEFENSE MECHANISMS

For no apparent reason John pushed the other fourth grader who was waiting in line in the cafeteria. It was clear that he was trying to goad Kyle into a fight. The other children barely took notice of the incident; they were accustomed to this type of behavior from John. He was the class bully and "tough guy." He was also the worst student.

At a very early stage in their development, children acquire an awareness of their own strengths and weaknesses. In kindergarten and first grade, they begin to compare their performance with that of their classmates and quickly develop a sense of their relative intelligence, athletic ability, social acceptability, and academic potential.

When a child consciously or unconsciously perceives a weakness or inadequacy in himself, his natural instinct is to protect himself from this real or imagined vulnerability. The child learns early in life how to insulate himself from frustration, failure, ridicule, or rejection. If he recognizes that he is unpopular, he may respond by becoming shy and self-effacing, or he may become loud and aggressive. If he concludes that he is dumb, he may become a clown, a troublemaker, or a bully.

Genetically programmed with a powerful survival instinct, a vulnerable child will defend himself as best he can, especially if he unconsciously concludes that his deficiencies are a threat to his emotional survival. The child struggling to read, play baseball, or make friends is forced to confront his inadequacies each day. Although his defensive and compensatory

---

[1]Chronic cheating or lying may be symptomatic of an emotional problem that requires professional counseling.

behaviors may help him cope with his limitations and the consequences of these limitations, they also ironically accentuate the very deficiencies that the child is trying to camouflage. The unpopular child who becomes a class troublemaker to get attention is not going to win many friends with his behavior. The child's unconscious defence mechanism is also, ironically, a self-destruct mechanism.

Parents who wish to help the learning disabled child relinquish his self-defeating defense mechanisms must somehow establish a reasonable balance between demanding too much and demanding too little from the child. Although the child's counterproductive behavior and defense mechanisms may be transparent to perceptive parents and teachers, they will not be transparent to the child. If the child is convinced that he cannot survive without his defensive behavior, he will be compelled by fear to resist self-examination and change. By controlling his environment and, to varying degrees, the people in it, he is also attempting to control his own fear. The child creates an illusion of security behind his protective wall. By not doing his homework or by procrastinating, he is able to avoid dealing with his math difficulties. By playing the victim and by accusing his teacher of being unfair, he may be able to avoid confronting his English deficiencies. In this way, the child learns to run away from his responsibilities and postpones the day of reckoning.

Specific defense mechanisms vary from child to child. Some of the most common include:

1. Irresponsibility
2. Indifference
3. Excuses and rationalizations
4. Laziness
5. Procrastination
6. Playing the role of victim
7. Resistance
8. Emotional outbursts
9. Untruthfulness

Parents and teachers who frontally "assault" a child in their attempt to force him to give up his defense mechanisms should prepare themselves for almost certain defeat. The more they push, lecture, threaten, and cajole, the more resistance they are likely to encounter. When parents and teachers insist that a child relinquish protective behaviors without offering the child viable alternatives, they increase the probability of a showdown in which there are no winners.

Until a child becomes convinced that he can survive without protecting himself, he will hold onto his defensive behavior for dear life. In this respect a child is no different from an adult who smokes because he feels more socially at ease with a cigarette in his hand. Lacking confidence in his ability to communicate, the person becomes habituated to using cigarettes as a social crutch. In time, his emotional reliance on smoking becomes increasingly entrenched. Convinced that he is incapable of functioning in social situations without a cigarette, he integrates into his self-concept the image of himself smoking and feeling secure. Before such a person would willingly change the behavior, he would need to examine his perception of himself. He would have to begin to see himself as a nonsmoker, and he would have to be sufficiently motivated to cope with the effects of breaking his physiological and psychological dependency.

It is, of course, reasonable for parents to desire that their learning disabled child relinquish his counterproductive defense mechanisms. This desire, however, must be tempered by reality. The parents of a child with severe learning problems may be able to identify their child's defense mechanisms. They may also recognize that these mechanisms are complex and deeply entrenched, and that these coping behaviors are seriously impeding the remediation process. Despite these insights, the parents may feel frustrated and thwarted as they attempt to get their child to relinquish his self-defeating behaviors, to take ownership of his problems, and to make a commitment to overcoming them.

Before a child realistically can be expected to accept help and become actively involved in the remediation process, he must believe that he can prevail over his learning problems. A seemingly irreconcilable paradox is created. To overcome his learning problems, the child must be willing to give up his defense mechanisms, but to give up his defense mechanisms, he must be convinced that he can overcome his learning problems. Parents can reconcile the paradox by demonstrating conclusively to their child that he is capable of learning. Quality learning assistance must be combined with an extra measure of support, love, understanding, patience, and sensitivity.

The learning disabled child whose school experiences have been especially bad may perceive his poor academic performance as conclusive evidence of his hopeless inadequacy. Given his history of negative school experiences, he may be sorely tempted to give up whenever he encounters any frustration or setback. Such encounters are, of course, inevitable. A child may have actually begun to make significant gains, but his self-esteem may be so fragile and his memories of past failures and frustration so vivid that he will cave in each time he encounters an impediment. Each setback, however minor, can cause the child to reexperience a demoralizing sense of futility.

The potential for setbacks increases significantly when a child is being asked to master particularly demanding skills. For example, a child with poor visual memory skills may diligently study his assigned spelling words. Despite his efforts and his conviction that he had mastered all of the assigned words, he does poorly on the weekly spelling test. Confronted with another failure, the child withdraws into a protective cocoon. Trying to insulate himself from the pain of feeling incompetent, he mobilizes all of his psychological defense mechanisms. He convinces himself that the learning assistance program isn't working and is a waste of time and money. Wanting to run away from the reality of his learning problems, he attempts to manipulate his parents into permitting him to quit the program.

MANIPULATIVE BEHAVIOR

A natural instinct impels parents to protect their child from experiencing pain. Reconciling this instinct with an equally compelling responsibility to resist a child's self-defeating, manipulative behavior can demand extraordinary insight and emotional fortitude. Parents who allow their child to quit or shut down when he is thwarted by a barrier which can and should be surmounted are unwittingly allowing the child to fail. There is a cumulative effect to quitting. With practice, it becomes easier and easier to do. Although parents may delude themselves that they are helping their child by repeatedly rescuing him, they are actually reinforcing the child's already tenuous self-esteem.

When a child confronts a difficult challenge and cries, he is venting his sadness, anger, and frustration. His emotional system is cleansing itself. Once purged, the child can get on with the business of solving his problem, assuming that the child is capable of solving it. If help is required, it can be provided without the parents taking ownership of the problem.

Crying serves a therapeutic function. It can be a safety valve that frees a child from the debilitating effect of imploding emotions such as frustration and anger. Although witnessing a child cry can be a heart-wrenching experience for parents, the crying may signal that the healing has begun. By expressing his pain, the child is able to liberate himself from the control that these emotions exert on him.[2]

When parents acknowledge their child's emotions, they affirm that it's all right for him to feel sadness, anger, or frustration. By encouraging the child to express his feelings, parents support the development of an emotional release system vital to the child's mental health. They are, in effect, helping their child accept himself and the legitimacy of his emotions. The child who learns to accept himself and who feels safe expressing his feelings will feel less guilt about having feelings. He will also feel less need to sanitize his legitimate emotions.

Although parents may encourage their child to express his feelings, they are not necessarily obligated to accept or respond to all of them. The child who uses his anger as a bludgeon or his tears as a means of controlling others must be dissuaded from relying on this behavior. If he is not dissuaded, he will integrate this behavior into his personality. The child who learns to use his emotions to manipulate his parents into doing what he wants has learned a lesson that he may reenact throughout his life with other people. The behavior is a time bomb that can destroy friendships, marriages, and careers.

Unless they are vigilant, the parents of a manipulative child may be drawn into the scripted behavior patterns. They may attempt to protect their child from any experience that might trigger his anger, or they may attempt to rescue him whenever he gets upset. By providing him with a payoff in the form of attention, acknowledgment, and nurturing, such parents are reinforcing their child's nonadaptive and self-sabotaging behavior. Like too much ice cream, this reinforcement is a payoff the child may be convinced he wants, but one he should not get.

The child must realize that his right to express anger or sorrow to his parents does not guarantee that they will acquiesce to being controlled. Indeed, those parents who realize that they are being manipulated and who resist being drawn into their child's script are serving their child.

---

[2]There are many reasons why children cry. When parents sense that their child's crying is the result of profound fear or sadness, they should alert themselves to the possibility of an emotional problem which may require professional treatment.

When parents recognize that their child is attempting to use anger or some other feeling to be manipulative, they might respond with a simple statement: ''I can see that you are angry, but I cannot allow you to disregard the family's rules simply because you are angry. If you wish, you may go to your room and be as angry as you want. When you are ready to talk calmly with me about what's bothering you, you can come out.'' Children who discover that temper tantrums are an effective means for getting what they want will probably continue to use this or other types of controlling behavior throughout their lives.

Parents should attempt to examine carefully and objectively the behavior and the feelings of the manipulative child. Children who continually resort to manipulation are signaling their unhappiness and confusion. As long as these underlying feelings persist, the behavior will persist.

Obviously, parents cannot disregard their child's pain and sadness when he experiences a defeat or a setback. Nevertheless, they must help their child understand that he cannot be permitted to quit or shut down every time he is sad, angry, or frustrated. Although the child may be upset with his parents for insisting that he persevere, ultimately he will appreciate that they cared enough to risk his wrath by demanding that he persist and prevail over his problem. The alternative is to allow the child to quit continually. If parents permit this to happen, they should not be surprised when quitting becomes a habit.

When the learning disabled child expresses his pain in a catharsis of unhappiness and tears, the catharsis could signal a turning point. The child may finally be getting in touch on a visceral level with his resistance, fear, anger, and feelings of inadequacy and may be ready to get on with the job of resolving his learning problem.

The child with learning problems must be helped to understand that it's all right if he fails an exam, but that it is not all right if he doesn't study or if he gives up after failing an exam. His grade is of secondary importance. What is important is that the child learn to persevere. At this critical juncture, he must be convinced that his parents and teachers are there to provide encouragement, understanding, support, and love. If he stumbles or becomes discouraged, he will need extra support. When he makes a breakthrough, he will need to be lavishly acknowledged and praised.

Once the learning disabled child realizes that learning assistance is not something that is being done *to* him, but rather, something that is being done *for* him, he will become less resistant. He can begin to relinquish his defense mechanisms and manipulative behavior and take a more active role in the remediation process. Major academic gains should follow.

COMPENSATORY MECHANISMS

The children at the class picnic had finished their lunch. The boys went to the softball field to choose sides for a game. The girls went to the volleyball net, chose sides, and began to play. Tim picked up his book and wandered off. He knew that if he played softball, he would be chosen last. Everyone knew that Tim was the worst athlete in the class.

A child who perceives real or imagined inadequacies or limitations in himself has four basic options:

1. He can develop defense mechanisms.
2. He can accept his limitations.
3. He can develop compensatory mechanisms.
4. He can attempt to overcome his limitations.

The choice that a child makes when forced to confront his weaknesses seldom reflects a conscious, analytical process. Usually, the child responds without thinking, and his response is a window into his inner feelings about himself.

Compensatory mechanisms are frequently reality-based and reflect a rational response on the part of a child to perceived limitations. When a child develops an adaptive compensatory mechanism, he is making a conscious or unconscious choice to develop an area of strength and to avoid an area of weakness. The child who learns to compensate for a weakness by developing a potential area of strength is choosing the arena in which he wishes to function and compete. This selection process is directly linked to a natural survival instinct. The process is rational and pragmatic, assuming that the child is not choosing to avoid other arenas in which he must also be able to function.

Just as reasonable challenges must be differentiated from unreasonable challenges, so, too, must healthy or adaptive compensatory mechanisms be differentiated from unhealthy or nonadaptive ones. Under certain circumstances, a child's acceptance of his limitations may be realistic and practical. The converse, however, may also be true. A child's unwillingness to confront and prevail over real or imagined limitations may signal a lack of self-esteem and/or psychological problems. Unfortunately, the demarcation line between healthy and unhealthy compensatory mechanisms can be difficult for parents to discern. One fact is inescapable: How a child chooses (and/or is guided) to respond to his deficiencies can establish behavior patterns that can profoundly affect the future course of the child's life.

The child who attempts to overcome his limitations is expressing confidence and faith in himself. He is asserting his power to control his destiny. Usually, such a child is an achiever and, perhaps, an overachiever. Children with an extreme form of this personality trait are compelled to test themselves constantly. They typically evolve into the men and women who climb mountains, sail around the world, break athletic records, discover new wonder drugs, and build financial empires.

DISTINGUISHING DEFENSE MECHANISMS FROM COMPENSATORY MECHANISMS

Despite some overlap, compensatory mechanisms can and should be differentiated from defense mechanisms. Although both can provide real or imagined emotional and physical protection, compensatory mechanisms generally serve a productive function. Defense mechanisms, on the other hand, inhibit a child's growth and development and are invariably counterproductive.

Like their adult counterparts, children will mobilize their psychological resources to protect themselves from as much pain as possible. This "circling of the wagons" may manifest itself as either a defense mechanism, an adaptive compensatory mechanism, or a nonadaptive compensatory mechanism. This latter behavior is exemplified by the learning disabled athlete who assiduously avoids academics in order to concentrate on sports.

Secure children usually have a realistic sense of their strengths and weaknesses. They tend to accept their limitations and they strategically compensate for these limitations by developing other skills. The child who concludes in first grade that he cannot sing very well may decide never to volunteer to sing in public. If he has the good fortune to be competent in sports or science, he may quite reasonably attempt to compensate for his singing deficiencies by developing these talents. This behavior must be distinguished from defensive behavior of the poor reader who, upon concluding that he will never be able to read well, decides to avoid reading. The salient difference is that a child does not need to be able to sing, but he does need to know how to read. Although the poor reader's attempt to insulate himself from frustration is understandable, the behavior clearly has horrendous educational, vocational, and psychological implications. A poor singer may decide not to sing in public with impunity. A poor reader does not enjoy the same impunity.

Defense mechanisms are invariably fear-based. They represent a desperate attempt on the child's part to exert control over himself, and his environment. By their very nature, defense mechanisms are restrictive, and the protection they afford is at best illusory.

CORY: REBELLING AGAINST TOO MUCH PARENTAL INVOLVEMENT

The mother sitting across the table from me looked desperate. As she struggled to keep from crying, her lips trembled involuntarily. For approximately six months, her son had been receiving learning assistance at our center. Although Cory was bright, charming, and outgoing, his mother was convinced that he was intentionally driving her crazy.

Cory's learning problems were relatively severe—perhaps a 6 on a scale from 1 (subtle) to 10 (severe). His academic deficits were compounded by the fact that he was extremely strong-willed and hadn't yet decided whether he was ready to resolve his learning problems. It was obvious that he liked the attention he was getting from his classroom teacher, his tutor, and his mother.

Cory's mother was a single parent and had been divorced for three years. His father, an engineer living in another state, saw his son only four weeks each year during the summer. Remarried, he and his second wife had a seven-month-old-daughter. Despite the infrequency of his visits with his son, the father was quite concerned about Cory and had written me several times to inquire about his son's progress. His relationship with his ex-wife, however, was strained and there was little direct communication between them about Cory.

Cory's mother had moved to northern California from Connecticut. In Connecticut, Cory had been diagnosed as learning disabled and had been placed in a special education program. When she enrolled her son in his new school in California, the mother requested that he be provided with special learning assistance. The work-up by the school psychologist confirmed that Cory required special help. The child was placed in his school's resource program and received one hour of assistance each day from the school's reading specialist. In addition, he attended our center for two hours per week of specialized learning assistance that focused on developing his perceptual processing skills.

Because of his tendency to be irresponsible, Cory's classroom teacher and his resource specialist suggested that his mother monitor him to make sure that he completed his assignments. They also recommended that she help him at home with his reading, math, and spelling. Having accepted this recommendation, Cory's mother began spending ninety minutes each evening helping her son with his schoolwork. Unfortunately, Cory was not cooperating. He overtly resisted all of her efforts and would work only if he was threatened with a punishment. The mother was usually exhausted when she came home from work, and she had begun to dread the nightly ritual of arguing, cajoling, and threatening.

Cory's mother had unwittingly permitted herself to be drawn into a power struggle with her son. The struggle was destroying their relationship. In desperation, she had begun to consider whether it might not be best to allow Cory to live with his father. She was convinced that her son needed more discipline, and she knew that she could not possibly be more stern with him than she was already.

I asked Cory's mother if she had experienced serious discipline problems with Cory prior to becoming his "tutor." She replied that she had not. I then asked her if she wanted to continue tutoring her son. She responded "no." She indicated, however, that she felt compelled to continue. If she didn't, she was certain that he would make no progress in school. I then inquired if Cory had shown any improvement since she had started helping him. She replied that he had not. He had actually regressed. At this point, I gave her "permission" to discontinue tutoring her son. Upon hearing this, she breathed an audible sigh of relief.

Having accepted the recommendation of her son's teachers, Cory's mother had reluctantly become a tutor. It was a role for which she was neither emotionally nor academically suited. Inasmuch as Cory was receiving assistance in school and at our center, it was redundant and counterproductive for her to tutor him. If her son was acting irresponsibly in class, there were better options for correcting the problem than forcing the mother to play tutor.

I suggested to the mother that we design a system which would permit her to get daily feedback from Cory's teachers. This report would indicate whether Cory was completing his assignments. We agreed that her son would be responsible for informing his resource teacher or his learning therapist at our center when he was having difficulty with his assignments. Otherwise he would be held responsible for completing his work. A system of rewards and consequences was also designed and carefully explained to Cory. If Cory was irresponsible, he would lose privileges such as watching Saturday morning TV. His mother agreed to discontinue helping him, unless Cory specifically requested assistance.

Four weeks later, a far less anxious woman entered my office. She was smiling and eager to share with me the progress that Cory had made in school. All of the tension at home had disappeared. Her son was now completing his homework and keeping up with his class. His reading had improved significantly. Although there were periodic lapses into irresponsibility, Cory accepted the consequences for such behavior. The most significant improvement involved the quality of the relationship between the child and his mother. The two were getting along again. The clinic staff also saw a dramatic improvement in Cory's academic skills. He had begun to participate actively in the process of resolving his learning problems, and he was picking up momentum. We were all certain that his learning problems would soon be resolved.

THE PARENT AS A TUTOR

Children tend to resist and resent parental involvement in their schoolwork, especially those who are defensive and sensitive about their learning deficits. Most parents do not understand how children learn or how to teach them most effectively. When they help their children with their schoolwork, they often insist on "closure" or total mastery. Some become quite upset if their child does not appear to be "getting it" or forgets something he had already seemingly mastered. This desire for closure can trigger resistance and work at cross-purposes with the resolution of the child's learning problem.

For obvious reasons, the emotions of parents are deeply enmeshed with those of the child. When a parent expresses his or her disappointment that the child is not mastering the material being studied, a powerful message is sent to the child. This message may be construed as a rejection and as verification of the child's inadequacies. Most struggling children are understandably insecure and anxious about their academic deficiencies. They can be quite threatened by their parents' intense desire for mastery of the academic material. The more intense parents become in their attempts to help their children resolve their problems, the more the children may resist by doing sloppy work, procrastinating, or shutting down. If the children's associations with their parents' "assistance" are extremely painful, they may develop profoundly negative associations with school and with learning. Ironically, this aversion is the very thing the parents were trying to avoid.

Parents and children communicate on many different levels. The communication system involves both verbal and nonverbal cues and responses. A look of dissatisfaction or exasperation can trigger an emotional chain reaction from a highly sensitive child who already lacks self-esteem. The resulting anxiety may cause the child to forget what he has already learned, and his fear or anger may cause him to appear especially resistant or "dense."

Relatively few parents are emotionally and educationally equipped to function successfully as their child's tutor. Unless there are no other options, most parents should resist being forced into this role. This advice is particularly relevant in the case of the learning disabled child. Parents who tend to lose their patience and to overexplain or overdrill should not be surprised when their child reacts negatively to them and to the material being taught.

Most children want their parents to be parents and their teachers to be teachers. Parents and children tend to bring their preestablished scripts, their behavior patterns, and their emotional entanglements to the tutoring sessions. Parents who have a tendency to become exasperated—even those who are teachers by profession and quite unflappable in their own classrooms—are apt to become upset during the tutoring sessions. Although the parent may have the best intentions, he may find himself responding with frustration and anger if he perceives resistance, distractibility, laziness, procrastination, and/or sloppiness. Such reactions are invariably counterproductive.

Sometimes parents have no recourse but to become their child's tutor. A family may live in a rural area and not have access to a qualified tutor. Another family may not have the funds to engage a tutor. If the parents are the only ones who can provide assistance for their struggling child, they have no choice but to do the best job they are capable of doing.

Avoiding the role of tutor does not mean that parents should not review spelling words with their child or assist him with a difficult math problem. Helping a child occasionally with his homework is not the equivalent of becoming a child's regular tutor.

Parents who do decide to help their children might consider the following guidelines:

1. The tutoring sessions should be short and to the point. Children with learning problems have a limited attention span. If they conclude that the child needs a great deal of help, they should break the sessions up into relatively short instructional segments.
2. Parents should not expect or demand "closure." Some children need several explanations before they understand a concept, and they need several exposures before they master a skill. Other children appear to have mastered a skill and may then forget what they have learned.
3. Parents should discipline themselves to be patient.
4. The sessions should be discontinued when parents perceive that their child or they are becoming frustrated or impatient.
5. Parents should review the basics before they expect their child to master more advanced material. For example, if a child does not understand how to multiply fractions, he may not understand the concept of fractions. This should be reviewed before expecting the child to do more advanced material.
6. If parents do not understand something such as "12 to the base 4," they should admit it. They should advise their child to get help from the teacher, or they should hire a tutor.
7. Parents who do not want to function as a tutor and parents who recognize that they have a tendency to lose their patience should discuss their feelings openly with their child. They should consider hiring a tutor or a qualified high school or college student.

8. If one parent is able to work more successfully with a child than the other parent, that parent should be given the job of providing occasional learning assistance.
9. Children with learning problems may not respond to tutoring. They may require professional learning assistance, especially if they have underlying perceptual or concentration problems. Parents must accept their child's and their own limitations.

While some children resent and resist their parents' efforts to help them, others can become overly dependent on this help. A symbiotic relationship may result. This dependency must be discouraged. The alternative is to undermine the child's capacity to work independently.

Some parents unconsciously encourage their child to become dependent on them. A parent, for example, might actually do all of her child's math problems or write his book report under the guise of "helping." Although these parents may rationalize their actions by contending that their child could not possibly do the work on his own, they unwittingly perpetuate their child's dependency. If a child is so confused or lacking in skills that he cannot do the work expected of him, he should be excused from doing the work until he has been taught the requisite basic skills. Alternative homework should be assigned until the child is capable of doing the regular work. Despite good intentions, parents do a disservice to their child when they do his work for him.

Genuine concern may motivate parents to become involved in their child's schoolwork. Under the proper circumstances, limited crisis intervention is, of course, justified. A child may need his parent to drill his spelling words or ask him review questions before a test. Continual intervention, however, can defeat the basic objective of education; namely, to train children to develop their own intellectual resources.

Parents who become overly involved in their child's schoolwork and assume ownership of his problems often have difficulty separating their child's performance from their own. A common example of this phenomenon is seen in the case of parents who identify so strongly with their children's athletic achievements that they cease being parents and become stern, demanding, and, often, relentless coaches.

Although some parents can successfully tutor their own children, they are relatively rare. When other viable alternatives exist, they should be considered seriously.

TAKING OWNERSHIP OF
A LEARNING PROBLEM

A critical point on the remediation process is reached when a child begins to take ownership of his learning problems. The child's active and voluntary participation can significantly facilitate the remediation process. Achieving this involvement is one of the major goals of any well-conceived remediation strategy.

Although parents can and should take an active role in their learning disabled child's education, they must establish appropriate limits. Their primary contributions should be in the areas of procuring learning assistance, monitoring improvement, and providing emotional support. Parents can best resist the temptation to take ownership of their child's problem by continually reminding themselves that their child's problems belong to him and *not* to them.

A clue that parents have become excessively involved in their child's problems is reflected in comments such as: ''*We* have a reading problem,'' or ''*We* studied our spelling words last night.'' The use of the plural pronoun is a clear signal of excessive parental involvement. When parents do take ownership of their child's learning problem, they create dependencies that discourage the child from developing his own emotional resources and problem-solving capabilities.[3]

Children can become easily addicted to excessive parental nurturing. The addicted child may feel quite threatened when his parents attempt to withdraw or modify the support system. If he perceives himself as hopelessly incompetent or inadequate, he may become convinced that he cannot possibly survive without continual assistance. Recognizing either consciously or unconsciously that once his learning problems are resolved, he will no longer receive attention, he may defeat attempts to help him overcome his problems.

The parents of a struggling child are on the front line. They cannot escape having to deal with the emotional fallout that results from the child's learning problems. Despite their desire to protect their child from pain, they cannot totally eliminate the struggle. At best, they can only provide their child with the means by which he can solve his problems.

---

[3]See *Parent Effectiveness Training* by Thomas Gordon (McKay, 1970) for an excellent analysis of parent/child communication strategies, problem ownership, and problem-solving techniques.

Parents, of course, cannot disregard their responsibility to help their child deal with unhappiness, frustration, anger, and despair. Handling this responsibility demands extraordinary patience and sensitivity. For example, a struggling child may begin to take out his frustration on his little sister. Although his parents may be sympathetic and understanding, they obviously cannot permit him to continue teasing or hitting his sister. They may be unable to help their child resolve his learning problems immediately, but they must, at least, address the immediate, critical problem of the child abusing his sister. By buying a punching bag and encouraging their son to use it, they can provide a safe means for the boy to vent his frustration. They must also communicate clearly to their child that his behavior is making them unhappy and is unacceptable. Establishing clearly defined behavioral guidelines is essential. The child must accept that there are certain basic rules of behavior which cannot be disregarded. He must learn that it is OK to hit the punching bag when he is angry, but it's not OK to hit his sister. If he continues to hit his sister, he must realize that he will be punished. At the same time, the child's parents should help him examine his frustration and his feelings about school. In the case of chronic frustration and anger, professional counseling may be advisable. The ultimate solution, of course, is to help the child resolve his learning problems so that he will be less frustrated and angry.

STRUCTURE AS THE CORNERSTONE OF RESPONSIBILITY

All children need structure in their lives. Bedtime, mealtime, chores, homework, playtime, school, church—these formatted periods provide a child with a sense of order, security, and stability. Learning disabled children in particular have a special need for structure at home and in school. Preoccupied with coping with his academic deficits, the learning disabled child may have a very difficult time managing and controlling the variables in his life. If he is faced with too many choices and options, he can easily become overwhelmed. Uncertainty about rules, expectations, and structure accentuates the classic patterns of inattentiveness and disorganization characteristic of many learning disabled children.

By establishing structure in a child's environment and by clearly defining a framework of family values, rules, and expectations, parents communicate where they stand on important issues such as honesty, effort, and commitment. Their attitudes and values provide the child with a frame of reference and a schema that helps him evaluate the many options with which he is faced each day. Should he take one more at bat and be late for dinner? Should he study an extra half hour for the Spanish quiz? Should he reread his essay one more time before handing it in? The values and the structure inculcated by his parents provide a primary standard for making these decisions. In a very real sense, these values and structure help to define the child's sense of identity.

When parents insist that their child do his homework, they are establishing a system of guidelines and standards that the child will either internalize or, to varying degrees, reject. The internalization process is directly linked to the formation of character and the development of a value system. For example, when parents insist that their child write neatly and legibly, they are encouraging the development of responsibility. Their expectations impress on the child that he had better not expect a free ride through life. The child learns that he will be judged by others on the basis of his effort and performance. The youngster who is not expected to conform and adjust to the values of his family will probably have a difficult time conforming and adjusting to the values of his society.

At an early stage in his development, a child begins to assimilate the rules, guidelines, values, priorities, and expectations of his family and his society. Toddlers are taught not to eat dirt. Three-year-olds are taught not to run into the street. Four-year-olds are taught not to interrupt. Six-year-olds are taught to look both ways when they cross the street, and eight-year-olds are taught to call home if they decide to go to a friend's house after school. Toddlers who do not learn that they are expected to obey the rules probably won't obey them as teenagers, and six-year-olds who do not learn that they are responsible for their actions will probably continue to feel that they are not responsible for their actions when they become adults.

Structure in the form of externally imposed controls provides the foundation upon which a child begins to build his own internal regulatory system. A first grader learns that it is against the rules to cheat, to steal, or to bully. A high school sophomore learns that it is against the rules to take the family car without permission. The internalization of external control forms the foundation for the development of self-control and self-discipline. The child who does not acquire these attributes will have difficulty learning to function in any context where he must regulate himself, be it the classroom or the playing field.

The lack of self-discipline often associated with learning disabilities may manifest itself in the form of inattentiveness, disorganization, or inconsistency. The learning disabled child who does not attend to such details as neatness, deadlines, punctuation, following instructions, completing assignments, and planning projects generally requires more externally imposed structure than does the nonlearning disabled child. By establishing structure at home and in school and by clearly defining acceptable standards of behavior and performance, parents and teachers provide the child with a functional support and guidance system.

The school performance of the learning disabled child must usually be more closely monitored than the school performance of the nonlearning disabled child. Until he is able to demonstrate that he has acquired sufficient internal control, the typical learning disabled child will probably require extra external control. He may need to have his academic assignments and objectives clearly defined by his parents and teachers. He may need to have them tell him precisely where in his notebook his assignments are to be written. He and his parents may need to agree upon a specific amount of time that he will spend on his homework each evening. (This assumes that the child is assigned homework, which, unfortunately, is not always the case.)

Parents who establish structure for their learning disabled child usually have fewer parenting problems than those who do not. Creating a structured environment, however, does not mean that parents need to be dictatorial or autocratic. Excessive parental control can result in emotional alienation or dependency. Highly authoritarian parents who attempt to control every aspect of their child's life are denying their child the opportunity to become an independent, fully functional adult.

To the extent to which they are capable, children should participate in the process of establishing family structure. For instance, the child who wants to be on the Olympic swim team must be willing to get up each morning at 5:30 to practice. If being on the swim team is important to her, she will have to agree to the structure and rules established by the coach. The rules might include eating no sweets and going to bed early. Because the child has voluntarily made the choice to be on the team, she will probably be willing and eager to comply with the rules. Had she been forced to join the swim team, she probably would have resisted the rules. Voluntary active participation invariably decreases incidences of the resistant child phenomenon.

Younger learning disabled children in particular need rules to help them learn to govern themselves. For example, when parents unequivocally communicate to their child that they expect him to do a minimum of one hour of homework each evening, they are clearly defining their position on the issue of homework. Rather than dictate when he must do his homework, however, his parents might consider giving the child some choices so that he can participate in the process of formatting his study schedule. For example, his parents might offer the child the option of doing his homework right after school, before dinner, or after dinner. The family rule about homework is thus clearly established. At the same time, the child is given some control over his own life.

Parents should explain family rules so that their child can understand the rationale for them. They should also encourage their child to express his feelings and objections. If he feels that an hour of homework each evening is unfair or excessive, he deserves an explanation about the reason for the rule. The child must understand that his parents have a responsibility to establish family rules. He must also understand that although he may not always agree with these rules, he is expected to comply, unless he can present compelling reasons for not complying.

Rules must be fair. If a child offers a rational, nonmanipulative argument for reconsidering an established rule, he deserves to have his position considered. If his parents do not accept the child's position, they should do so in a carefully reasoned, nondemeaning way.

Parents should not be afraid to back down when their child can present a non-manipulative, logical argument for reconsidering a particular rule. Contrary to popular belief, parents do not undermine their authority or their child's respect when they alter their position. On the contrary, they are actually modeling a rational problem-solving attitude that their child probably will model someday for his own children. For example, the family rule may be that the child spend a minimum of one hour each evening on homework. The child, however, may be able to prove that his teacher doesn't assign that much homework. If the parents are committed to having him spend an hour doing homework each evening, they would either have to request that the teacher assign additional homework to their child, or they themselves would have to create extra educational projects.

Another option is for the parents to change their rule about how much homework is required.

Reasonable and consistent rules provide an important sense of security for a child. Conversely, rules that are not clearly defined, consistently applied, and reasonable cause children to become confused and insecure. This lack of definitiveness can create emotional stress.

Children who know and accept the limits are invariably happier than those who do not know what the limits are or those who refuse to accept the limits and continue to test them. It is quite common for children who have become habituated to testing to become temporarily resistant when their parents begin to apply the rules consistently. Once they realize that the guidelines are meant to be obeyed, most children usually stop testing. Children desperately want their parents and teachers to define the guidelines and to tell them what they are and are not permitted to do. After all, it's better that the limits are defined by the child's parents and teachers, and not by a judge in a juvenile court.

TRANSFERRING RESPONSIBILITY

Parents play a pivotal role in the process of helping their child develop responsibility. They must, however, accept that their prerogatives to monitor and regulate their child's behavior and performance become more limited as he matures.

One of parenting's primary obligations is to prepare a child to assume responsible control of his own life. Parents cannot be with their ten-year-old as he rides his bicycle to the store. They can only trust that he will be careful and not take unnecessary risks. They cannot be with their fifteen-year-old when he takes his history exam. They can only trust that he was conscientious when he studied for the exam and that he will do his best while taking it.

One of the major milestones in the process of transferring control to a child occurs on the first day of kindergarten. It is then that the child learns that he will be held responsible for his actions and performance by adults other than his parents. He learns that he is expected to obey the teacher's rules, and he learns that he has to deal with the consequences of his actions. If he decides to put paste in someone's hair, he discovers that he probably will be punished. On the other hand, if he does something well, he discovers that he probably will be praised. Making this transition from answering exclusively to his parents for his actions to answering to strangers is a vital step in the child's development.

The first manifestation of a child's physiological and emotional drive to become independent can be seen in the impelling need of a toddler to explore the nooks and crannies of the house. As the child grows older, he will concurrently crave independence and parental support. This paradox is an inherent component in the process of a child's emotional and physiological development.

Knowing when to support and monitor and when to back off and allow a child to make choices for which he must assume responsibility can pose a serious dilemma for parents. This dilemma is particularly acute when parents recognize that their child is making a poor decision and yet realize that the child must be permitted to make the mistake so that he can learn from it. Parents, obviously, cannot allow their child to make life-threatening mistakes, but they must accept the fact that making mistakes is an essential part of the child's learning process. If they are ultimately to become thinking, independent, and fully functional adults, children cannot be shielded from all mistakes. As parents wrestle with whether or not to allow their child to make a particular mistake, they must rely on their intuition, discretion, and past experience.

The way in which parents transfer control to their maturing child can have a dramatic impact on whether or not a child develops responsibility. As they transfer control, parents must consider both the child's chronological age and his level of maturity. What may be appropriate to permit one fourteen-year-old may not be appropriate for another fourteen-year-old. To the extent to which they are capable, *all* fourteen-year-olds should be encouraged to take responsibility for their lives and their actions.

By the time a child becomes a teenager, his capacity to function with age-appropriate independence should be fairly well established. Although teenagers still require guidance and support, they should have by now acquired the ability to make responsible decisions. They should also have come to the realization that they are responsible for their decisions and actions. The process of transferring control will, of course, continue during the teenage years, but the foundation for making responsible choices should be in place. For example, they should know how much time they need to allocate to studying and to doing homework. They also should have developed a realistic sense of their abilities and should be developing a sense of their priorities and goals.

Responsibility is an attitude about oneself and about life. Children who realize at an early age that they are answerable for their behavior become responsible adults. Those who realize that they must apply themselves and must struggle to prevail over challenges become responsible adults.

The degree to which a child is willing to assume responsibility for his life is directly linked to how the child feels about himself. The child who takes charge of his life and considers himself accountable for his actions is signaling that he possesses self-esteem and self-confidence. These qualities will imprint themselves on all of his actions.

A child's basic attitudes about himself, about responsibility, and about life are acquired during childhood. Insightful, fair, decisive, supportive, and loving parents dramatically affect the development of these attitudes. Parents who are willing to work at developing their parenting skills significantly improve the odds that their child will ultimately become an achieving, responsible adult.

CHAPTER 9

Dealing with the Emotional Fallout

KEVIN: CHOOSING AMONG THREE OPTIONS

Kevin was visibly upset with his instructor, and the instructor was equally upset with him. The thirteen-year-old had been given a specific language arts assignment to complete during the one-hour tutoring session. When I entered the classroom, I could hear the instructor telling Kevin that he was dissatisfied with the work he had done during the first forty minutes of the session. The seventh grader responded that he had written only four sentences because he had been thinking. The teacher was skeptical. He told Kevin that he had observed him spending most of the period playing with his pencil and looking out the window. He then advised Kevin that if he didn't increase his output during the final twenty minutes, he would have to stay an additional hour to complete the work. Kevin's facial expression mirrored his anger. He told the teacher that he felt that he was being unfair. The teacher, however, was adamant. The assignment would have to be completed, and the work would have to be up to the standards previously established by the tutor.

Perceiving that Kevin was about to go into a shut-down mode, I felt it appropriate to intervene. Although I knew that the teacher normally had a great deal of patience with distractible children, I could see that he was becoming exasperated. I asked Kevin to come into my office. As he sat down across the table from me, the teenager looked very glum.

LJG: You are really upset with the teacher.

KEVIN: I wasn't goofing off. I was thinking about what I was going to write, and he started to get on my case. He always does that. He never lets me think.

LJG: Do you feel that writing four sentences in forty minutes is a reasonable output?

KEVIN: I don't know.

LJG: Were you playing with your pencil and doodling on your paper?

KEVIN: Yeh, I suppose.

LJG: Let's assume that you were the tutor, and a student wasn't doing his work. Do you feel that you would have a responsibility to the student and his parents to come down on him?

KEVIN: Maybe.

LJG: Do you feel that a teacher has the right to get on someone's case when the student's work is sloppy and illegible?

KEVIN: I guess so.

LJG: This is your paper, Kevin. It represents forty minutes of work. Describe it for me.

KEVIN: It's not very long.

LJG: And?

KEVIN: It's sloppy.

LJG: Is this the best work you can do?

KEVIN: No.

LJG: Let me ask you a question. Does your dad have a boss?

KEVIN: Yeh.

LJG: Does he have to do good work in order to please his boss?

KEVIN: Yeh.

LJG: Well, your tutor answers to me. I am his boss. He knows the standard that I expect from our students. Kids are expected to put out 100 percent when they are at the center. Your tutor is pushing you because he knows the rules. If those rules are unfair, they are unfair because I made them, not the tutor. Now, *you* know the rules. Can you accept them?

KEVIN: Yes.

LJG: Good. Kevin, I am going to give you three choices. Choice one: you can decide to complete the work in class. Choice two: you can come for an additional hour of learning assistance when you do not complete the required work. Choice three: you can take the assignments home to complete. Let's be clear about the quality of work that is expected: complete, grammatically correct sentences that are neatly written and legible. Do you feel that the options I have given you are fair and reasonable?

KEVIN: Yes.

LJG: Kevin, if the tutor and I weren't certain that you could meet this standard, we would not expect it of you. You have the skills. We want to make certain that you get in the habit of using them. Now, I want you to think carefully about your choices. The quality and quantity of your work during the next session will tell us which choice you have made.

I knew that the language arts assignment the instructor had given Kevin was reasonable and that Kevin had the skills to complete the work within the allotted time. Kevin was habituated to procrastinating and pressing adults' "hot buttons." His teachers reported that he manifested the same counterproductive behaviors in his regular school.

As a child, Kevin had discovered that whenever he appeared upset, his parents would bend the rules. He learned that his scowl was quite intimidating, not only to his parents but also to many of his teachers. Like his parents, the teachers frequently would back down and accept the minimum amount of effort from him. The behavior had served Kevin so well that he now used it whenever he wanted to avoid work. He had become quite adept at playing the role of angry victim. If he were permitted to continue doing so, he probably would play this role throughout his life.

Although the tutor had resisted backing down, he nevertheless had been pulled into the script. Kevin was a master at using excuses as a smokescreen. He realized that he could press the tutor's "hot button" whenever he wished. His behavior also served another function: It guaranteed attention.

Before Kevin could make any significant academic progress, the dynamics of his script would have to be changed. To defeat his manipulative behavior, clear and consistently enforced performance standards and consequences would have to be defined. The three options I gave Kevin permitted him to exercise *legitimate*, *nonmanipulative control* over his life. He would have to make a choice, and he then would have to assume responsibility for that choice. Game playing would not be tolerated.

The following week, Kevin completed his assignments in class. The work was neat, legible, and beautifully written.

RELINQUISHING
MANIPULATIVE BEHAVIOR

To avoid the pain of having to confront their limitations, learning disabled children can become very adept at manipulating their parents and teachers. For example, a child with a learning disability may say or imply that he doesn't have any homework when, in fact, he does have homework. He may use this subterfuge because he does not want, or may not be able, to cope with additional schoolwork. Although the child is misrepresenting the truth, he actually may have convinced himself that he doesn't have homework because this is what he wants to believe.

Expecting a child to relinquish entrenched behavior without a struggle is unrealistic. Nevertheless, the behavior *must* be actively discouraged. The child who realizes that he can manipulate himself out of having to deal with his learning problems probably will begin using this behavior whenever he encounters any type of difficulty. With sufficient practice, he may become so adept at controlling his parents and his teachers that the trait could become an integral part of his personality. Unless the behavior is reoriented during the formative years, the highly manipulative child will probably evolve into a highly manipulative adult.

As previously stated, manipulative behavior may be unconsciously perceived as a basic survival mechanism by a child who feels inadequate and vulnerable. To the child, the behavior may be the path of least resistance. Finding a way—any way—to avoid a seemingly inevitable defeat can be very tempting to a struggling child.

Manipulation can assume many forms. Some children become quite charming and use their charm very effectively to get what they want. Others throw temper tantrums or slam doors when they don't get their way. Like Kevin, these children discover that they can control others through intimidation.

The spectrum of manipulative behavior ranges from outright lying, blaming, and rebelliousness on the active end of the spectrum to indifference, irresponsibility, and laziness on the passive end. Ironically, most manipulative children are not consciously aware that they are being manipulative.

There is a payoff for every manipulation. The payoffs may range from being permitted to stay up past bedtime to getting Mom's attention by making her angry. When a child perceives his parents or teachers to be slot machines, he has a powerful incentive to keep on playing the game.

He will learn that all he has to do to get a reaction is to keep on pulling the handle. As most gamblers can attest, slot machines tend to become very addictive.

The key to convincing a child to give up his manipulative behavior is to convince him that the behavior will not work. Parents can best accomplish this by not buying into the child's behavior. A parent reading this statement might respond: "Easier said than done!" Indeed, resisting being manipulated by a consummate manipulator can be one of parenting's greatest challenges.

The first step in developing a strategy for dealing with manipulative behavior is to obtain accurate information about what is happening in the child's life. This information will permit parents to discern truth from fiction. If they are to obtain accurate data, parents must establish an effective communication system with their child's teacher. The teacher's feedback will alert parents to how the child is doing in class and precisely what the teacher expects from the child. A good communication system also reduces the risk of the parents discovering in April or May that the teacher is recommending that their child be retained. Parents who request periodic parent-teacher conferences are alerting the teacher that they want their child's performance closely monitored. Regularly scheduled conferences also allow the teacher to alert parents when they need to monitor their child's homework more closely. (See Chapter 7.)

Manipulative behavior is usually well scripted. A child who gets into the habit of blaming others when he does poorly in school may discover that his parents respond quite predictably to this behavior by immediately taking his side or by rescuing him. The child making this discovery would be very tempted to continue being manipulative.

If parents are to resist being manipulated, they must figure out the script. Were their child to tell them that he failed an exam because his teacher asked unfair questions, they have several response options:

1. They can automatically accept their child's excuse.
2. They can disagree with their child's explanation.
3. They can accuse their child of being untruthful or lazy.
4. They can discuss the issues and attempt to determine why their child feels his teacher was unfair.
5. They can request a conference with the teacher to discuss their child's perceptions.

Response #1 (automatic acceptance) probably indicates that the parents are caught up in a rescue script. Although it is possible that the child is correct and that the teacher did indeed ask "unfair" (or unexpected) questions, the parents need more information before they can reasonably support their child's position. The child who concludes that his parents will respond with carte blanche support for his excuses is being encouraged to make excuses whenever he encounters difficulty or frustration. Children can become very adept at manipulating their parents into providing support for their irresponsible behavior.

Response #2 (disagreement) sets the stage for an argument. The child may react by feeling even more victimized. He may shout, "You never believe me or take my side!" To reject a child's contention of unfairness without an objective examination of the issues encourages distrust and disrespect. The child may focus on his disillusionment with his parents' lack of support for his position, and may fail to look at the basic issue— confronting and resolving the learning problems. By responding in this way, his parents join the ranks of his teacher and have become "oppressors."

Response #3 (accusation) creates an even more emotionally charged adversarial context. With justification, the child will perceive himself as being attacked and will mobilize his defenses. He may become withdrawn and sullen, or he may become angry. If the parents' reaction triggers a showdown, the resulting conflict will deflect attention from the problem and divert the energy necessary to resolve the problem. The child will simply become more resistant and intransigent.

Response #4 (parent/child discussion) creates an opportunity for the family to explore the issues underlying the child's poor performance on the exam and his response to his poor performance. Although the child's excuse may be accurately identified by the parents as an attempt to absolve himself from any responsibility for his performance, the child, nevertheless, deserves an opportunity to express his position and feelings. By functioning as a sounding board, the parents can help him sort out the issues and understand his responses. The way in which parents orchestrate the discussion is critical. If they respond to their child's feelings judgmentally, they risk turning him off. However, if they encourage him to express his perceptions and use this discussion as an opportunity to clarify the issues, they can help him attain greater insight. The following dialogue models one possible strategy.

PARENT: What did the teacher do that was unfair?

CHILD: She gave us a math test, and she didn't ask us the things we were supposed to study.

PARENT: What did you think you were supposed to study?

CHILD: Fractions.

PARENT: What was on the test?

CHILD: Word problems.

PARENT: Give me an example.

CHILD: I'll show you one from the test. If $\frac{1}{4}$ of the class of 32 students went to the football game and $\frac{1}{4}$ of those students bought popcorn, how many bought popcorn? That's an unfair question!

PARENT: Does that problem involve fractions?

CHILD: Yeah, I guess so, but she didn't ask fair questions.

PARENT: Do you think the teacher was trying to find out if you really understood how fractions work?

CHILD: Maybe. But her questions were not like the problems in the book. We had tons of problems with fractions. We practiced adding them, subtracting them, and multiplying them.

PARENT: Do the other students in the class also feel the test was unfair?

CHILD: I guess some do.

PARENT: Could you have been confused about how to use fractions?

CHILD: Maybe.

PARENT: Do you think it is possible that the teacher felt she was being fair?

CHILD: Well, she might think she was fair, but I still don't think she was.

PARENT: Perhaps the teacher really wasn't trying to trick you. Perhaps she was just trying to find out if you really understood the material. Think about it. In the morning, if you are still convinced that you have been treated unfairly, I recommend that you discuss your feelings with the teacher.

By suggesting alternative ways to look at the problem, the parent is helping the child gain a new perspective on what may be a recurring behavior problem—the tendency to blame others for his failure. At the same time, the parent carefully resists the temptation to judge the child and refrains from trying to solve the problem for him. The process models an analytical, strategic, problem-solving approach that should serve the child in good stead throughout his life.

The child who predictably reacts to academic setback by blaming his teacher usually responds in the same way to setbacks in other situations. Parents who refuse to buy into this behavior are discouraging the child from being manipulative. At first, the child may be frustrated by this change in the dynamics of the family system. When he discovers that his parents are not responding in the scripted way, he may be confused and unsettled. In time, however, the child will learn to adjust and will become more aware of the consequences of his actions. As he becomes acclimated to a more honest communication system, he will begin to appreciate the fact that he can no longer be manipulative. Children who wield too much power are invariably unhappy and confused. Although they probably would not admit it, they are unconsciously relieved when their parents reassert their legitimate authority. Should the child become excessively unsettled by changes in the family system, professional advice should be sought.

Response #5 (parent-teacher discussion) represents another option. The child may have been correct, and the test actually may have been unfair. If the child is convinced of the accuracy of his perspective and can present plausible justification for his position, he should be given the benefit of the doubt. To attempt to convince him that he is wrong or to discount his perceptions a priori is unfair. A parent-teacher conference will permit the teacher to present his side. By inviting the child to participate in the conference, parents afford him an opportunity to express his feelings. Parents, however, must recognize that the conference may be quite intimidating for the child, and, despite their encouragement, he may choose not to participate. Nevertheless, by inviting him, the child realizes that his parents support his right to "have his day in court."

Most classroom teachers are receptive to scheduling conferences with parents and children. Encouraging a child to communicate openly and frankly with an authority figure is an invaluable learning experience. If the child's perceptions about the teacher are accurate, the teacher should have this input. If the child's perceptions are inaccurate, the child requires clarification. If the child is being manipulative, he needs to recognize that this behavior will not work.

The transition from manipulative to authentic behavior can be painful for everyone in the family. Children tend to hold onto their manipulative behavior. The letting-go process must proceed in stages. During the transition, parents must provide support, understanding, sensitivity, firmness, and love. Once the child becomes convinced that he can succeed without having to resort to manipulative behavior, he will be far more receptive to the idea of relinquishing his manipulative behavior.

MARK: RUNNING AWAY FROM HIS ANGER

From my office window, I could see Mark storm out of the classroom. The thirteen-year-old went to a bench in front of the center to wait for his mother. I knew that his class would not end for another hour. Although I could see that the teenager needed some time to cool off, I also knew that it was important that he return to class. I let him sit on the bench for five minutes, and then I walked over to him.

Later, in my office, Mark explained with barely contained fury that the teacher had corrected him repeatedly when he had been doing the activity correctly. Because he was so upset with how unfair she was, he decided to leave the classroom. He told me that he had decided to drop out of the program.

From past experience, I knew that whenever Mark became upset, he would remove himself from the situation responsible for his upset. He could see nothing wrong with this behavior. He explained that when he became angry, he became *very* angry. At such times, it was best for him to go off by himself.

I asked Mark if he would quit his job if someday a future boss unjustly corrected him for a mistake that he felt he hadn't made. He replied emphatically that he would. I then asked him if he would do the same thing if his next boss did something he felt was unjustified. This time he responded with more reluctance that he would still walk out. I then inquired what he would say to the next employer who was thinking of hiring him. Would he tell why he quit his last two jobs? Mark didn't respond.

During the next ten minutes, Mark and I talked about anger. I described some of the things that made me angry, and he described the things that made him angry. We also discussed the choices a person has about how to handle anger. Finally, we discussed how Mark had chosen to handle his anger.

Mark and I made a deal. If he could figure out a way to hold onto his anger until after class, he could then tell any of the teachers on my staff precisely what his feelings were without fear of getting into trouble. Walking out or blowing up in class would violate the agreement, and he would have to attend a makeup session.

I then informed Mark that it was time to go back to class and that I would work with him for a while. When he realized that he was not being given a choice in the matter, he agreed to accompany me back to the classroom. We began working together, and I could see immediately why the instructor had been correcting him. Mark was doing the assigned activities incorrectly, primarily because he was impulsive and wasn't concentrating. With some prodding on my part, he began to attend to the task. When I left the classroom to return to my office, Mark was doing fine. In fact, he had one of his best days at the center. After class he came into my office with a big smile on his face. He wanted me to know that he jumped rope thirty-two times while blindfolded and while spelling his name backwards. The activity demanded absolute concentration. Three weeks previously this distractible, overweight, poorly coordinated teenager hadn't been able to jump rope at all!

Mark hadn't been permitted to run away this time. He learned that he could choose how to handle his anger and that he would have to deal with the consequences of his choices. If he chose to get angry at the teacher during class, he would have to attend a makeup class. The same consequence applied when he left the classroom without permission.

Terrified by his own anger, Mark felt a compelling need to orchestrate all situations so that he could remain in control of himself and the situation. He would accomplish this by running away whenever he experienced any frustration. In so doing, Mark was able to delude himself into thinking that he was acting responsibly. My immediate job was to convince him that he could manage his anger without having to run away and that he could not use anger as an excuse for giving up.

I had no illusions about having made any significant inroads into the source of Mark's hostility during our short session together. It was clear that he would need a therapist to help him examine and sort out the feelings that were triggering his intense emotions. The sooner he began the process of delving into the source of his anger, the sooner he would be able to release himself from his fear of his own anger.

Upon my recommendation, Mark's parents agreed to have their son evaluated by a child psychologist. I was certain that therapy would permit

Mark to discover that his fury was not nearly as devastating as he feared. Once he realized this, he could stop running away from himself.

HANDLING FAILURE AND FRUSTRATION

Sensitivity to failure is a very human reaction. Even the most emotionally healthy child can begin to doubt himself and his abilities when faced with a series of successive failures. Most children, however, are able to bounce back from setbacks if their self-esteem is basically intact and if they recognize that the setbacks are temporary.

The child with a history of failure often lacks the requisite emotional resources to rebound from defeat because his self-esteem is fragile and because he realizes that he will undoubtedly encounter further setbacks. A child's life experiences must inevitably color his perceptions and perspective. Failure invariably produces negative self-esteem, attitudes, and expectations. Although a child may actually be making progress in resolving his learning problems, he may remain convinced that he is hopelessly inadequate. With each new defeat, real or imagined, his self-esteem becomes more tenuous and his psychological defense mechanisms more impenetrable.

Rarely does a child with a serious learning disability say: "Today was a terrible day, but I know that tomorrow things will be better." For the struggling child who never experiences even a minor victory, there is an excellent chance that tomorrow will be an equally terrible day, unless he is fortunate enough to receive meaningful learning assistance.

The learning disabled youngster is the victim of a vicious cycle. Because he has failed so often, he never develops a positive mental attitude. Without a positive mental attitude, he cannot develop the necessary willpower and determination he needs to be able to succeed.

Parents and teachers can best help the child with a learning problem break the failure/poor self-esteem cycle by assuring him of their support for his efforts and their resolve that he prevail. This resolve and support will serve as an interim surrogate for the resiliency, willpower, confidence, and positive mental attitude that the child himself has not yet acquired.

A child who has learned how to rebound from defeat has acquired an important survival skill. Resiliency in the face of failure is an invaluable emotional resource. Unfortunately, there is no magic system for teaching a child how to handle setbacks.

Although some children voluntarily will talk to their parents about their feelings when they encounter a setback, others will have difficulty sharing these emotions. Those who feel guilt, embarrassment, sadness, frustration, or anger may need extra support and time before they would be willing to take the first tentative steps toward sharing their innermost feelings.

Some children become guarded because they feel that if they admit they have failed at something they would profoundly disappoint their parents. They may try to hide their defeats with rationalizations, lies, or half-truths. Usually, children who are willing to talk about their feelings cope with setbacks more effectively than those who repress their feelings. A sounding board can be very therapeutic when a child's feelings and self-confidence are badly bruised.

Communicating effectively with struggling children demands exceptional parenting skills. Before an emotionally vulnerable child would be willing to express his pain and unhappiness, he would need to trust his parents. He must be certain that they will listen to him without passing judgments, blaming, or taking ownership of his problems.

Effective communicators can sense when they need to give their child sufficient time and space to mull over the issues and his options. They possess the patience and forbearance to permit the child to wrestle with his feelings. They know when it is appropriate to make a suggestion and when it is appropriate to remain silent. They sense when to commiserate over a disappointment and when to resist their child's manipulative behavior.

Parents lacking "natural" communication skills need not be disheartened. Communication skills can be improved if parents are motivated to improve them. The first step in the process is to make a concerted effort to understand and empathize with their child's perceptions and perspective. Parents must also be willing to examine objectively their own emotions and behavior. If they conclude that they have been responding in a way that discourages trust and communication, they must be willing to modify their counterproductive behaviors. If they feel incapable of doing this on their own, they should seek professional help.

Disappointment is a natural consequence of defeat. If the disappointment is a recurring phenomenon in the child's life, it inevitably will jade his attitude, perspective, and behavior. A major negative threshold is crossed when the child begins to accept that disappointment and sadness are inescapable facts of life. Anticipating pain, embarrassment, and failure, the child begins to construct elaborate and all but impenetrable emotional defenses. He may attempt to protect himself from the anticipated pain of defeat by surrendering, shutting down emotionally, or turning off academically. There is another possibility: he may become angry.

ANGER

Anger is a natural by-product of failure and frustration. This anger may be overt and explosive, or it may be repressed and implosive. When it is explosive, the anger usually manifests itself in aggressive or destructive behavior. When implosive, it typically manifests itself in shyness, passive aggression (teasing or put-downs), depression, or emotional withdrawal.

Anger can be terrifying for a child, especially when he feels that it is wrong for him to feel angry. The child may respond to his anger by attempting to repress the unpleasant feelings. Anger directed toward parents can be particularly insidious because it often triggers guilt and depression, especially when the anger is unconsciously felt and repressed. Knowing that he "should" love his parents, the child's unconscious realization that he actually harbors negative feelings toward them can be devastating.

For obvious reasons, the child who is hostile toward his parents often has difficulty acknowledging and accepting his anger. If he concludes that his innermost feelings are "bad," he probably will conclude that he himself is bad. To cope, he will attempt to deny, repress, screen, or deflect the unwanted emotions. Despite these efforts, the child must inevitably discover that he cannot escape from his emotions. At best, he can only create an illusion of being all right. Like an untreated cancer, unresolved feelings of anger and guilt inevitably metastasize and begin to eat away at a child's self-acceptance, self-esteem, and self-confidence.

One of the unfortunate consequences of a child's attempts to deny and repress his anger is that in the process other feelings are also denied and repressed. The child is at risk of becoming increasingly detached from his emotions. This emotional detachment may create temporarily an illusory sanctuary from the disowned emotions. To perceptive parents, the child's attempts to camouflage his anger with sarcasm, passive resistance, or passive aggression should be quite transparent.

Parents must inevitably frustrate their child from time to time. There are occasions when they must override his wishes, impose their guidelines, and reprimand him for misbehavior. On these occasions, their child will naturally feel a certain amount of resentment and hostility toward them. Parents must remind themselves that anger does not preclude love, and that love does not preclude anger. At the same time, they must realize that their child lacks their perspective and experience and that during his fit of pique he may think and act unreasonably.

Parents serve their child when they help him understand his anger and upsets and when they encourage him to express his feelings. There are, of course, limits. The angry child cannot be permitted to break the lamp in the living room or hit the dog or his younger sister. But he can be encouraged to blow off steam in his room or to hit a punching bag.

Parents also serve their child when they help him realize that he can be angry and still love them, just as they can be angry and still love him. Parents, however, who perceive that their child's anger is excessive, chronic, and/or manifests itself in destructiveness or uncontrollable aggressiveness are justified in feeling concern and are advised to consult a mental health professional.

When anger is repressed and implodes, it frequently causes depression. Depression can also be produced by exploding anger, especially when the anger triggers guilt. The two reactions can be represented graphically:

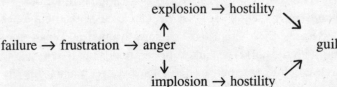

From a mental health perspective, the open expression of frustration or anger is preferable to the repression and implosion of anger, assuming the anger is not highly destructive or chronic. When angry feelings are expressed, they can be examined, and, if necessary, treated. Parents, however, must recognize the danger signals that a child's anger is symptomatic of serious underlying psychological distress. The child consumed by rage is indicating through his behavior that he is unable to cope with his underlying emotions. In the same way the child consumed by indifference is also signaling underlying emotional turmoil. The frustrated child who goes beserk and the frustrated child who retreats into an impenetrable shell are waving red flags. Both are crying out for help, and their behavior cannot be disregarded.

The recurring explosion or implosion of powerful emotions underscores the need for intervention. The nature of the child's behavior and symptoms will determine the appropriate type of intervention. In less extreme cases, a better family communication system or more clearly defined behavior standards may be all that is required. In more extreme cases, psychotherapy may be the most appropriate treatment. Nonadaptive, destructive, and self-sabotaging behaviors do not go away of their own accord. Children who are not helped to deal with these behaviors are in serious jeopardy. Many end up in prison or in mental institutions.

Identifying a child's underlying problems and providing appropriate therapy are the most effective means to protect a child from serious emotional damage. There is no stigma when parents admit that they lack the skills to help their child with a particular problem. In fact, such an admission testifies to the parents' concern, honesty, and wisdom.

Fortunately, anger and nonadaptive behavior tend to dissipate when a child begins to examine his unconscious feelings under the guidance of a skilled therapist. If parents perceive that their child's emotional turmoil and anger are causing the child pain and if they conclude that the underlying problems are too complex for them to handle, they have a responsibility to seek outside assistance. Acknowledging that they need help is not a sign of weakness or inadequate parenting, but rather a sign of wisdom and concern. The role of a therapist is to assist the child unlock the doors to his unconscious feelings so that he can deal with them on a conscious level. Because the therapist is specially trained and less emotionally entangled with the child, he can exercise greater objectivity while helping the distressed child sort out the feelings that are causing his unhappiness.

In cases of less chronic anger, parents may be able to function as their child's guide. The ideal time for them to intervene is when the child's frustration first begins to manifest itself. A simple observation or a simple question may be sufficient to open the emotional floodgates. For example, a parent might comment: "Honey, I can really see that you're upset about not doing well on that spelling test." Or the parent might ask: "Would you like to talk about how you are feeling right now?" By helping the child get in touch with his emotions and by communicating that the child will not be judged, reprimanded, or told what to do, parents can activate a vital safety valve. Of course, the ultimate goal is to show the child how to activate the safety valve himself when he senses that he is becoming angry or depressed.

The first step in communicating with a child about emotions is to listen to what the child is saying. Were a child to say he's upset about the grade he received on a test and were his parent to reply: "Well, you're just going to have to study harder," the child might never again be willing to discuss his academic performance with that parent. The child did *not* ask his parent what he needed to do in order to get a better grade. He simply volunteered to tell what he was feeling. He wanted the parent to listen and perhaps offer some sympathy. An appropriate response might have been to ask the child what he thinks he needs to do to solve the problem. If he replies that he doesn't know and asks for suggestions, the parent might respond, "Well, perhaps there's a better way to study. Maybe you can try a new approach. Let me know if you want to brainstorm some ideas with me." In responding in this way, the parent lets the child know that he or she is available to help him develop a more effective study strategy. The next move is up to the child.

Parents who recognize that they cannot work with their child because they become impatient or because they have limited knowledge about the subject matter should consider hiring a tutor. Parents must remind themselves that their child owns his problems and his emotions. They serve their child far better by providing support and guidance than they do by taking ownership of the problems and emotions.

In limited doses, the experience of failing can actually serve a positive function. Failure can be an impetus for the child to develop the skills he needs to succeed the next time around. For example, the child who goes into a batting slump but who, nevertheless, continues to practice in an effort to overcome the problems is demonstrating a basic belief in himself and his ability. By continuing to struggle and by ultimately prevailing, he is learning to face life's challenges. Had the child become emotionally distraught every time he struck out and had he quit the team in frustration, he would be internalizing a very different modus operandi. In time, the habit of running away from life's challenges would become increasingly entrenched in his personality. His surrender in the face of frustration would express his lack of faith in himself and his abilities, and this behavior would probably persist throughout his life.

Parents who model problem-solving strategies and who discourage their child from giving up when faced with a setback are helping their child transform the negative energy of failure into positive, growth-oriented energy. Striking the proper balance between protecting a child from excessive, demoralizing failure and frustration and allowing him to experience a controlled amount of failure and frustration can be one of parenting's most challenging assignments. Parents have no recourse but to rely on their intuition and instincts.

THE EFFECTS OF LEARNING PROBLEMS ON BROTHERS AND SISTERS

Whenever a child is on the receiving end of a great deal of attention, there is the possibility that the other children in the family may resent the extra attention that their brother or sister is receiving. Because the child with a learning problem is an obvious source of concern for his parents, his problems can quickly become the focus of the entire family's emotional energy.

It is common for the frustrated, demoralized child to act out. This counterproductive behavior can sorely test the patience and the endurance of everyone in the family. During the remediation process, the brothers and sisters of the learning disabled child may also require additional emotional support, especially if they are on the receiving end of the acting-out behavior. Parents will need to explain to them why their brother or sister is being given special attention and why he or she might require extra love and patience from everyone in the family until the learning problem is resolved.

Periodic family council meetings can offer an excellent opportunity for everyone to express any resentments, frustrations, hurt feelings, or misunderstandings. The expression and the nonjudgmental acknowledgment of these emotions can be an invaluable safety valve for the entire family. Being sensitive and understanding, however, does not preclude parents from providing negative feedback. The child who is responding inappropriately must be apprised of this by his parents. Guidelines that establish acceptable and unacceptable ways of expressing frustration and anger may be required.

Although children have a right to their feelings, even if these feelings are negative or unpleasant, they don't have the right to misbehave to the extent that they are making everyone miserable. Other members of the family also have rights. An unhappy ten-year-old who is frustrated in school cannot be permitted to have a tantrum in the middle of a restaurant, nor can he be permitted to terrorize his four-year-old sister. When the child's feelings create tension or unpleasantness, the feelings must be addressed. Although negative emotions sometimes dissipate of their own accord, they generally recur until the source of the negative feelings is identified and treated.

Sometimes the siblings of the learning disabled child will also act out. They may resent the attention their brother or sister is receiving, and they may tease or make fun of him. Such behavior can only magnify the child's distress and intensify his need to resort to counterproductive defense and compensatory mechanisms. Parents who perceive that their children are intentionally hurting each other through their words or deeds have an urgent need to examine and realign the family dynamics. Unless the resentments are discussed openly, they will continue to fester.

THE EFFECTS OF LEARNING PROBLEMS ON PARENTS

Many children with learning problems do not develop behavior problems. This is especially true when the learning problems are not severe or when they are identified early in a child's life. If meaningful remedial treatment begins in kindergarten or first grade, it can often prevent much of the emotional scarring that is typically a by-product of a learning problem.

Disagreement between parents about whether or not a child has a learning problem can cause a great deal of family stress and dissension. One parent may be more aware that a child is struggling in school than the other parent, or one parent may be more willing to accept the evidence than the other. Generally, fathers have more difficulty than mothers acknowledging that their child has a learning problem. This tendency in part may be attributable to the fact that mothers not employed outside of the home are on the front line. They are the ones who must often deal with the emotional and behavioral consequences of the child's academic difficulties. Teachers also tend to communicate more often with mothers about classroom or homework problems than with fathers.

Some fathers let their own ego needs affect their better judgment. They may deny that their child has a problem despite incontrovertible evidence. For such parents, admitting their child has some sort of problem is tantamount to admitting that they or their child is defective or inferior. This denial can have profoundly negative academic and emotional consequences for the child and can postpone the onset of much needed learning assistance and/or counseling.

Families who can discuss openly and forthrightly the emotional strains the family is experiencing have a distinct advantage over families who do not share such problems. Parenting the struggling child is infinitely easier when parents have each other's support.

Unfortunately, single parents of learning disabled children do not have as ready access to an emotional support system. This is especially true when the child's other parent is deceased, living in another geographical area, or on unfriendly terms with the parent who has primary custody. Because single parents may not have anyone with whom to share the tribulations, they must often shoulder a heavy burden.

Single parents may discover parent support groups in their community that are associated with their church or with local mental health organizations. Sometimes social organizations for single parents and their children provide support groups. If not, parents may wish to form their own group.

Even when there are two parents in a family, one frequently assumes the primary responsibility for dealing with the learning disabled child's needs at home and at school. The burden of responsibility can be very heavy when one parent is doing the work that should rightfully be shared by two.

FEELING GUILTY

Acknowledging that a child has a learning problem can be painful and threatening for some parents. With acknowledgment comes the responsibility for finding a means to resolve the problem.

Parents who are confused or guilt-ridden may attempt to protect themselves emotionally by denying that their child has a problem. This denial may take the form of refusing to look at the evidence which clearly documents their child's learning problem or of blaming others for their child's difficulties.

Parents who choose to deny that their child has a problem may give only marginal support to those who are attempting to provide help. They may go through the motions of giving the learning assistance "a try," but if the assistance does not quickly produce results, they may pull their child out of the program or they may look for a scapegoat. They may attribute the child's lack of immediate progress to the learning disabilities specialist, the program, the classroom teacher, the school, or the educational system.

The child who senses his parents' lack of commitment to the teacher or the remedial program will also lack commitment. Without parental support, the learning assistance program is probably destined to falter and perhaps fail.

Some parents feel that if they admit that their child has special needs, they are admitting that he is defective. Others react to their child's learning problem with excessive or unwarranted concern. This intense concern often interferes with their judgment and can cause them to overreact. For example, they may attempt to monitor their child's performance by volunteering to help out in the classroom. Although their ostensible and professed goal is to aid the teacher, their real objective may be to keep tabs on their child's progress. These same parents may also enroll their child in an outside learning assistance program and then request permission to observe each session. On an intellectual level, they may recognize that their concern is creating an unhealthy situation, but on an emotional level they are not prepared to allow their child to own his problems, nor are they prepared to trust those who are providing help for the child.

An excessively concerned mother who is intent on overseeing her child's school performance may become quite threatened when it is suggested that she not help out in the classroom. Convinced that her child would be incapable of surviving in school without her support and unwilling to acknowledge that she is creating an emotional dependency which is actually undermining the child's self-concept, she may offer all sorts of rationalizations for her taking ownership of her child's problems.

It is not uncommon for a barrier to develop between a learning therapist and excessively concerned or denial-oriented parents. The learning therapist might, for instance, recommend that a child would benefit from being placed in a special learning assistance program. Denial-oriented parents, or those whose own ego needs prevent them from admitting that their child has a problem, might regret this reasonable recommendation. To justify their position, they might argue that the formal identification of their child's learning disability would cause him to be permanently labeled as handicapped.

Schools do not use their records in the same way that the police use a "rap" sheet. Children with learning problems are identified for one purpose only: so that they can be helped. Those who overcome their learning problems are not barred from colleges because they received learning assistance in elementary or junior high school. They compete for admission on the basis of their ability, and they are judged on their academic record, their recommendations, their scores on entrance exams, and their interviews. Parents who deny their struggling child learning assistance because they fear that some day he will be discriminated against are doing their child a disservice. Without learning assistance, the child has virtually no chance of gaining admission to college. A college admissions officer is interested in a child's demonstrated level of performance, not whether he went to the resource center in fifth grade. Ironically, it is more probable that if the student chooses to reveal that he once had a learning disability and overcame it, he would actually score points with the admissions officer. His success clearly testifies to his grit and determination.

Parents who fear that their child will be indelibly branded can easily dispel their concerns. By law, they have the right to demand access to their child's school records, and they can challenge the inclusion of any information that is biased, inaccurate, or not relevant.

Guilt is one of the primary sources of excessive parental concern. In their attempt to cope with guilt, parents may act quite irrationally and counterproductively. Fearing that they are in some way responsible for their child's problems, they may respond by denying reality or by becoming excessively concerned.

Children whose parents had learning problems do have a greater statistical chance of developing those same problems. The cause and effect link, however, between learning problems and genetics is not absolute and there are countless exceptions. Many parents of learning disabled children did not have learning problems. And many parents who did struggle in school produce children who are highly successful students.

The transmission of genetic traits is an inescapable reality. Visual acuity, height, musculature, facial features, and motor skills are among the many traits that are passed from parents to child. Given the complex mix of genetic characteristics that a child inherits, it is all but inevitable that some less than perfect traits will be transmitted. Parents who conclude that they have inadvertently passed on the genetic trait responsible for learning problems must remind themselves of the many other far more devastating afflictions that a child can suffer.

Few reasonable parents would feel guilty if their child is nearsighted or if he later becomes bald. There is nothing parents can do to prevent the genetic transmission of less-than-perfect eyesight or pattern baldness. The same is true in the case of a learning disability. A child's need for eyeglasses, a speech therapist, or a tutor is a small price to pay for providing a child with the gift of life. All parents can do is to provide their children with the appropriate assistance when assistance is needed.

Parental guilt feelings are often based on misinformation. A parent may feel responsible for her child's learning problem because she smoked during pregnancy. Another may fear that her child's learning problem was caused by her going back to work soon after the child was born. Smoking may damage an unborn fetus, but no direct link between smoking and learning problems has been documented, nor has any direct link between child care and learning disabilities been documented. The child of an employed mother who receives love and is provided with adequate sensory stimulation is no more likely to become learning disabled than a child raised at home by his mother.

As many as eight million children in the United States are struggling in school. This staggering population of children represents the potential for creating sixteen million guilt-ridden parents. If they wish, parents can choose to feel guilty about something which they could not prevent from happening, or they can choose to provide their child with the means for resolving his problem. Those providing quality assistance and emotional support serve their child far better than those who allow guilt to waste, divert, or mutate their energy.

CHAPTER 10

Communicating with Your Child

CRAIG: HE COULD HANDLE THE TRUTH

I was totally charmed by the redheaded, freckle-faced nine-year-old. As he progressed from task to task, his expression ranged from intense seriousness to sparkling joy.

Craig was giving total effort as he worked on each subsection of the diagnostic test. When I began showing him letters and numbers to determine if he could recognize and remember them, I could see absolute concentration mirrored in his face. Despite his intensity, the third grader was clearly enjoying himself, and he proudly informed me that his special teacher in school had done many of the same things with him.

Craig's enthusiasm quickly disappeared when I began to assess his auditory processing skills. He had great difficulty with any task that required auditory memory. As he struggled to keep track of the number of beats and the rhythm of the patterns I was clapping, he became increasingly frustrated and discouraged. Distinguishing the different vowel sounds was very difficult for him. This difficulty could not be attributed to a hearing impairment, as the nine-year-old's hearing had recently been tested by his pediatrician and was within the normal range. It was clear that Craig had a perceptual dysfunction. Other specific learning deficits supported the diagnosis of a sensory processing problem: poor phonics and visual tracking skills and reading and math skills that were approximately two years below grade level. Given this wide spectrum of symptoms, it did not surprise me that Craig's reading was highly inaccurate and labored and that he was struggling desperately to keep up in school.

Despite Craig's blatant learning deficits, none of his teachers had ever suggested to his parents that he had a learning disability. His parents, however, could see that their son was not learning properly, and they insisted that he be evaluated by the school psychologist. The diagnostic work-up confirmed their suspicions. Craig had a relatively severe learning disability. Ironically, his positive attitude, pleasing personality, and conscientiousness had worked in his disfavor. He was so nice and so cooperative that his teachers had chosen to overlook his learning problems. Now that he was falling further and further behind, his academic deficits could no longer be ignored.

When he entered third grade, Craig was enrolled in a full-time learning disabilities program. According to his parents, he had made virtually no academic progress in this program.

My diagnostic evaluation revealed nothing that would suggest an organic neurological disorder (see Chapter 3 for a discussion of the symptoms of neurologically based learning disabilities). Craig's gross- and fine-motor coordination were good, and he did not appear to have any difficulty paying attention. Although I did not administer an intelligence test, I was certain that the boy's IQ was in the normal range. On a scale from 1 to 10 (1 representing a very subtle learning problem and 10 representing a severe problem), I assigned the third grader a score of 7.

Craig's parents told me that they had been reluctant to bring him to the center because they feared that he might become demoralized. He had only recently begun his special program in school, and his parents felt that he might conclude that there was something profoundly wrong with him if they enrolled him in another learning assistance program. Craig's parents were also concerned about putting too much pressure on him.

Although I knew from past experience that the learning assistance program at Craig's school was basically sound, I felt that he would benefit from additional help in the area of auditory processing (see Chapter 3 for a discussion of perceptual processing deficits). Because of the seriousness of his auditory problems, I did not concur with Craig's parents that an additional two hours of intense learning assistance would be an unfair burden to impose upon him. Rather than add to the pressure he was experiencing, I felt that the additional help would actually reduce the pressure and considerably speed up the remediation process.

I presented the idea of receiving additional help in very positive terms to Craig. I assured him that the program would make school much easier and would help him to become a better student. Sensing that Craig liked challenges, I wanted to capitalize on his fighting spirit.

When I explained to Craig why he was struggling in school and why he was having difficulty remembering what he heard, I could see his relief. Despite his positive disposition, the child was painfully aware of his learning deficits. Now he finally understood why he was struggling. I explained that his learning problem could be corrected, if he was willing to work with us. I also assured him that having a learning problem did not mean that he was dumb. From my experience, I knew that this secret—and in some cases the not-so-secret—fear of many learning disabled children had to be addressed directly. Despite my attempts to allay his fears, I had no illusions that Craig fully believed me when I told him he was intelligent. Only a pattern of academic achievement would ultimately convince him of his intelligence. Our responsibility was to orchestrate this pattern of achievement.

I was not surprised when Craig readily agreed to my proposal that he receive extra help. Like most struggling children, he desperately wanted to succeed in school. His parents' fears about his becoming demoralized or overburdened were unwarranted.

HONESTY: THE FIRST STEP

Children are rarely oblivious to the fact that they have a learning disability. Although they may not be willing to admit to themselves or their parents that they need help, they *know* they are having difficulty learning. They need only look around the classroom to see how much easier it is for their classmates to master the material with which they are struggling.

When parents explain to their child that he has a learning problem and that with special help the problem can be corrected, they are lifting a great weight from the child's shoulders. The issue is out in the open and can now be dealt with constructively. By confronting the problem forthrightly and positively, parents communicate to their child that they understand the struggle and they are there to provide support and encouragement.

Children become confused when their parents intentionally avoid discussing a learning disability. Although these parents may have the best of intentions and may be attempting to spare their child from having to confront something unpleasant, they are actually compounding the problem by shrouding it in mystery. Deprived of information and feedback, the child may conclude that his deficiencies are more serious than they actually are, or that his parents are too embarrassed or ashamed to discuss the issue with him.

Some parents hesitate to discuss the learning problem openly because they fear that to do so would cause their child to feel "defective" or "different." Compelled by excessive concern, and perhaps guilt, they expend a great deal of emotional energy trying to insulate their child from reality. As they build a protective, and essentially ineffective, shield around their child, they create the illusion that everything is OK. Although their motives may be good, the net effect of their efforts is to impede the remediation process.

Parents who believe they can protect their child from pressure or from feeling inadequate by avoiding any discussion about the learning problem or by pretending it doesn't exist are deluding themselves and are not helping their child. This denial of reality only delays the day of reckoning.

The "truth" can be a double-edged sword, depending upon how the truth is used. The way in which parents communicate the facts about their child's learning problems can profoundly affect how the child responds to the challenges he faces. When parents communicate positive expectations, they usually elicit a positive response. Conversely, when they express their frustration, exasperation, and anger they usually elicit a negative response. The father who tells his procrastinating learning disabled child that he will never be able to get a decent job unless he stops being lazy may be telling the truth as he perceives it. Although he is upset and angry about his child's irresponsible behavior, he should not be surprised if his son reacts to his statement by becoming defensive and resistant. Being honest with a child does not mean using the truth as a bludgeon. Parents who frontally assault their child with the "facts" invariably trigger fear, anger, resentment, and/or rebellion.

A parent can be honest and still emphasize the positive and de-emphasize the negative. Parents can tell their child that he has a learning problem and, at the same time, assure him that his learning problem can be resolved with appropriate assistance and effort. By using the truth positively and supportively, they affirm their faith in their child's capacity to prevail over his difficulties, and they invite his active participation in the remediation process. Children can sense when their parents are expressing confidence in them. This expressed confidence can be a pivotal factor in determining the ultimate success of the remediation program.

Parents should not be surprised if their child attempts to run away from his learning problem. A child who is struggling may feel compelled to deny that he is having difficulty in school for the same reasons that an adult might feel compelled to deny that he has a drinking problem or a gambling problem. Admitting a problem can be threatening and frightening to anyone with a poor self-concept and tenuous emotional resiliency. By pretending that his problems do not exist, the child is desperately trying to delude himself that everything is OK.

A highly defensive child who denies that he has a problem may be emotionally unable to accept reality. To insist that the child confront the "facts" and change his behavior immediately could cause unnecessary psychological stress. Understanding the facts, sorting out feelings, and mobilizing emotional resources requires time. Parents must realize that their child's reluctance to engage himself in the remediation process is usually a reflection of uncertainty and fear. They may need to initiate several discussions before their child can accept the realities of his situation and get on with the job of prevailing over the problem.

Children who persist in denying that they have a problem despite compelling evidence may need to be gently coerced into accepting help. An eight-year-old who is not ready to accept that he has a learning problem may reject the idea of learning assistance. Because they cannot risk waiting until the child becomes overwhelmed by his academic deficiencies, his parents may need to act unilaterally and without the child's approval. Once the child realizes that he is making progress, his initial resistance and trepidation usually will dissipate.

The response patterns of children to confronting their learning problems can vary significantly. Older children with a long history of academic difficulty can be quite resistant to accepting help (see Chapter 11, "Dealing with Learning Disabled Teenagers"). After years of frustration, the teenager's defense mechanisms and feelings of inadequacy are often very elaborate. Parents may need to tap into their own emotional reserves in order to find the requisite patience and resolve to persist on a course that their intuition tells them is correct.

Teachers must also confront the challenge of discussing the "facts" with the learning disabled child in terms he can understand. Not only must they communicate with honesty and sensitivity, but they must also figure out how to improve the child's learning skills, build his confidence, and motivate him. Realistic goals, expectations, and guidelines must be established. Should the child falter, his teacher must then find the means to get him untracked. These are awesome responsibilities.

The attitude of the classroom teacher and the resource specialist plays a key role in the remediation equation. The way in which they present the issues invariably influences the child's response to the learning assistance program. Teachers who clearly communicate their expectation that the child will prevail are expressing a vital vote of confidence in the child. This vote of confidence can be one of the most important factors in determining the success or failure of the assistance program.

There is no single, ideal strategy for examining a learning problem with a child. Whatever approach parents or teachers select, they should make sure that the approach is congruent with their personalities and that of the child.

The use of analogies and metaphors can be a very effective resource in helping a child understand his learning problem and accept assistance. Two examples of how this method might be used are modeled here. The analogies are oriented toward children in grades one through six. "Upgraded" analogies could be used with equivalent effectiveness in communicating with teenagers.

The Race Car Analogy

LJG: Do you know what a Ferrari (or a Porsche or a Trans Am) is?

CHILD: Yeah, a car.

LJG: What kind of car?

CHILD: A fast car.

LJG: Yes, a fast car with a super engine. What happens when the car isn't running well?

CHILD: You take it to a garage.

LJG: That's right. You take it in for a tune-up. In a way, you are just like a car. You also have a super engine. This engine is in your brain. But just like a car sometimes needs a tune-up, you also need a tune-up. The tune-up will help you to run better and do well in school. You don't want to run like an old stationwagon when you have a Ferrari engine, do you?

CHILD: No.

LJG: This tune-up is special. Instead of adjusting your carburetor like a mechanic might do with a car, we need to work on your concentration, your reading, your spelling, and your handwriting. When we're done giving you a tune-up, you'll run like a race car. School will be easier for you because you will no longer have learning problems. How does that sound?

CHILD: Good.

LJG: Do you want us to help you do better in school?

CHILD: Yes.

LJG: Are you ready for a tune-up?

CHILD: Yes.

LJG: Super! Let's start next week.

The Athlete Analogy

LJG: If you wanted to be on the U.S. Olympic swim team, what do you think you would have to do?

CHILD: I'd have to practice.

LJG: That's right. You would have to get up really early every morning and swim laps in the pool. And your coach would give you exercises to improve your speed and to make you a stronger swimmer. Do you think it would be hard doing all that training?

CHILD: No. Well, maybe.

LJG: Do you know how to swim?

CHILD: Yes.

LJG: Even though you already know how to swim, do you think the coach might want to help you learn to swim better so that you could make the team?

CHILD: Yes.

LJG: Well, we want to show you how to learn better so that you can do well in school. Of course, you already know how to read, but we feel that we can help you improve your reading. Just like the swimming coach, we're going to train you to become a better student. We will give you things to practice so that your reading, math, and concentration improve. It will be hard work, like swimming laps can be hard work. But I know you're smart and you're tough, and you can do it. Soon you'll find that the hard work is paying off. You won't have to struggle as much in school. You'll be keeping up with the class and getting better grades. How does that sound?

CHILD: Good.

LJG: Great! We'll start the program next week.

Parents can choose from among many possible metaphors and analogies. These can be used not only to help the child understand his learning problem but also to encourage him to become actively involved in the process of resolving it. When children form meaningful associations with information, they generally have far less difficulty comprehending and remembering the issues. Metaphors and analogies have another advantage. If a child should falter during the remediation process, his parents can refer to the metaphor or analogy again and use it to rekindle and sustain the child's effort and commitment.

Communicating with a defensive, frustrated, resistant, or unhappy child can be extremely challenging. Through trial and error, each parent must develop a communication strategy that feels comfortable and natural. Confronting the truth and accepting the facts may be painful for the child at first, but the sooner the child deals with the reality of his situation, the sooner he can get on with the job of resolving the problem.

Learning disabilities have the potential to create serious strains in the family. Parents who confront the situation openly, seek advice when necessary, agree on a remediation strategy, support each other, and communicate openly with their child can significantly improve the chances of prevailing over these strains.

COMMUNICATING VS. LECTURING

Being on the receiving end of a lecture is a passive experience for a child. Although certain children respond positively to lectures, most simply shift into cerebral "neutral" when they are being admonished. The child's primary concern is to get the lecture over with as quickly and painlessly as possible.

Under certain circumstances, however, a lecture may be the most appropriate remedy. Parents who emphatically tell their five-year-old that unless he is ill he is not to disturb them on weekend mornings before eight o'clock are communicating a reasonable rule of the house. Although parents may find that the admonition approach works, they may also find that they can achieve their objective more effectively by using a strategy that empahisizes reasoning to communicate the house rules to their child. Such a strategy is modeled here:

PARENT: After you go to sleep at night, do you know what mommy and daddy are talking about, or what we might be watching on TV?

CHILD: No.

PARENT: Why can't you tell what we are doing?

CHILD: Because I'm sleeping!

PARENT: Do you think you would be happy if we woke you up to tell you it was raining outside?

CHILD: No.

PARENT: Would you be mad?

CHILD: Yes.

PARENT: Do your think mommy and daddy would wake you up to tell you it's raining?

CHILD: No.

PARENT: You're right. We love you, and we know that it would make you unhappy if we woke you up to tell you something that is not important. Well, on the weekends mommy and daddy like to sleep until it's time for us to get up. Now, you can read the number "8" on the clock in your room. When you see that the number 8 is the first number, you can knock on the door and come into our room. We know that you love us as much as we love you. And we also know that you wouldn't want to make us unhappy by waking us up when we are trying to sleep. Is that true?

CHILD: Yes.

PARENT: What do you think you could do in the morning if you get up before we do?

CHILD: I could play in my room.

PARENT: Yes, you could. Or you could go into the living room and watch TV. And if you're hungry you could go into the kitchen and have a banana or a glass of milk. Does that sound OK?

CHILD: Yes.

PARENT: Good. Let's see if tomorrow you can take care of yourself until we get up. I'm betting that you can!

This dialogue represents a communication strategy that actively involves the child in the process of recognizing, understanding, and modifying his unacceptable behavior. The approach represents an alternative to the more traditional responses to a child's misbehavior: a command, a lecture, or a threat of punishment for noncompliance.

The command/lecture/threat method can, of course, be effective. A young child can usually be easily intimidated by his parents. Some children, however, respond to highly authoritarian parents with passive resistance. Although children do not have as much overt power as their parents, they do have covert power. The child who is intent on using this covert power to thwart his parents can make life miserable for everyone in the family.

Children usually react on a reflex level to an upset parent. In the face of anger, the typical reaction is: "Uh, oh, I'm in trouble again, and I'm going to get punished." Although the child's behavior may change because of the threat of punishment, he is essentially responding out of fear. The impact of this type of behavior modification tends to diminish when the threat of punishment is overused.

Family systems based on parents having all of the power are tenuous. Parents must recognize a basic fact of life: As their child matures, the power base begins to shift. A six-year-old may have little real power, but a sixteen-year-old has a great deal of power. If he so desires, he can take the family car without permission, drink beer with his friends, or take drugs. His parents, of course, can punish him, but they have relatively few options to control him if the teenager refuses to obey them. They cannot go to his parties with him, or monitor him when he is in school. The overuse of autocratic parental power is like bluffing in a poker game. The person who bluffs too often is ultimately going to be "called."

Parents who show consideration for their child's feelings are encouraging their child to be considerate of other people's feelings. Knowing how to communicate disapproval for a child's behavior without eliciting a power struggle, resentment, or resistance is a vital parenting skill. By helping a child understand why a particular behavior is unacceptable, parents increase the likelihood that he will be more receptive to changing his behavior. Introspection usually produces insight, and this insight can lead to a greater appreciation for the rights, feelings, and sensitivities of others.

At 6:00 A.M., it may be both appropriate and effective to yell "Quiet!" to a five-year-old who is making too much noise. It may also be appropriate and effective to tell him unequivocally and emphatically the family's rules about noise on Saturday morning: "If you get up before mom and me, you can either stay in your room and play, quietly watch TV, or go to the kitchen and get something to eat. Unless you are sick, you are not to wake us.'' The rules are the same as those described in the previously modeled dialogue. The difference is that in the dialogue an attempt is being made to help the child understand the rationale for the family rule. In the second scenario, the misbehavior has already occurred, and the parent is expressing his anger after the fact.

The ideal objective in disciplining a child is to help him recognize the reasonableness of the behavior being demanded. Strategic, nonconfrontational communication can usually achieve this objective far more effectively than angry, threatening communication.

The same communication strategy used to help children appreciate the effects of their behavior on others can also be used to examine the implications of a learning problem. Actively involving the child in the process of examining the realities of his school situation is the key to making the strategy work. By eliciting and acknowledging the child's feelings and perceptions, parents can help him take ownership of his learning problems. For example:

PARENT: I want to check in with you about how things are going in school.

CHILD: They're going OK.

PARENT: No major problems?

CHILD: Well, I'm having some trouble with spelling.

PARENT: How about your other subjects?

CHILD: They're all OK.

PARENT: You know that I just had a conference with your teacher. She indicated that you're having some difficulty in reading and math. Are these subjects difficult for you?

CHILD: A little.

PARENT: Do you have any idea what needs to be done?

CHILD: Study harder, I guess.

PARENT: That probably would help, but maybe something else needs to be done. Any ideas?

CHILD: Maybe I need extra help.

PARENT: That probably would take some of the pressure off you, wouldn't it?

CHILD: Yeah.

PARENT: What do you think about taking some diagnostic tests so that we can find out what the problem is? If you don't know why you're having difficulty, you may study harder, but you may be studying the wrong thing. That wouldn't help very much, would it?

CHILD: No.

PARENT: You agree to accept the idea of taking these tests?

CHILD: Yes.

PARENT: Good. I'll call the school tomorrow and request that the school psychologist do some testing.

Honest, nondemeaning communication enhances the relationship between parents and children. Parents who involve their child in the process of examining and finding solutions to problems encourage analytical solution-oriented thinking. This capacity to think strategically is a vital survival skill in a competitive society. When parents reason with their child, they teach him to respect the power of reason. Overcoming a learning problem becomes far less awesome when a child understands the challenges and recognizes that his family is betting on his capacity to prevail.

The following checklist is designed to help you evaluate the effectiveness of your family parent-child communication system.

PARENT-CHILD COMMUNICATION CHECKLIST

	YES	NO
I am willing to express my feelings openly to my child.	☐	☐
I am willing to permit my child to express his/her feelings openly to me.	☐	☐
I am willing to listen.	☐	☐
I am willing to make the effort to understand my child's feelings and perspective.	☐	☐
I am willing to admit that I am wrong.	☐	☐
I am willing to examine objectively and nonjudgmentally my child's opinions and feelings.	☐	☐
I am willing to discuss with my child ideas and feelings that contradict my own.	☐	☐
I am willing to accept context-appropriate compromises.	☐	☐
I am willing to work at improving the family communication system.	☐	☐

I am willing to be patient.	□	□
I resist being highly critical or judgmental.	□	□
I do not demean my child.	□	□

Interpreting the Checklist

A pattern of ''yes'' answers to the statements suggests that you are communicating productively with your child. A pattern of ''no'' answers indicates deficient communication. If you desire to improve the quality of your communication with your child, you must be willing to work at it. The more you and your child communicate, the more competent you will become.

FEEDBACK: A TWO-WAY STREET

Expressing feelings or thoughts can be risky, especially if the person recognizes that the content of what is being expressed has the potential to trigger a negative or defensive reaction. No one enjoys hurting someone they love.

Being on the receiving end of negative input can be equally risky. This input nevertheless is vital to the development of a good family communication system. Feedback is like a ping-pong ball—it needs to bounce on both sides of the net to be in play. Without feedback, what appears to be communication is simply monologue, lecture, or diatribe.

Parents who have established a highly authoritarian relationship with their child may consciously or unconsciously discourage their child from expressing contradictions, anger, criticism, or intense emotion. If the parents' sense of propriety is rigid, they may perceive the open assertion of feelings as a threat to their position and authority. The more inflexible the parents' attitudes, the more difficult it may be for them to tolerate statements that might challenge their sense of propriety and order. Parents who ascribe to such attitudes as ''Children should be seen and not heard'' or ''Spare the rod and spoil the child'' will tend to have difficulty handling the open and frank expression of emotion.

To communicate openly with a child, parents *must* be willing to listen.

They must value the sharing of feelings, and they must be prepared to create a safe environment where the child is certain that he will not be punished or degraded for expressing himself. Feeling safe is a requisite to candid communication.

It demands courage for a child to tell his father about how unhappy it fortihmakes him feel when the father always criticizes him. Imagine the fortihude required for a child to say: "You know, Dad, you never compliment me when I do something well. All you do is get upset with me when I make a mistake." The child making such a statement is taking a chance, especially if he had never before dared to express such feelings to his father and if he knows that his father is not accustomed to receiving this type of feedback. Were the child's father to respond by getting angry ("I am the parent in this house! I have the right to correct you. You do not have the right to correct me!") or were he to respond by putting the child down ("Well, it's not very often that you do something that's worth complimenting"), it is unlikely that the child would ever again venture to share such feelings with his father. With his response, the father has clearly signaled that he does not desire honest and open communication with his son.

Another parent given the same feedback from his son might have reacted quite differently. Recognizing the risk his child was taking, the father affirms his appreciation for the child's courage and honesty. "Son, perhaps you are right. I frankly wasn't aware that I was not giving you compliments when you deserved them. I apologize. Now that I am aware of how you feel, I will be more conscious of acknowledging your achievements." With this sensitive, nurturing response, the father signals that he is willing to look objectively at his own behavior. The message is clear: "Thanks, son, for sharing your feelings." By modeling a reasonable response to criticism, the father creates the framework for an interactive communication system. His reaction also affirms that feedback is a two-way street and that he will expect his son to respond with equal reasonableness to valid criticism.

Parents who reject all criticism or who become defensive or autocratic invariably create major barriers to communication. Those who are highly critical of their children or who place certain subjects off limits for discussion discourage intimacy. Even under the best conditions, children can have great difficulty expressing and understanding their feelings. Those who conclude that their parents are harshly judgmental, insensitive, or unresponsive are candidates for becoming distrustful and resentful.

Parents own the primary responsibility for creating an atmosphere conducive to communication. Because children have had limited life experiences, they tend to lack perspective, insight, and objectivity. They may not recognize or admit when they are acting defensively or unreasonably. Parents must sensitize themselves to the behaviors and attitudes that indicate a communication impasse (see parent-child communication checklist on page 223). If parents conclude that a communication impasse has developed, they must shoulder the responsibility for restructuring the family communication system.

Although parents wanting to communicate with their child should resist the inclination to be judgmental and highly critical, they nevertheless must retain their prerogative to examine issues, draw conclusions, and, when appropriate, make recommendations and/or impose injunctions. How parents express their perspective and position on key issues can strongly influence whether or not their child becomes defensive and resistant. Communication breakdowns are unavoidable when parents and children are intent primarily on defending their respective positions. Parents who react judgmentally or critically to everything their child says convey a lack of respect for the validity and legitimacy of their child's position, and, by implication, for the child himself.

The potential for effective communication increases significantly when parents and children have established a habit of expressing respect for each other's position and perspective. This does not mean that parents and children must necessarily always agree with each other's position and perspective. Disagreements that are expressed in an open, honest, non-demeaning, and nonthreatening way can actually enhance family communication. Children must learn, however, that there are behavioral guidelines for expressing disagreement and that everyone in the family is expected to conform to these guidelines. They must also accept that if they fail to convince their parents of their position, they must bow to their parents wishes.

Even if a child respects and trusts his parents, he may still be unwilling to discuss certain subjects and feelings. For example, many adolescents have difficulty discussing their sexuality or their social life with their parents. Such reluctance to communicate about specific subjects does not mean that parents have failed as communicators. The adolescent may simply wish to keep these subjects off limits. There is nothing intrinsically ''unhealthy'' about a teenager's reticence in this area, and the adolescent's unwillingness to enter into a discussion about sex should be respected. Appreciating the child's discomfort does not preclude parents wanting to explore important matters such as pregnancy and sexual responsibility with their child. Parents who are patient and sensitive and who work at developing their communication skills often discover that in time their reticent child will feel less and less discomfort exploring matters that were previously off limits.

Parents must examine periodically their own response patterns. This introspective process can afford them an opportunity to assess how their reactions to their child's actions and statements are affecting the family communication system. An important distinction, however, must be made between expressing legitimate anger and upset, and using anger as a hurtful weapon. Whereas the occasional open and "clean" expression of anger can stimulate family communication and intimacy, the chronic, tyrannical expression of anger can cause irreparable damage to the family system. Belittling or antagonistic feedback invariably destroys the potential for effective communication.

Highly traditional parents may have an especially difficult time dealing with the open expression of resentment or hostility. Although venting these emotions may be very therapeutic for the child, the conveyed feelings may be quite unsettling and painful for the child's parents. Despite the discomfort that the interaction may cause, parents should make every effort to deal with the feelings and the underlying issues. Parents who recognize that they are uncomfortable with the open expression of feelings and with emotionally charged situations are advised to seek the assistance of an objective mediator or family counselor.

The quality of a family's communication hinges on several major factors:

1. Parents and children acquiring insight into their respective feelings and reactions
2. Parents and children taking the risk to express their feelings and reactions
3. Clear guidelines that avoid "guilt trips," put downs, and expressed or implied threats
4. An environment that is supportive, nurturing, and loving

Improved family communication invariably leads to improved family relationships.

JIM: LEARNING TO DECIDE FOR HIMSELF

It was all but impossible to establish eye contact with the handsome four-teen-year-old sitting across from me. Although the ninth grader had been receiving special help at our center for approximately three months, he had remained distant and uncooperative. His relatively severe learning problems were compounded by a profoundly negative attitude about school, about life, and about himself.

Jim's learning problems had been diagnosed in second grade by the school psychologist. Because Jim and his family had moved several times, he had received only sporadic learning assistance during elementary school. Each time the family moved, the child had to be reevaluated and placed in another special education program. During the inevitable waiting period before being tested at each new school, Jim was usually placed in a regular mainstream academic program where he would struggle for two to ten weeks. After the testing was completed, he would then be assigned to a resource program. Over the years, Jim had derived little from this cycle of testing, temporary mainstreaming without learning support, and patchwork learning assistance.

Jim had initiated the meeting in my office. The previous week, he had asked his learning instructor at the center if he could discontinue a component of the learning assistance program that he did not like. The instructor suggested a conference with me and his parents to discuss the request.

From past experiences, I knew that Jim's desire to discontinue the program was consistent with his behavior. Whenever he encountered difficulty, he would either attempt to flee the problem, or he would blame others. From having tested Jim and from having observed him at the clinic, I knew that the teenager had great difficulty concentrating, following oral instruction, paying attention to details, and remembering visual and auditory information. Conferences with our clinical learning therapist and Jim's regular classroom teachers had confirmed these impressions. The teenager manifested a classic profile of learning deficits consistent with an attention-deficit disorder. It did not surprise me that the part of the program that Jim wanted to discontinue specifically focused on correcting his concentration deficiencies. He was being challenged in a deficit area, and true to form, he wanted to flee.

We obviously could not force Jim to continue the program. It was equally obvious that if we simply tutored him in specific subject areas, we would not address his underlying perceptual processing deficits or his concentration problem. Before Jim could achieve in school, he needed to learn how to pay attention.

The following is an approximate recounting of my conversation with Jim during the conference in my office.

LJG: Jim, give me an update on what's happening in school.

JIM: I'm having problems in some of my subjects.

LJG: Which subjects?

JIM: English, history, and math.

LJG: Any ideas about what's causing the problems?

JIM: I guess I'm just not a very good student. What I need is tutoring in those areas. I don't need any of this other stuff. These memory and concentration activities are a waste of time.

LJG: I agree that you need tutoring in your specific academic subjects. But I'm also concerned about some other problems. I just received teacher evaluation forms from all of your teachers. Every teacher has indicated that you are having difficulty concentrating in class and that you don't follow instructions. The teachers also say that you are not handing in your assignments on time and that your work is sloppy. Here, you can take a look at the forms. Are the teachers' observations accurate?

JIM: Yeah, I guess. But one of the teachers is mean. She's always yelling at me and getting on my case. I tune her out just like I tune out my mom when she starts yelling at me.

LJG: Tuning out the teacher and your mother makes the yelling more tolerable.

JIM: Yes! I just can't take any more yelling.

LJG: It makes you sad.

JIM: Yeah.

LJG: And angry?

JIM: I guess so.

LJG: Do you think tuning them out solves the problem?

JIM: Yes.

LJG: I assume that you feel your teacher and your mom are being unfair when they yell at you?

JIM: Yes. They yell at me when I'm not really doing anything wrong.

LJG: Do you think you might be doing things that press your parents' and your teachers' hot buttons?

JIM: Maybe.

LJG: Well, not wanting to be yelled at is a legitimate feeling. I'd like you to tell your mom how you feel. Tell her directly.

JIM: (Turning to his mother) You're always yelling at me.

LJG: Would you please respond to your son.

MOTHER: I get upset with you because you don't do your work.

JIM: You get more than upset. You yell.

MOTHER: All right. I yell. But you get me very exasperated with your procrastination.

JIM: I don't procrastinate!

LJG: It's clear that you both have lots of feelings that you need to express to each other and examine. Telling another person about how you are feeling can clear the air of resentment. Even getting mad can be beneficial if everyone "fights fair." Sometimes expressing real feelings can be scary, and parents and kids may need someone who is specially trained to help them learn how to communicate more openly. I feel strongly that both of you would benefit from family counseling. But right now some decisions have to be made about where we go from here in the learning assistance program. Jim, how do you feel about receiving learning assistance?

JIM: I don't know. I'm not sure I need help with that concentration stuff or basic reading and math.

LJG: Jim, let me ask you a question that may not appear to be related to what we're discussing. Are you interested in sports?

JIM: Yes.

LJG: Do you follow professional football or tennis?

JIM: I like football.

LJG: If you were a professional football player and had difficulty concentrating when you played, do you think that this could hurt your game?

JIM: What do you mean?

LJG: Well, I'm sure that you've heard TV announcers comment about how the receiver was able to make a seemingly impossible catch because his concentration was excellent. Have you ever heard them say that?

JIM: Yes.

LJG: Do you agree that concentration is important in football?

JIM: Yes.

LJG: What do you think the role of the football coach is?

JIM: He teaches his team how to play better.

LJG: Right. He helps them win. If a coach has a good player who has difficulty concentrating, he would have to teach the player to concentrate better if he is to help him become a superstar. That's the coach's job. He puts the player through certain types of drills to develop his skills, timing, *and* concentration. You've seen your high school team practice. Am I correct in what I am saying?

JIM: Yes.

LJG: Well, that's precisely what we are doing with you during the perceptual training part of the program. We are your coaches, and we are training your mind in much the same way that the football coach trains his players' bodies. We are teaching you to concentrate, follow instructions, and remember. We are training you to become a better player in the classroom. But we can't help you to become a good student unless you want to be one and unless you believe in us and are willing to work. Does that make sense?

JIM: Yes.

LJG: Do you know what a game plan is?

JIM: A plan a coach makes up for winning a game.

LJG: Exactly. Tell me, do you have a game plan?

JIM: What do you mean?

LJG: Do you feel that you have a plan that will allow you to win in school?

JIM: I guess not.

LJG: I am convinced that you have the potential to be a good student, perhaps even a superstar. But you do not have a winning game plan. You are using most of your energy to tune people out—your teachers in school, your mother, your instructors here at the clinic. If this is what you choose to do, you can defeat our efforts to help you and in the process defeat yourself. Without help, there's a real danger that you could lose the game in school. It's sad when someone allows himself to fail. Do you understand what I am telling you?

JIM: Yes.

LJG: You have to make a very important decision now. You have to decide whether you are also going to accept us as your coaches, or reject us. You are going to have to decide whether or not you trust us and think we know what we are doing. You're too old for us to force you to do what you don't want to do. And if we tried to force you, you obviously have the power to make us fail and yourself fail. I need to tell you two more things. I truly believe that you can overcome your learning problems. But I also believe that if you don't make the necessary effort now while you are a freshman in high school, you will probably continue to struggle for the next four years. Your problems will not go away of their own accord. Your problems belong to you. You cannot blame others for your difficulties in school. Jim, the ball is in your court. Do you want to run with the ball, or do you want to concede the game and simply give up?

JIM: Well, I guess I'd be willing to stay in the training portion of the program for six more weeks.

LJG: I really don't know if that will be enough time for us to help you overcome your concentration problems. But I'm going to have to accept this compromise because I think that's the best deal that I can get from you right now. I know that if you give 100 percent for the next six weeks, you could make tremendous strides. We'll have another conference in six weeks, and we'll take a look at how you're doing. But if we're going to work with you for the next six weeks, we're going to need total effort from you. No complaining. No blaming. Just hard work. Is that a deal?

JIM: It's a deal.

LJG: Good. We have a deal.

Jim's avoidance system consisted of resisting help, blaming others, feeling sorry for himself, and giving up. The system allowed him to cope with his deficiencies, fears, and insecurities. When things became difficult, Jim would simply take off. His unwillingness to accept responsibility, to commit himself, and to complete projects had become an integral part of his personality.

Although Jim had relatively severe learning problems, he could overcome them with appropriate learning assistance and sustained effort. The assistance program would have to provide more than a band-aid. It would have to address the teenager's underlying inattentiveness, irresponsibility, and perceptual processing deficits.

My objective was to encourage Jim to make a commitment to resolving his learning problems. I knew that his decision to continue or discontinue the learning therapy would have a profound impact on the future course of his life. If he made the wrong choice and decided to run away once again, he might never escape from the cycle of self-sabotage and failure. To make an intelligent and informed decision, Jim needed to understand *why* he was struggling in school, *what* he had to do to correct the situation, and *how* to get the job done. He also needed to recognize the implications of his choice to quit or to persevere. Had I attempted to lecture, coerce, scare, or dictate, I would only have increased his resistance.

The conference produced a compromise with which I was not fully satisfied, but then compromises are rarely completely satisfying. If he were forced to remain in the program against his will, Jim could have made life so miserable for his parents that ultimately they would have withdrawn him. He would have thus failed one more time.

Had he been a seven-year-old, I would not have permitted Jim to make such an important decision unilaterally. Jim, however, was fourteen, and it was obvious that he would derive little from the learning assistance unless he agreed to participate actively. In agreeing to a compromise, I was taking a calculated risk. Fortunately, Jim made significant headway during the six weeks and he agreed to continue in the program. When he completed the school year eight months later, he was receiving C's and B's in all of his courses.

SCRIPTED BEHAVIOR

In families where communication patterns have become scripted, specific words and gestures trigger highly predictable responses. For example:

> CHILD: I can't find my homework, and the bus will be here in one minute!
> MOTHER: You've misplaced your homework again! You're so irresponsible. You are always losing things.
> CHILD: I know someone moved my folder from the table! People are always moving my things.

Preprogrammed scripts function like a security blanket. They provide the struggling child a constant in his life. He knows that if he does or says a certain thing, someone will respond in a highly predictable way. The script provides the child with certainty in a world that might otherwise appear frightening and uncontrollable. By refusing to make a serious effort, by misplacing things, by failing to complete his projects, the chronically irresponsible child is able to exert control over people and events. This control creates an illusion of security and permits the child to insulate himself from his fears, vulnerabilities, and deficiencies.

Human beings are instinctively programmed to flee from danger or pain. Before they can find the strength and the courage to resist the temptation to flee, they must feel that they can survive the confrontation with the danger.

The prospect of facing a defeat can be terrifying to a child with tenuous self-esteem. Each failure forces the child to confront his limitations and inadequacies. By scripting those aspects of his life that are threatening, he is able to protect himself. Acting or reacting in a certain way can permit him to sidestep danger, pain, stress, and depression.

To the child who feels undeserving of success and who is accustomed to failure, the prospect of achievement can actually be a source of stress and fear. Although he may not be consciously aware of the implications of success, the child often realizes unconsciously that the dynamics of his life and his relationships would change if he were to begin to achieve. Success would affect the perceptions of all of those with whom he interacts. He might fear that once his parents and teachers realize that he is actually capable of achieving, they would begin to expect continued success. This new need to produce could have a paralyzing effect. The child might also fear that once his nonachieving friends begin to see him succeed, they may become envious and reject him. Success might necessitate having to make a whole new set of friends.

The child's own perceptions about himself would also change. His success might engender the expectation of continued achievement. By striving, the child inevitably exposes himself to the possibility of defeat. To a child whose self-concept is based on the expectation of failure or marginal performance, an achievement-oriented script might be very unsettling.

The child who chooses to take responsibility for his actions, to establish goals, and to work toward achieving those goals places his ego on the line. If he fails, he can no longer blame others. If he succeeds, he must deal with a new set of unpredictable variables. In electing to reach for the brass ring, the child has crossed a symbolic threshold. His efforts and achievement will testify to his talents, and he will be judged on his merits. The child has allowed himself to become accountable.

Parents cannot reasonably expect a struggling child with a long history of defeat to take a lot of risks. Failure and frustration inexorably wear down a child's willingness to expose himself to threatening situations. To counteract this reluctance to take risks, parents must patiently and ingeniously create repeated opportunities for the child to succeed. As he begins to realize that he has the power to affect his destiny without having to resort to manipulative behavior, the child will develop greater confidence and self-esteem. Thus armed, he can make his first tentative steps toward assuming increasing responsibility for his life.

COMPROMISES

An important distinction must be made between reaching a compromise, compromising oneself, and being compromised. The person who compromises himself makes a choice to capitulate. He may do so because giving in is the easiest or most expedient thing to do. For example, a parent may feel strongly about the value of honesty but may permit, or even encourage, his child to do something dishonest. Although the parent may rationalize his decision, he has voluntarily compromised himself and his child.

The parent who allows himself to be compromised by his child is permitting himself to be coerced, forced, betrayed, or manipulated into doing something that is against his wishes. For example, a parent may state that homework must be done before his teenage child can take off on Sunday with his friends. Under pressure, he may relent. If the parent ultimately establishes a pattern of giving in on the rules, he has compromised himself and the rules.

Reaching a compromise with a child is quite distinct from being compromised. Under the appropriate conditions, compromises are an important parenting resource in the resolution of disagreement and conflict.

There are four primary prerequisites to reaching an effective compromise. The parties involved must be

1. open-minded
2. willing to acknowledge the other's person's thoughts, feelings, and perspective
3. willing to work creatively at finding solutions to mutually shared problems

Although context-appropriate compromises are an important resource, they must be used selectively and judiciously. Parents who continually compromise risk undermining the family rules and standards. Compromising with a child each time there is a disagreement can establish a terrible precedent. Clearly, not all issues are negotiable. When appropriate, parents must be prepared to make unilateral decisions, even if these decisions do not meet with their child's approval. For example, a child who is misbehaving may need to be sent to his room as a punishment or simply because he needs some time out to think about his behavior. To compromise with the child under these circumstances undoubtedly would cause confusion about the family guidelines for acceptable and unacceptable behavior.

Parents who compromise and negotiate too frequently are sending a message to their child that all of the family rules are flexible. Children who conclude that they can barter and bargain with their parents whenever they want something frequently become manipulative and unwilling to accept authority. These tendencies usually persist into adulthood.

Parents should be able to sense intuitively when it is appropriate to reach a compromise with their child. For example, a mother who makes a deal with her child and allows him to go to the movies with his friends after he completes his homework is negotiating a reasonable compromise. By agreeing to the arrangement, the parent acknowledges the child's basic need for recreation. At the same time, she affirms the importance of the family's position on studying.

Parents who are able to reach reasonable, context-appropriate agreements which do not compromise them or their child usually find themselves involved in far fewer power struggles. The distinctive negative, counterproductive energy produced by unnecessary conflict is thus avoided.

ESTABLISHING EDUCATIONAL GOALS

Before the learning disabled child can be expected to participate actively in the remediation process, he needs to know what his problems are, how he is doing, and what he must achieve before he can be considered "cured." Once he acquires this data, he can then be guided toward establishing realistic performance objectives and standards for himself. These objectives are like rungs in a ladder. For example, a student struggling in English might be encouraged by his parents to establish very basic initial performance objectives for himself. These might include writing a legible book report with a minimum of spelling and syntactical errors. Other performance objectives could then be established: reducing spelling errors on each subsequent report, improving syntax, and improving writing style. This series of incremental interim goals will provide the means to achieve a realistic long-term goal which might be a B or even an A in the English course.[1]

It is vital that parents involve children in establishing their short- and long-term goals. A method for achieving this objective is modeled here.

PARENT: Your teacher showed me the results of the achievement test you took in September. The test indicates that your reading level is approximately one and a half years below grade level. Does this surprise you?

CHILD: Not really.

PARENT: Do you feel that the scores are accurate?

CHILD: I guess so.

PARENT: Any ideas about what might be causing the problem?

CHILD: I'm having difficulty reading my textbooks. The words are too hard. And I'm having trouble remembering the information.

PARENT: The teacher is convinced that the problems could be corrected if you received extra help. She thinks that you could probably catch up by the beginning of school next September. What do you think?

CHILD: I don't know.

PARENT: Would you be willing to accept extra help?

CHILD: Does that mean extra homework?

PARENT: Perhaps some.

CHILD: I guess I'd be willing to get extra help if there's not a lot of extra work.

PARENT: I think that's a fair request. I know you have a lot of homework already. The teacher has recommended a private reading specialist. I'll call her tomorrow. It's now October 1. How many months' improvement would you like to make in your reading by Christmas?

CHILD: Half a year, I guess.

PARENT: That sounds like a good goal to shoot for. I'll tell you what. If you achieve your goal and improve six months in your reading by Christmas, you and I can celebrate by going skiing the first weekend in January. Just the two of us. Do we have a deal?

CHILD: Yeah!

[1]See my book *Getting Smarter* (David S. Lake Publisher, 1985) for practical activities designed to help students to establish goals. Also see *Kids Who Underachieve* (Simon & Schuster, 1986) and *Smarter Kids* (HP Books, 1987) for a comprehensive examination of the function of goals in orienting children toward achievement.

PARENT: OK. Tell me in your own words what the deal is.

CHILD: I will improve my reading scores by six months by Christmas. If I do, you and I will go skiing the first weekend in January.

PARENT: Okay. We have a deal. I will ask the school to test you in three months to see if you have achieved your objective. We're going to need to get you a good reading tutor. She'll be able to tell us what you'll need to do to reach your goal. We're going to need to get you a good reading tutor.

By involving a child in the process of resolving his own problems, parents can dramatically improve the prospects for remediation. By keeping the child informed about how he is doing and by encouraging him to participate in establishing goals for himself, they can significantly accelerate the rate of progress.

AVOIDING IMPASSES

Resistance can assume many forms. Active resistance may manifest itself as defiance, irresponsibility, temper tantrums, or chronic misbehavior.

Passive resistance is often more difficult to identify than active resistance. One child may express his resistance by sabotaging himself. A second may shut down, and a third may go through the motions of doing what is expected of him without making any commitment to doing a first-rate job.

Occasional periods of resistance are not uncommon during the remediation process. These episodes are a yellow flag that could indicate burnout. This behavior often occurs when a child has worked very hard for a protracted period of time and can see only minimal improvement in his learning skills. Chronic resistance is a red flag and is more problematic. The behavior usually reflects an underlying, psychologically based problem that needs to be identified and treated. Because active and passive resistance waste vital energy and are invariably counterproductive, the behaviors must be addressed and resolved through improved family communication and, if appropriate, professional counseling.

A child's concept of time is very different from that of an adult. To a learning disabled child, the prospect of devoting an entire year to resolving a learning problem can seem like an eternity. To expect an eight-year-old to remain enthusiastically involved in a seemingly endless process is unrealistic, especially if the child has a significant learning problem and there are snags along the way. Parents must be prepared for periods of discouragement. Keeping their child informed about his progress and status is the most potent antidote to this discouragement.

To avoid shutdowns, resistance, letdowns and impasses, parents must develop their capacity to "read" their child and the specific challenges the child is facing. They must discover through a process of trial and error when to exhort, when to back off, when to give a pep talk, and when to commiserate. A simple mannerism or statement may reveal their child's mental state. The ability to identify and interpret the clues can be developed by parents who are willing to make the effort.

It is not uncommon for a child at a critical stage in the remediation process to decide that he no longer wants or requires learning assistance. The child may be quite convinced of his perceptions and may argue emphatically, "I'm doing fine now!" or "That stupid class isn't helping me at all!" Obviously, the child's parents must reconcile his perceptions with those of their own and with those of his teacher. Parents who conclude that their child is attempting to manipulate them into allowing him to quit because he is tired, or because he is at a challenging or threatening phase in the remediation process, must find the emotional resolve to resist the manipulation. Some children are terrified of crossing the final threshold and relinquishing their learning problems. At this critical juncture, their parents must hang tough.

Parents can plan in advance how they will deal with periods of resistance and burnout. Those who are unprepared may find themselves being conned into making deals with their child which are not in the child's best interests. Some negotiated compromises may be reasonable and appropriate. Others may be very damaging to the child's prospects of ultimately prevailing over his learning problems. Allowing the child to take the easy way out can establish a dangerous precedent.

The desire to terminate a process that is painful or demanding is quite natural. Like a patient in a hospital who is anxious to be released, the child receiving learning assistance may press for a specific date when the learning assistance program will be finished. Because remediation rarely conforms to a predetermined timetable, providing the child with such a date is often impossible. Three critical factors must be taken into consideration before permitting a child to terminate his remedial program:

1. the child's performance in school
2. the child's performance on standardized achievement tests
3. the child's performance in the learning assistance program

Although a resource specialist may speculate that it might require approximately eight to fourteen months to remediate a child's learning deficits, no teacher can state definitively that a child's learning problems will be corrected by May 26.

When parents and teachers keep the child apprised of how he is doing, what he has accomplished, and what still needs to be done, they are helping him make the transition from passive to active participation in the process of resolving his learning problem. The simple act of listening to a child express his frustration can effect an emotional catharsis that may permit a stalled program to proceed.

Ironically, some children become most resistant just as they are about to make a major breakthrough. Usually, such children have become habituated to their learning problems and addicted to the ongoing help and attention they are receiving.

If a child is to prevail over his learning problems, he will need to acquire more than academic skills. His perceptions of himself and his abilities must also change. Parents and teachers play instrumental roles in helping the child achieve these positive changes in perception.

CHAPTER 11

Dealing with Learning Disabled Teenagers

MIKE: A FRIGHTENED TOUGH GUY

Mike swaggered into my office looking tough and streetwise. With his demeanor, body language, and scowl, he achieved the desired effect: I knew that he was at the clinic under duress. As soon as he sat down, the fifteen-year-old informed me that there was nothing wrong with him. The only reason he was flunking in school was because school was "dumb," and the only reason he was talking to me was because the judge had ordered him to be tested.

Mike had been arrested three weeks previously for drinking beer in front of a movie theater. Because he had also been picked up on two other occasions for truancy, he was facing the possibility of being sent to the "ranch," a minimum-security facility for youthful offenders. As a court-imposed condition of probation, the judge had instructed Mike's parents to have me evaluate the teenager to determine if he had a learning disability. The parents had been directed to submit my written summary of the test results to the court.

After talking with Mike and his parents for a few minutes, I realized that his tough image was an affectation. The teenager came from a professional, middle-class home and had access to virtually anything he wanted. Prior to being assigned to a continuation high school, Mike had attended a local suburban high school where juvenile delinquents were in the district minority. Set apart and isolated by his behavior, Mike seemed intent on calling attention to himself. Now that he was attending an inner-city school where there were real tough guys, he felt all the more compelled to maintain his carefully cultivated image. Despite his swagger, it was obvious that the tenth grader was angry, insecure, unhappy, and frightened.

The teenager's anger toward his parents was palpable, and they were obviously intimidated by him. Whenever they said something that displeased him, he became hostile, sarcastic, or argumentative. His parents would then apologize and back down, desperately trying to avoid a confrontation.

My diagnostic assessment revealed that Mike could barely read at a fourth-grade level. He manifested a classic learning disability profile: poor visual and auditory processing skills, poor phonics, and poor word-attack skills. He was also highly impulsive, distractible, and disorganized.

Although I recognized that the fifteen-year-old desperately needed learning assistance, I had serious misgivings about working with him. His anger, defensiveness, and resistance were too intense. After years of working with hundreds of defeated, seriously learning disabled teenagers, I had no illusions. If Mike refused to cooperate, he would derive nothing from our program. Even with his cooperation, there would be no magic cure. The remediation process might require two years, and from Mike's demeanor and attitude, I was certain that he would never agree to such a long-term commitment.

Before Mike could make any inroads into resolving his learning problems, he would have to be willing to accept help. Basic learning assistance would not be sufficient. Mike had to begin examining his behavior and his anger. He would also have to establish some specific goals for himself. If he refused to make a commitment to this process, he would remain on a course that I feared might someday lead to prison. His reactions during our session together signaled that he was terrified of introspection. Without professional counseling, academic progress would be impossible.

Although I had not administered an IQ test, my instincts told me that Mike was quite bright. Stymied and frustrated by his hostility, I was willing to grasp at straws in an attempt to help him. I hoped that if I could present Mike with conclusive evidence of his potential ability, this evidence might motivate him to begin looking for the keyhole in the barricaded door that separated him from his emotions.

When I proposed to Mike that he take an IQ test, I could sense his initial resistance. True to form, he attempted to camouflage his feelings with an ''I couldn't care less'' expression. He reluctantly agreed to take the test, and it was scheduled for the next day.

We met again the following week. Mike looked at me incredulously when I informed him that his IQ was 130. I then told him that he was bright enough to succeed at any college in the country, and I could sense his mixed feelings of pride, fear, and confusion. Although clearly proud of the score he had achieved, he was at the same time frightened and uncertain about the effect this new and unexpected information would have on his life.

Manifesting the classic behaviors of a defensive, insecure teenager, Mike devoted most of his energy to hiding from his self-doubts and compensating for his vulnerabilities. He did this by strutting, blaming, intimidating, making excuses, and affecting toughness. Mike, of course, was not consciously aware of why he acted the way he did. He had relied on rationalizations and pretenses for so many years that these affectations had become an integral part of his personality.

Mike's bravado was his security blanket, and he carried this blanket with him wherever he went. The blanket shielded him from his fears. The fierce scowl provided additional protection. Mike unconsciously was convinced that his ritualized intimidation act was his only means of survival.

Participation in a court-imposed learning therapy program would clearly be a waste of time. Mike could easily sabotage any program that we might design, and in so doing, he would fail once again. The last thing in the world Mike needed was another failure.

Despite my misgivings, I had a professional responsibility to ask the teenager if he wanted us to provide him with academic assistance. As I expected, he adamantly informed me that he didn't need or want help. I then urged him to consider counseling, but he again refused. During this exchange, I could see the look of resignation and despair mirrored in his parents' faces. All I could do was tell Mike that the door to the center was open and that if he agreed to cooperate, we would make every effort to help him. I once again urged him to consider counseling, and I gave his parents the name of a very talented therapist who specialized in working with learning disabled teenagers. As he was leaving my office, I asked Mike to call me when he was ready to start working on resolving his learning problems. The call never came.

CONFRONTING REALITY

Convincing a defensive, emotionally scarred, and resistant learning disabled teenager that he would benefit from learning assistance can be a monumental test of one's parenting skills. Years of defeat and frustration can cause a child's protective walls to become all but impenetrable.

Of course, not all learning disabled teenagers become hostile and self-sabotaging. Some manage to emerge from the educational system relatively unscathed. Despite their academic difficulties, they are motivated and conscientious. In most instances, such students have subtle to moderate learning problems and have received quality learning assistance and counseling support in elementary and junior high school.

The majority of learning disabled teenagers do not progress through the system unscathed. They are badly bruised and scarred by their negative school experiences, and their wounds may never completely heal. If untreated, these wounds can fester, and the resulting infection may afflict them throughout their lives.

Learning disabled teenagers deal with their distress and insecurity in different ways. Some flaunt their inadequacies and emotional scars by acting out and by developing delinquent or bizarre behavior. Others attempt to hide their pain and uncertainty by retreating into a protective cocoon. If not freed, these shy and insecure children ultimately become shy and insecure adults.

Despite the wide range of coping and defense mechanisms employed by teenagers to protect themselves, there are common denominators including poor self-esteem, resistance, discouragement, self-doubt, defensiveness, and poor motivation.

The child whose learning problems are not resolved by the time he reaches high school is in considerable jeopardy. Once the learning disabled student becomes convinced that he is hopelessly inadequate and that his situation is futile, his fate is all but sealed. Demoralized and defeated, he will either give up completely or simply go through the motions of being educated. At the extreme end of the demoralization spectrum can be found the tens of thousands of learning disabled high school students who are so discouraged by their academic experiences that they make no pretense about the fact that they are marking time until they are legally permitted to drop out. Lacking skills and confidence, these teenagers have virtually no vocational prospects. They are academically and psychologically unprepared to compete for jobs in a society that now primarily requires skilled workers. As they become increasingly disillusioned with themselves, their prospects, and life in general, these teenagers become susceptible to drugs and prone to criminal behavior. To a child who is convinced that life is futile, escape can be very appealing.

Factors that influence how a teenager elects to deal with his learning problems include:

1. The severity of the learning problem
2. The type and quality of the learning assistance that the student has received during elementary school
3. The teenager's strengths and weaknesses in other areas
4. The quality of the communication system that exists between the teenager and his family
5. The amount of self-concept damage that has occurred
6. The teenager's personality
7. The type and quality of the learning assistance programs available in high school

As a general rule, teenagers with less severe learning problems tend to have less severe emotional scars and manifest less counterproductive behavior. There are exceptions, however. Some teenagers with subtle to moderate learning disabilities develop serious self-concept problems, while others with more serious deficiencies somehow survive twelve years of academic struggle with their self-esteem relatively intact. This latter phenomenon is rare. Without effective learning assistance and emotional support, most learning disabled teenagers shut down.

Learning problems do not necessarily affect high school students in all academic areas. A student may have great difficulty in one academic subject and little or no difficulty in other subjects. Usually, however, learning disabled students tend to struggle in most subjects, especially if they have significant underlying perceptual processing and concentration deficits.

Although some learning disabled teenagers manifest learning problems exclusively in the area of math, the majority have reading problems. Because reading is central to all academic subjects, inadequately developed reading skills can cause monumental and pervasive academic difficulties. A student who struggles to decipher, comprehend, and remember the material in his textbook inevitably has difficulty in social studies, science, English, and even math.

Although effective learning assistance during elementary school can significantly reduce the risk of subsequent academic difficulty and self-concept damage in high school, this assistance does not guarantee that a student will enter high school in good shape. Despite quality remedial help, highly dedicated teachers, and sensitive and supportive parents, elementary school children with severe learning disabilities may continue to struggle in high school from the residual effects of their learning problems. If they are to survive academically and psychologically, these students will require ongoing academic learning assistance.

DEVELOPING EFFECTIVE COMMUNICATION RESOURCES

Because the parents of learning disabled teenagers must often deal with the behavioral fallout produced by their child's academic struggle, they face special challenges. Communicating with an unhappy learning disabled teenager demands extraordinary determination, commitment, strength, patience, and sensitivity. In spite of the challenges, parents can create an effective communication system if they are willing to reach out to their child and persevere. There are, however, some requisites:

1. Parents must make a special effort to sensitize themselves to their child's feelings and perspective.
2. Parents must make a special effort to search beneath the surface symptoms (anger, laziness, procrastination, irresponsibility, strange dress habits, weird hair styles, etc.).
3. Parents must be willing to admit when they need professional help in dealing with recurring problems.

Life is not a textbook. Because they are human, parents inevitably make mistakes. From time to time, they will become justifiably angry and upset with their child, and they must give themselves permission to respond occasionally to stressful situations in a less than ideal way. Although parents do not have to be perfect, they do have a responsibility to be respectful, sensitive, fair, affirming, and open if they wish to establish an effective communication system with their teenager.

Parents should not be surprised when their demoralized teenager argues that school is "dumb," irrelevant, or boring. Although they undoubtedly will be distressed by their child's attitude, they must remind themselves that the teenager's words and behavior are a smokescreen that masks confusion, anger, fear, discouragement, and insecurity. Blaming the teacher or the system is simply a convenient way for the child to deflect pain, feelings of inadequacy, and inner turmoil.

Learning disabled teenagers are highly visible and vulnerable. They know that their poor academic performance stands in stark testimony to their deficiencies. Because they have limited options for hiding their deficits, they will seize upon whatever protection is available. They may affect nonchalance, toughness, shyness, learned helplessness, or antisocial behavior as protective armor. Once they strap on this armor, they will begin to seek out others who protect themselves in the same way. Because teenagers are so enmeshed in their own drama, they do not realize that the protection their armor affords is an illusion. Their fear compels them to defend themselves as best they can.

Until the struggling teenager becomes convinced that he can survive without his armor, he will refuse to relinquish it. Unless he is untracked, he will probably become increasingly addicted to its illusory security.

The parents of learning disabled teenagers have an especially compelling responsibility to create an effective family communication system. Unfortunately, those who attempt to do so often discover that their teenager is intent on repelling their efforts. Parents cannot allow this resistance to discourage them. They must remind themselves that their child is reacting instinctively. Human beings are programmed to flee from feelings that they sense are unpleasant and painful. The same fear that compels teenagers to avoid examining the source of their pain also compels adult overeaters and compulsive gamblers to avoid examining the source of their own behavior. A teenager's unwillingness to communicate should not be construed by parents as a personal rejection. The child may be too wounded, too guarded, or too ashamed to communicate openly about his feelings and about his tribulations in school. This barrier can usually be broken down with sufficient effort, patience, perseverance, practice, and, when appropriate, professional counseling. Once trust is established, productive communication generally ensues.

THE ROLE OF
THE SCHOOL COUNSELOR

The school counselor can play a vital role when parent-child communication is impeded or when a teenager is unwilling to communicate with his parents about his academic problems. The types of support that the counselor can ideally provide include:

1. Serving as an intermediary between the child, his teachers, and his parents
2. Providing emotional support
3. Functioning as a sounding board
4. Helping the teenager identify, sort out, and resolve academic problems which might appear overwhelming and insoluble

Quality, on-site school counseling is one of the key factors that can determine whether or not an emotionally fragile learning disabled teenager remains committed to the process of overcoming his learning problems. The services of a school counselor are especially critical when a student is not doing the work up to the classroom teacher's standard and is receiving continual negative feedback in the form of poor grades and derogatory comments. High school teachers may have only a marginal understanding of learning problems and may take the student's poor performance personally. They may begin to resent the student who hands in work that is chronically late, sloppy, and incomplete. The counselor's intervention can be crucial when a student's defense mechanisms manifest themselves in the form of negative attitude or misbehavior in class. A well-timed conference between the student, the counselor, and the teacher can often diffuse resentments and misunderstandings. Without this intervention, a struggling student might easily become demoralized and even psychologically and academically immobilized. The student also risks being suspended if the misbehavior is not addressed and corrected.

Despite their critical role in the remediation equation, many counselors are too overloaded with work to provide extensive, individualized support for the learning disabled teenager. Tragically, many school districts have been forced to cut back on their counseling programs for economic reasons. Parents who recognize that the on-site counseling support at their child's school is limited or inadequate will have to step into the breach. When appropriate, they may have to function as an intermediary between their child and his teachers. Parents who conclude that they cannot serve in this capacity must seek out an alternative counseling support before their child suffers serious psychological damage.

Effective family communication provides a vital emotional safety valve for a struggling high school student, especially when the school counseling is deficient. One of the most important functions of periodic family discussions is to offer the teenager an opportunity to vent the frustration, resentment, and sadness he might be feeling as a result of his struggle in school. Without this communication, the emotional pressure generated by setbacks and frustration can build to the point where it can implode or explode with potentially devastating consequences.

COPING WITH ANGER AND UNHAPPINESS

Human beings tend to build a wall between themselves and their anger. Teenagers are no exception. Those who are unhappy, frustrated, demoralized, and angry often express their inner turmoil by developing counterproductive and self-sabotaging behaviors.

Despite the walls that teenagers build to contain their anger and unhappiness, the emotions have a way of seeping through the cracks. In some instances, a child's anger may be overt and take the form of blatant hostility. In other instances, it may be covert and manifest itself as sarcasm or negativity. Sometimes, the anger is self-directed and assumes the form of masochism or nihilism.

Hostile teenagers are often terrified by the raw feelings lurking on the other side of their defensive wall. Given their fear, it is quite logical that they might feel threatened and upset by their parents' attempts to encourage them to examine their underlying emotions.

The origins of self-sabotaging behavior invariably can be traced to poor self-esteem, fear, and hostility. By refusing to give himself permission to succeed, the struggling teenager is making a profound statement about himself. Lacking self-respect and perceiving himself as a failure, he may begin to defeat himself intentionally. In this way, he confirms his negative self-perception. Parents are frequently mystified by this phenomenon. With justification and logic, they wonder why their child would intentionally orchestrate his own failure. To understand the behavior, parents must recognize that a struggling child who sees no way to prevail over his problems will often acquire a self-destructive mind-set. Repeated failure and frustration can cause the mind-set and the corresponding behaviors and attitudes to become integrated into the child's identity. Unless the teenager's self-concept undergoes a transformation, he may remain quite resistant to receiving help and to reorienting his behavior and attitudes.

The teenager who sabotages himself intentionally is expressing his anger by punishing himself. If he is angry at his parents, he may also use failure as a means of punishing them. Self-inflicted failure can be a powerful weapon that hurts not only the child, but also those who love the child. The child enmeshed in this type of self-defeating cycle requires more than basic learning assistance. Unless he is helped to identify the source of his poor self-esteem, his fear, his hostility, and his emotional discord, he will remain a nonachiever.[1]

PROVIDING SUPPORT SYSTEMS

It doesn't take long before the battle for academic survival begins to wear down a teenager's emotional resources. As their resources erode, many teenagers loose their capacity to bounce back from setbacks. By the time they enter high school, they may no longer possess the psychological resolve to continue battling against their learning problems.

Students who are provided with competent remedial assistance and counseling in elementary and junior high school are considerably less likely to become demoralized. Those whose problems have not been resolved and who are assigned to high school special education classes are often exposed to a very negative learning environment.

High school special education programs are generally filled with badly scarred, turned-off, and highly resistant teenagers who are embarrassed by having been assigned to such programs. In many instances these classes do little more than babysit students. The students in the special programs

---

[1]Behavioral psychologists advocate using behavior modification to deter the child from resorting to such self-sabotaging cycles. These psychologists would design a carefully structured system of positive and negative reinforcements (rewards and punishments) and would use this system to condition the child to abandon his counterproductive behavior. As a general rule, behavioral psychologists do not feel that it is necessary to understand the source of a child's negative behavior in order to change the behavior.

know this, and so do all of the other students in the general school population. Many learning disabled teenagers quickly conclude that their special classes are a waste of time. Unfortunately, many also conclude that they must be hopelessly ignorant and defective to have been placed in these classes.

Because of the psychological ramifications, the prospects of resolving a high school student's learning problems are poorer than the prospects of resolving the learning problems of an elementary school student. Nevertheless, most learning disabled teenagers can be helped with proper instruction and adequate counseling. The efficacy of the remediation program hinges on three primary factors:

1. The personality and skills of the teacher
2. The quality of the learning assistance strategy that he implements
3. The willingness of the student to participate in the program
4. The availability of on-site school counseling

Perceptive, sensitive, enthusiastic teachers can achieve miracles, sometimes even with students who are initially distrustful, resistant, and unmotivated. The key is to establish trust, to communicate positive expectations, and to set up students so that they succeed. For example, teachers might encourage their students with poor reading skills to read special high-interest material that are intentionally written at a lower reading level. Although the student's achievement may be modest at first, this achievement can be the catalyst that motivates the teenager to participate actively in the remedial program.

Learning disabled teenagers who develop alternative nonacademic interests and skills are fortunate. Their competencies in these areas can be a source of important ego support. A good athlete who doesn't do well in school will at least be able to gain acknowledgment for his athletic achievements. The pride and sense of accomplishment he derives from sports may be sufficient to blunt the negative effects of his frustration in school. By encouraging him to develop other proficiencies, his parents are helping the teenager acquire an important alternative emotional support system. A skill or a hobby can provide the struggling child with a comforting refuge from the academic storm.

The teenage years are difficult. Even teenagers without learning or emotional problems inevitably experience moments of insecurity and self-doubt as they make the first tentative steps toward establishing an adult identity for themselves. During the transition from childhood to adulthood, powerful social, physiological, and emotional pressures pull the teenager in many directions. A student whose self-concept is already tenuous because of learning problems may find the pressure exerted by these forces all the more debilitating and may become susceptible to negative influences.

Most learning disabled teenagers learn to protect their "soft spots" in whatever way they can. Their methods may vary, but they typically involve behaviors and attitudes which ironically magnify the deficits. For example, a child who considers himself to be unattractive may seemingly defy reason by dressing and acting in a way that accentuates his real or imagined unattractiveness. Acting out, cutting classes, avoiding studying, leaving assignments incomplete, and resisting help may represent the only means by which the struggling teenager can express his frustration.

Parents who must deal on a daily basis with their teenager's counterproductive behavior often find their own emotional resources sorely tested. Watching a fifteen-year-old make self-defeating choices can be one of parenting's most painful experiences. The experience is even more painful when the child adamantly refuses to accept help.

The perceptions of a teenager with significant unresolved learning problems are inevitably influenced by his experiences in life. Negative experiences tend to produce negative attitudes, behavior, and self-esteem. Although they may be discouraged by their teenager's behavior, parents cannot afford to give up because their child is resistant or unappreciative. The sooner they provide help, the sooner the teenager can begin the process of rebuilding his self-esteem, developing his skills, and altering his behavior. Conversely, the longer the child remains locked in the counterproductive loop, the more profound the emotional damage to the child and his family.

PEER PRESSURES

Demoralized teenagers usually seek out friends who are like themselves. Because these friends have had many of the same life experiences, they share many of the same feelings and attitudes. As individual negative energy is pooled, the peer group often begins to generate a collective negative energy that feeds upon itself and reinforces each group member's negative self-perceptions. In some instances, learning disabled students may band together, isolate themselves from the mainstream, and develop their own interests and social system. In extreme cases, unhappy learning disabled teenagers may express their frustration and anger with destructiveness, drinking, drugs, vandalism, or theft.

The value system of a peer group can easily influence a highly impressionable and insecure teenager. Parents recognizing the danger of their teenager's association with a particular group may want to intervene. Unfortunately, such attempts at intervention usually elicit resistance and resentment.

Parents who perceive that their teenager's peer group is reinforcing negative attitudes and behaviors may feel especially thwarted in their efforts to reorient their child. These parents should seek assistance of a skilled therapist who can help their child sort out his emotions and confront the underlying issues. The anger and frustration must be defused before the teenager can get on with the job of developing a practical strategy for resolving his learning problems. As he begins to feel better about himself, and more confident, the child will act and think more positively, and he will begin to associate with friends who act and think the same way.

PARENTAL OPTIONS

Parents are instinctively programmed to protect a young child from danger. This same instinct motivates them to shield their teenager from making mistakes that they feel could have immediate or long-range negative consequences.

Under certain circumstances, it may be totally appropriate and essential that parents intervene directly and even forcefully. This intervention and protection may save a teenager from doing something that could have calamitous implications. One situation may require that parents be tough and demanding, another may require that they be gentle and supportive. Although parents must confront the child who is stealing or taking drugs, they have many options about how to handle the confrontation. The way in which they respond can be instrumental in determining whether or not they are successful in dissuading their child from engaging in behaviors that are illegal and self-destructive. Deciding how to respond requires a judgment call, and parents have no alternative but to rely on their intuition. If they have doubts about how to deal with a particular situation, they must seek professional advice.

Sometimes intervention by parents may be inappropriate. For example, a teenager may be having problems with her boyfriend. Although she may be unhappy, she may not want her parents to become involved. If her parents are certain that she can handle the problem and that she is not in any emotional or physical danger, they may have to resist their natural inclination to provide protection, assurance, advice, and assistance. They might offer to serve as a sounding board, but they must respect their daughter's wishes if she insists on working through the problem herself. On the other hand, if the teenager is suffering and asks for help or clearly requires assistance, her parents must be available to provide this support.

Resisting the temptation to offer protection or to take ownership of a teenager's problem can sometimes demand every ounce of parental restraint. Parents must recognize that their offer to provide assistance may be rejected, and even if it is accepted, they may not be able to resolve their child's problems.

Teenagers must ultimately develop the capacity to sort out and resolve their own problems. The process of equipping them to do this is sequential and does not necessarily follow a prescribed timetable. At some point, however, teenagers must begin to make the transition from dependent childhood to independent adulthood. The continual, inappropriate offer of protection by parents can defeat this essential process. When a parent's offer of protection is enmeshed in a family script, the parent must be willing to look at this script. Unconsciously and unintentionally, the parent may be placing his or her own emotional needs to "mother" or to "father" above the needs of the child.

The warnings made in previous chapters about lectures and threats are especially applicable to teenagers. Parents who react to their teenager's self-defeating behavior with admonishments should prepare themselves for resistance and resentment. Defensive, insecure, frustrated, and angry teenagers tend to react negatively to hearing the "truth." The more parents attempt to impose their perception and attitudes, the more intensely their child will resist.

The most effective antidote for self-defeating behavior is communication. Ideally, this communication will lead to insight. Teenagers who are helped to examine and understand why they are behaving in a particular way tend to be less resistant to abandoning their counterproductive behavior.

The risk of an impasse, a showdown, or a shoot-out is especially high when teenagers and parents are intent primarily on defending their respective positions. Communication invariably breaks down when people become highly defensive. Parents must discipline themselves to listen, and they must make every effort to clarify the issues. In the end, the teenager must determine for himself what the truth is. Although parents must establish reasonable rules, they must also recognize that if the teenager is determined to break the rules, he will do so in one way or another. Parents cannot police their child twenty-four hours a day.

Parents involved in a dispute with their child have four basic options:

1. They can lecture their child.
2. They can threaten to take away privileges.
3. They can do nothing.
4. They can examine the issues objectively and empathetically.

Option #1

Teenagers seldom can be lectured into being responsible. They typically respond to this approach by tuning out what is being said or by resisting actively or passively. Usually, they have heard the lecture before, and it is unlikely that they will change their behavior simply because they are hearing it again.

Most teenagers recognize that they have less overt power than their parents, and they will deal with this power inequality in different ways. Some precipitate arguments. Others appear to acquiesce to their parents' wishes, but secretly do what they want to do. Those who are intent on disobeying their parents will find the means to do so. Whereas the actively resistant teenager may rebel, the passively resistant teenager may feel safer employing subterfuge or manipulation. He may simply "forget" to do what he was told.

Option #2

Threatening to take away privileges may serve as a deterrent, but such deterrents rarely change underlying attitudes. Threats of punishment may cause the teenager to alter his behavior temporarily. Usually, however, the undesirable behavior reemerges in a different form. Parents whose objective is to encourage their teenager to become more responsible can best achieve this by helping him appreciate the value of being responsible. Threatening to restrict access to the family car may work for a while, but in the long-term, this strategy will do little to change underlying attitudes. Usually, threats produce only bitterness and resentment.

Option #3

An alternative to threats, punishment, and denial of privileges is to do nothing about a teenager's misbehavior. Although doing nothing allows parents to avoid a confrontation, it also communicates to the child that his parents are either resigned to his self-defeating behavior or simply don't care. The message is clear: The teenager does not have to answer for his behavior. Teenagers who conclude that they can misbehave with impunity frequently collide with society's rules.

Option #4

The fourth alternative—exploring issues and conflicts objectively, empathetically, and constructively—offers a far more effective means for reorienting a teenager's counterproductive behavior. Parents who create a cooperative atmosphere can begin to communicate in a more meaningful way with their child about mutually shared problems. Such an atmosphere permits parents to hear and consider their child's perspective and conveys to the child that his perspective deserves consideration. This "examination method" is modeled in the following dialogue.

PARENT: I received a note today from your counselor. She says that you have not been completing your homework assignments in English. What's up?

TEENAGER: Why should I do them? I get bad grades on them anyway.

PARENT: The assignments are hard, I assume.

TEENAGER: They're stupid! What does it matter if I know the parts of speech? I speak OK. Why do I have to know whether *going* is a participle or an infinitive or who knows what? How's that going to help me get a job?

PARENT: Knowing whether *going* is a participle or an infinitive probably won't help you get a job. What would help you get a job?

TEENAGER: I don't know.

PARENT: What about your track record?

TEENAGER: What do you mean?

PARENT: Your history of success and failure.

TEENAGER: When I try to find a job after school, I won't have much of a history. It'll be my first real job.

PARENT: I imagine there will be lots of kids competing for those jobs.

TEENAGER: Yeah, I know.

PARENT: If you were the owner of an auto parts store, and you were going to hire an eighteen-year-old high school graduate, how would you decide which person to hire?

TEENAGER: I don't know. I guess I'd hire the kid I liked best.

PARENT: Me, too. Imagine if you had to choose between one student who had good grades and who was in the school band and who had good recommendations from his teachers and from his previous bosses, and another who had gotten D's in school. Which person would you hire?

TEENAGER: The first guy, probably.

PARENT: Yeah, so would I. Think about that when you choose not to hand in your assignments. Your grade in that course and your teacher's recommendation might mean the difference between getting the job and not getting the job. If you decide to go to college, the teacher's recommendation might be even more important. Sometimes a recommendation can make the difference between being accepted or not being accepted at the college of your choice.

In the preceding dialogue, the parent carefully avoids any tendency to berate or lecture. He makes his points succinctly and intentionally keeps the dialogue short. Because the teenager does not perceive that he is being attacked or demeaned, he does not respond defensively. Had the parent responded to his child's counterproductive behavior by threatening punishment, it is possible that the teenager might have agreed to be more responsible about his assignments. It is more likely, however, that an argument would have ensued. By means of active or passive resistance, the teenager could have defeated his parent's wishes.

Despite the parent's restraint, the resolution of the situation described here is not certain. The teenager may still choose to continue handing in incomplete English assignments. Under such circumstances, the parent might initiate another discussion or might try a different approach. Like their adult counterparts, teenagers rarely change their habits overnight.

The probability of an angry confrontation is especially high when a teenager is intent on contravening his parent's wishes. Many intransigent teenagers are willing to suffer the consequences in order to assert their right to do things their way. Although parents may succeed in forcing their child to comply with their wishes, the use of force rarely makes inroads into the attitudes responsible for the undesired behavior.

Parents must acknowledge a basic fact of life: Their power to control the thoughts and actions of their teenage son or daughter will diminish as the teenager gets older. The wise parent recognizes that reason and co-operation are preferable to threats and punishment. The wise parent also recognizes that reason and cooperation provide a far more solid foundation for an effective parent-teenager communication system.

When parents help their teenager achieve insight into his behavior, they are preparing him to meet the challenges of adulthood. Teenagers perceiving the cause-and-effect relationship between their choices and the consequences of those choices have a distinct advantage over teenagers who are oblivious to the role they play in determining the outcome of events in their lives.

The preceding dialogue models a method for relating to teenagers in a way that improves the chances that conflicts, disagreements, and contradictions in perception can be resolved. The communication strategy encourages the teenager to assess his situation, make rational choices, and exert legitimate control over his life. By encouraging their teenager to take responsibility for his choices and by permitting him to have a reasonable degree of control, parents facilitate the transition from childhood to adulthood. Avoiding "war" is in everyone's best interest. Parents who offer support rather than create confrontations can usually sidestep battles that no one really wins.

The following parent-teenager communication checklist is designed to help parents determine if they are prepared to communicate effectively with their child.

PARENT-TEENAGER COMMUNICATION CHECKLIST

	YES	NO
I calmly present my perspective and perceptions.	☐	☐
I encourage my child to present his perspective and perceptions.	☐	☐
I resist the temptation to lecture my child.	☐	☐
I resist being highly judgmental or critical.	☐	☐
I attempt to identify and explore objectively the issues when there are disagreements.	☐	☐
I keep the discussions relatively short, unless my child wants to continue the discussion.	☐	☐
I accept that immediate agreement or resolution of problems is unlikely. Several discussions may be required.	☐	☐
I give my child time to consider the issues.	☐	☐
I am willing to compromise when appropriate.	☐	☐
I encourage the expression not only of ideas and facts, but also emotions.	☐	☐
I postpone discussions when emotions are so intense that they interfere with the ability to reason.	☐	☐
I treat my child, his ideas, and his feelings with respect.	☐	☐
I am willing to seek professional assistance if an impasse develops which appears unresolvable.	☐	☐

Interpreting the Checklist

Parents who have answered "no" to even one of the statements might well benefit from examining their parenting attitudes and communication style. Communication flourishes when children are encouraged to express freely their feelings and thoughts. The tone and mood parents establish are pivotal factors in creating a context conducive to effective communication. The more insightful parents are about themselves, the more insightful they will be about their children, and the more effective and rewarding the family communication system will be.

DEVELOPING RESPECT

An adult who works for someone who continually denigrates his work undoubtedly would quit, unless, of course, he has no other alternative or is a masochist. No one wants to be made to feel incompetent and ineffectual, and no one wants to feel unappreciated.

For many teenagers with unresolved learning disabilities, life is a series of denigrating experiences. Those with serious problems usually encounter repeated defeat and frustration and must often resign themselves to little or no positive acknowledgment. If they conclude that they can never please their parents, their teachers, or themselves, they will probably develop increasingly elaborate defense mechanisms that can only serve to increase the family disharmony.

Children are not the only ones at risk. Parents also develop defense mechanisms. As they become increasingly resigned to their teenager's negative performance and counterproductive behavior, these parents may intentionally or unintentionally cease to provide any affirmation for their child. Those who do so intentionally may rationalize their behavior by arguing that their teenager does little that is worthy of positive acknowledgment. Their lack of affirmation can become an expression of anger or even a form of retribution.

In time, a teenager's pattern of negative attitude and negative performance can jade the perceptions of his parents. They may begin to perceive their child as a failure and lower their expectations accordingly. This tragic chain of events can be arrested. To do so, parents must make every effort to create opportunities for their child to succeed. They must recognize and acknowledge small or partial successes. They must affirm effort even when the child fails. They must develop patience and tolerance. They must say: "Laurie, you know that you have a problem in history. How can I help? And what are you prepared to do to solve this problem?"

A child's lack of respect for himself, when coupled with his parents' lack of respect, invariably undermines the potential for communication. The pattern of failure and counterproductive behavior can lead the teenager to become increasingly estranged from his parents. Unless parents take the initiative and effect changes in the family communication system, they may permanently jeopardize their relationship with their child.

There are no magic bullets for repairing the self-esteem or reorienting the self-defeating behavior of the learning disabled teenager. Nevertheless, parents who intentionally communicate positive expectations, provide emotional support, insist on quality learning assistance, monitor school performance, orchestrate opportunities for success, and convey respect *can* counteract the negative forces and help their struggling teenager rekindle the will to achieve.

CHAPTER 12

Building Self-Esteem

JIMMY: DANCING ISN'T ALWAYS FUN

As the third graders filed into the gymnasium, they were excited and apprehensive. Today was the day they were going to learn how to square dance.

The teacher divided up the boys and girls into couples and then arranged the children in squares of four couples each. She explained the steps, and the children practiced at first without the music. When the teacher turned on the music, most of the children responded to the commands of the caller as if they had been square dancing for years.

When the class was over, the teacher made an announcement. "Children, I have just learned that Jimmy has been accepted at Brookview Academy." She paused and then added in a slightly lower tone of voice, "They must have lowered the standards in his case."

Jimmy's cheeks turned crimson with embarrassment. His dancing partner, a little girl with black hair and freckles, stared at him, as did the other third graders in the gymnasium. It had never before occurred to Jimmy that there was something wrong with him. Now, for the first time in his life, he felt very different from the other children. The teacher had said he was dumb. The teacher couldn't be wrong.

As a private college preparatory school with classes from kindergarten through twelfth grade, Brookview prided itself on its academic excellence. The students were bright and, in many instances, brilliant. Because of the school's high entrance requirements, the teachers were able to accelerate and enrich the curriculum. Even the brilliant students had to work diligently.

Jimmy's third-grade teacher had actually been correct in her assumption that he had just barely passed the entrance exam. Jimmy had been anything but an outstanding student in her class. Nevertheless, he had been accepted at Brookview despite his marginal performance on the entrance exam and his less than exceptional performance in public school.

At Brookview, Jimmy struggled conscientiously to keep his head above water. The rigorous, highly traditional curriculum emphasized the 3 R's and the memorization of a great deal of information. Children in fourth grade and above were expected to do two to three hours of homework each evening. Middle school and high school students were expected to do three to four hours of homework each evening.

Unlike many of his classmates, Jimmy was not particularly adept at memorizing and retrieving data that was not relevant to him. Remembering the names of the phyla in biology or the dates of major battles in the Revolutionary War was very difficult for him. Although he had a highly analytical mind and was very articulate, his performance in math, language arts, Latin, French, and Spanish was marginal when compared to that of his classmates. (At Brookview, students were required to take French in grades 3 to 6, Latin in grades 7 and 8, and could choose Spanish, French, or Latin in grades 8 to 12.)

Despite working hard, Jimmy was consistently in the bottom quarter of the class. On those rare occasions when he did receive a B, the grade was the end product of total effort. His realization that even the most brilliant of his classmates had to work conscientiously made the drudgery more tolerable. He did his four hours of homework every night and never felt sorry for himself.

During Jimmy's senior year, Brookview hired a new headmaster who instituted major changes in the curriculum. In a move that was quite revolutionary for a conservative private college preparatory school in 1959, Brookview began to offer elective courses in psychology and philosophy. Jimmy was drawn to these subjects and found them fascinating. To his surprise and that of his teachers, he became a top student in these classes. For the first time in his life, he was receiving A's on his report cards.

Jimmy did well on his college board exams and scored in the ninety-ninth percentile on the National Merit Scholarship exam. Because of his performance on these exams, his teachers began to perceive him differently. It occurred to them that perhaps Jimmy was a late starter and that he might actually be quite bright. Jimmy also began to perceive himself differently. Was it possible that he actually might be as intelligent as his gifted classmates? Later, when he was admitted to a first-rate college, this suspicion was confirmed.

It was remarkable that Jimmy's experience in the gymnasium in third grade and his subsequent eight difficult years at Brookview did not jade his perceptions about himself and his abilities. His teachers knew he was working hard, and they had concluded on the basis of his performance that he was of average intelligence and ability. They never considered that he might be bright and simply learn differently than the other students at Brookview. Nor did they factor into their assessment the fact that Jimmy related better to ideas and concepts than he did to details.

Until his senior year, Jimmy's grades were in the C+ range. Although he periodically doubted his ability, he never accepted that he was intellectually inferior to his seemingly more gifted classmates. Perhaps he refused to accept the evidence out of stubbornness. Perhaps he persevered because his parents communicated that they expected him to persevere.

Jimmy was fortunate. During his years at Brookview, his parents never once expressed disappointment with his grades. They repeatedly assured him that all they expected from him was that he do his best. Recognizing that Jimmy was receiving little affirmation in school, they attempted to compensate by continually communicating their support for his efforts and their faith in his abilities. At the same time, they were very explicit about their own value system and priorities. They wanted their son to become the best person he was capable of becoming. They expected him to work hard and to give 100 percent. Whether he was an A student or a C student was not the crucial issue for them. What mattered was that Jimmy learn to appreciate the value of effort. They were confident that accomplishment and success would inevitably follow, and they conveyed this conviction to their son. Jimmy believed them. He graduated from college with a 3.6 grade-point average, went to an excellent graduate school, and ultimately became highly successful and respected in his chosen profession.

ENVIRONMENTAL AND PERSONALITY FACTORS

The reasons why some children fight and others give up is difficult to explain. Personality, environment, and perhaps even genetic factors can affect a child's reaction to negative ego-attacking experiences.

A child's self-concept is shaped and molded by his life experiences. Two basic axioms that influence this shaping and molding process are especially relevant to the plight of the learning disabled child and have served as major themes throughout this book:

1. The child who feels loved, accepted, and affirmed and whose social and educational experiences are positive usually develops a positive sense of self.
2. The child who feels unloved, rejected, and unaffirmed and whose social and educational experiences are negative usually develops a negative sense of himself.

Learning disabled children are especially vulnerable to the feedback they receive from adults. Although they may not appear to react to a negative statement from a parent or teacher, the experience can destroy the foundation of their self-concept.

Because of the support systems his parents created, Jimmy persevered in spite of his continual academic struggle. Many children in similar circumstances either would have given up or would have erected an elaborate system of defense and compensatory mechanisms.

The gratuitous comment of Jimmy's third-grade teacher violated every tenet of sound teaching theory and appropriate adult behavior. Although she may have believed what she was saying or felt that she was simply being funny, the teacher had no right to make a public pronouncement about her perceptions of a student's ability or potential. Unfortunately, such insensitive, nonprofessional behavior on the part of some teachers occurs with more frequency than it should.

Negative experiences have a cumulative psychological effect. Derogatory or depricating statements are especially virulent. These statements are like germs that invade the body. The child's reaction may be immediate and may register as pain, anger, or shame, or the emotional reaction may be delayed. A child may appear to be unaffected by a snide remark or a put-down, but this lack of an obvious emotional response can be deceptive. The effects may not manifest themselves until months, even years later. Such a delayed response actually can be far more debilitating than an obvious or immediate response. The spectrum of potential effects includes depression, anger, misbehavior, self-doubt, manipulative behavior, stress, irresponsibility, and generalized emotional disharmony.

Parents and professionals are often mystified by the different ways in which children respond to environmental stimuli. Despite making every effort to assist and positively reinforce a learning disabled child, parents and teachers may discover that one child retreats into a defensive shell while another perseveres and struggles to prevail over his learning problems. The treatment of both children may be essentially the same. When the children's behaviors are analyzed, two characteristics that differentiate the "fighter" from the "capitulator" can usually be identified: self-esteem and self-confidence. For reasons that are often difficult to explain, one child somehow manages to survive his learning disability with his confidence and self-esteem relatively intact; the other child does not. Despite equally severe learning problems, the persistent child prevails over his deficits and evolves into a confident and achieving adult. This disparity in responses suggests two possibilities:

1. Subtle, hard-to-define environmental factors and parental cues may have almost as significant an impact on behavior and the development of personality and temperament as the more obvious, tangible factors.
2. Inherited personality factors may also affect the development of personality and temperament.

The influence of genetics on children's temperament and responses is now being examined scientifically. This research is focusing on the source of childhood inhibition and fear. According to studies conducted by Jerome Kagan, a Harvard developmental psychologist, 10 percent of all children are born with the personality trait of shyness. Another 10 percent tend to be outgoing, spontaneous, and effervescent. Kagan has suggested that inherited neural circuitry may cause certain children to be more reactive to stress. Inhibited (fearful) children have been found to have elevated levels of the hormone cortisol in their saliva at all times. Cortisol is normally secreted in response to fear and is produced when the hyperthalmus stimulates the pituitary gland which in turn stimulates the adrenal cortex. This fear also causes the muscles to tense. While this is happening, the automatic nervous system is causing changes in the heart rate and in the size of the pupils of the eyes. The fact that the level of cortisol in the inhibited child's saliva is continually elevated strongly supports the theory that a child inherits metabolic characteristics that affect his personality.

Although children often react with a high degree of predictability to specific environmental conditions in school and at home, their responses sometimes defy predictions. For instance, a child who is very short may respond by becoming a bully or a tyrant. A second child who is also short may become shy, self-conscious, and withdrawn. A third child may simply accept his shortness as a fact of life and show no psychological ill effects.

Human beings do not react like chemicals in a laboratory experiment. Although a scientist can predict with absolute certainty what will happen when he combines two chemicals at a specific atmospheric pressure, a social scientist cannot be as certain about how human beings will react. Children are complex. This complexity and the multiplicity of the environmental stimuli to which they are exposed produces a wide range of responses. The additional factor of inherited personality traits further complicates the response patterns. Because of these variables, human behavior does not always conform to predictions based on sociological and psychological tenets. Although a physically abused child has a significantly higher statistical chance of becoming an abusive parent, he may defy the sociological model and may respond to his own negative childhood experiences by becoming a gentle and sensitive parent. It should be noted, however, that such a response to being abused is atypical.

Although a positive, loving family relationship may not guarantee that a child will be emotionally adjusted, there certainly is a great deal of evidence documenting the positive effects of a healthy home environment on a child's emotional adjustment. Inherited personality traits and complex human reactions to environmental stimuli notwithstanding, a child's personality development is unquestionably affected by the quality of the family bonding. The more healthy the parent-child relationship, the more positive the child's emotional adjustment. The nature and quality of the bonding process invariably influences in one way or another the development of a learning disabled child's personality and the nature of his perceptions about himself and his abilities.

The parents of a learning disabled child have a special responsibility to do everything in their power to enhance the quality of their relationship with their child. This relationship can provide security and refuge during the storms that a learning disabled child will inevitably experience.

SUPPORT SYSTEMS

The child with learning problems is typically found at the bottom end of the self-acceptance/self-appreciation spectrum. This is especially true if the child's learning deficiencies have persisted for years. Like acid, school failure can eat away at the foundation of the child's self-concept. The learning disabled child whose problems remain unresolved is at risk of never developing a sense of his own power and efficacy.

The role played by parents in the development of self-esteem cannot be overemphasized. Parents who create a family environment that supports the child emotionally while he is struggling to resolve his learning problems can usually dramatically reduce the risk of permanent damage to the child's self-concept.

The role played by teachers in the development of a child's self-esteem is equally crucial. By creating a positive environment in the classroom, by providing the learning disabled student with an opportunity to experience success, and by acknowledging the child for his accomplishments, the teacher can significantly reduce the danger of self-concept damage.

Parents and teachers working in tandem and intentionally creating opportunities for the learning disabled child to succeed can be a powerful force in the process of rebuilding the child's self-acceptance, self-confidence, and self-esteem. Unfortunately, parents and teachers do not always work as a team.

Ideally, if either the parent or teacher support system fails to function adequately, the other system can compensate. Teachers who realize that the parents of the learning disabled child are not acknowledging and affirming the child must do everything in their power to make up for this deficiency. They must provide extra nurturing and support for the child in school. At the same time, they must attempt to impress upon the child's parents the necessity of providing emotional support at home.

Parents who perceive that the teacher is not making an effort to bolster the learning disabled child's self-esteem must do everything in their power to make up for this deficiency. They will need to supply extra positive strokes at home, and they may also need to provide private learning assistance or tutoring. During parent-teacher conferences, they must attempt to impress upon the teacher the necessity for creating opportunities for their child to experience academic success and acknowledgment.

IDENTIFYING SELF-ESTEEM DEFICITS

Parents may unintentionally overlook the blatant symptoms of poor self-esteem. A child's behaviors, attitudes, and actions are windows into his innermost feelings. Often these windows have the shades pulled down.

In some instances, the symptoms of a child's self-esteem may be too subtle for parents to identify. A child may become so effective at compensating for his deficiencies and camouflaging his vulnerabilities that he may prevent his parents from recognizing behavioral and emotional signals of his distress and self-esteem deficits.

A child's need to camouflage his feelings may reflect his desire to gain or maintain his parents' approval. An insecure, struggling child may consciously or unconsciously fear rejection if he were to reveal his weaknesses and vulnerabilities. Such a reaction is especially prevalent in homes in which a child perceives his parents as being highly judgmental and disapproving. It is also possible that a child may feel compelled to hide his emotions because he is frightened by the anger that is linked to these emotions. Children are often frightened and/or ashamed of their hostility. In the process of denying and hiding it, they often deny and hide all of their emotions.

Parents can also slip into a denial mode. Some may dismiss their child's blatantly nonadaptive behaviors as a personality quirk. Other parents may flee from confronting irrefutable evidence that their child is experiencing internal discord and feelings of inadequacy. These parents may react in this way because they suspect that they might be responsible in some way for their child's disharmony and may feel guilty. Others may feel threatened by any situation that demands self-examination and self-confrontation.

Parents who disregard the red flags that signal possible emotional disharmony and lack of self-esteem are courting disaster. They must intervene, or their child may ultimately be forced to pay a very high price for their disregard.

The following checklist is intended to help identify some of the specific behaviors that might signal a child's lack of self-esteem.

SELF-ESTEEM INVENTORY

Code: 0 = Never   1 = Rarely   2 = Sometimes   3 = Often   4 = Always

My child has difficulty establishing eye contact.   — —

My child is reluctant to experience anything new, different, or unexpected.   — —

My child is shy with people that he knows.   — —

My child is shy around strangers.   — —

My child has difficulty relating or playing with other children.   — —

My child has difficulty making friends.   — —

My child feels that he is unpopular.   — —

My child feels that he is dumb.   — —

My child is convinced in advance that he will fail or have difficulty with new challenges.   — —

When asked to draw a picture of a person, my child's picture is very small.   — —

My child is generally fearful.   — —

My child has difficulty expressing his emotions.   — —

My child is resentful and/or jealous of his siblings.   — —

My child has difficulty accepting compliments or praise.   — —

My child is derogatory of other people.   — —

My child is derogatory of himself.   — —

My child is frequently angry or hostile.   — —

My child appears depressed.   — —

My child is often withdrawn and emotionally detached.   — —

My child is a "loner."   — —

My child is defensive about his deficits.   — —

My child has chronically poor posture.   — —

My child tends to blame others for his problems.   — —

Interpreting the Checklist

A pattern of 3s and 4s in response to the statements suggests that your child is manifesting symptoms of low self-esteem. Although a learning disability might account for many behaviors that are associated with low self-esteem, the disability may not be the exclusive source of the child's poor self-concept. Other factors that can cause low self-esteem include family problems, emotional problems, and problems associated with the advent of adolescence.

When low self-esteem is the direct result of learning disability, the esteem deficits may become less pronounced as the child begins to respond to learning assistance. Symptoms which persist despite competent learning assistance could reflect an underlying psychological problem. This problem may be directly related, tangentially related, or unrelated to the child's learning disability. Chronic anger, jealousy, resentment, isolation from friends and family, and depression are clear signals that a child needs to be evaluated by a mental health professional.

SELF-ASSESSMENT SCALES

The impressions and emotional responses of a child to his struggle invariably imprint themselves on the child's psyche. Unfortunately, the learning disabled child often has difficulty expressing how he is feeling about school and about himself. In his innocence, the child may attempt to deny, repress, or hide his negative emotions in the hope that the feelings will go away. This unconscious process of denial is usually ineffective. The repressed emotions inevitably manifest themselves in one form or another.

Although children may not be consciously aware of their underlying feelings, they nevertheless are controlled by these feelings. Before they would risk examining their emotions and admitting to themselves or their parents that they are hurting and unhappy, most children require a great deal of encouragement. Parents must establish trust, and they must respond to their child with patience and sensitivity.

Parents desiring to help their learning disabled child identify and express his feelings may find the following self-assessment scales useful. The scales are designed to facilitate parent-child communication about school and about the feelings produced by academic setbacks and frustration. The scales are not sacred, and you are encouraged to change them or add to them as you see fit. Be cautious about overusing the method. If overused, your child may begin to perceive the system as gimmicky.

A strategy for using the scales is modeled here.

PARENT: I'm curious about how things are going in school. I'd like to try an experiment. Which is your best subject in school? Let's write it down.

Best Subject: _____

PARENT: Now, which is your worst subject?

Worst Subject: _____

PARENT: Okay. Now let's take a look at these assessment scales. Notice that the title says "Quality of Work in Best Subject." You indicated that your best subject is _____. Let's write it down again on the line. Now notice that at one end of the line is a sad face. At the other end is a happy face. Do you see how the numbers run from 1 at the "sad" end to 10 at the "happy" end? Let's say that number 1 is the worst student in your class in this subject and number 10 is the best student. What number best describes how good a job you do in this subject? Are you a "10" or a "9" or are you in the middle? Perhaps you feel your score should be lower. Circle the number which describes you. (More detailed explanation about how to use the number scale may be required with very young children.)

QUALITY OF WORK IN BEST SUBJECT
Subject: _____

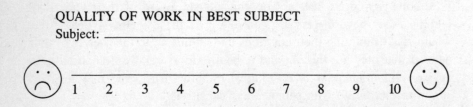

PARENT: Good. Now, let's do the same thing with your worst subject.

QUALITY OF WORK IN WORST SUBJECT
Subject: _____

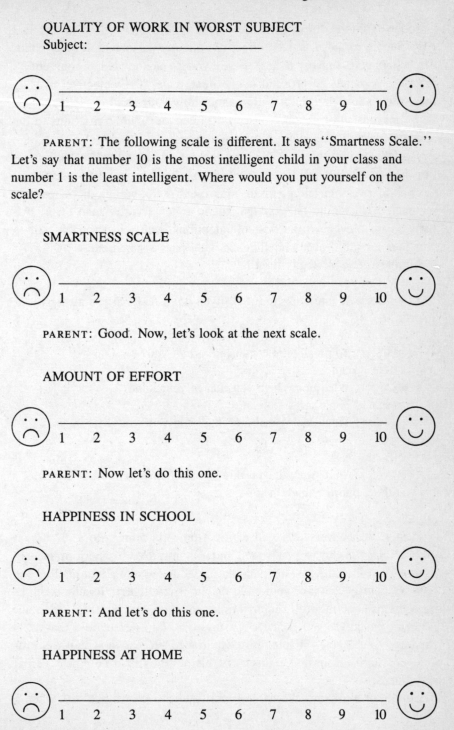

1   2   3   4   5   6   7   8   9   10

PARENT: The following scale is different. It says "Smartness Scale." Let's say that number 10 is the most intelligent child in your class and number 1 is the least intelligent. Where would you put yourself on the scale?

SMARTNESS SCALE

1   2   3   4   5   6   7   8   9   10

PARENT: Good. Now, let's look at the next scale.

AMOUNT OF EFFORT

1   2   3   4   5   6   7   8   9   10

PARENT: Now let's do this one.

HAPPINESS IN SCHOOL

1   2   3   4   5   6   7   8   9   10

PARENT: And let's do this one.

HAPPINESS AT HOME

1   2   3   4   5   6   7   8   9   10

You may choose to discuss each scale before proceeding to the next one. Such a strategy can be effective, but may also inhibit your child. The alternative suggested here is for you to acknowledge your child's response and then to proceed to the next scale. The objective of using the scales is to obtain information about how your child is feeling. Once you elicit this information, you can explore your child's reactions to the specific scales during subsequent discussions.

While examining your child's responses, you should resist the temptation to take ownership of the problems or the feelings. For instance, if your child gives himself a 2 on the smartness scale, you might be tempted to react: "Oh, come on, Johnny. You're much smarter than that!" Although you may have the best of intentions, you will probably fail to convince the child of his intelligence with such a statement.

An alternative strategy might be:

PARENT: It sure looks to me that you don't feel that you are very smart.

CHILD: I'm not.

PARENT: You really are convinced, aren't you?

CHILD: Yeah.

PARENT: What might help you change your mind?

CHILD: I don't know.

PARENT: Would doing well in school convince you that you are smart?

CHILD: Yeah.

PARENT: Well, what do you think would help you succeed in school? Do you think tutoring might help?

Ideally, the conversation will evolve from this point into a discussion of possible ways by which your child can improve his performance in school. You should not expect that an initial discussion about intelligence will necessarily convince your child that he is intelligent. To alter a child's perceptions about himself requires time, patience, and strategic planning. Before your child's self-concept can improve, he must believe that he is capable of achieving. Helping him experience success in school can provide far more persuasive evidence of his abilities than countless verbal assurances.

Parents should resist the natural inclination to give a pep talk when a child expresses doubts about himself or his abilities. Although they should provide assistance when appropriate, parents must remind themselves that a child's feelings belong to him.

The self-assessment scales are designed to help children examine their perceptions, identify their feelings, and ventilate their frustrations. If the emotions revealed appear highly distorted or if you do not feel equipped to deal with what is revealed, you should not hesitate to seek the assistance of a qualified mental health professional.

You may want to use the scales periodically to measure improvement (or deterioration) in your child's self-concept. For instance, you may want to compare how your child feels about himself before beginning his learning assistance program, midway through the program, and after completing it. Ideally, your child should begin to feel better about himself as he makes inroads into resolving his learning deficits. If you observe no improvement, you should discuss the situation with a counselor.

BREAKING THE FAILURE CYCLE

The origins of self-esteem and self-confidence are not very mysterious. The equation that yields a happy, confident, harmonious child is comprised of love, acceptance by others, self-acceptance, and success.

Genetics must also be factored into the equation. For example, a child with intellectual limitations or a physical handicap must learn how to overcome and/or accommodate himself to his disabilities. Many children with genetically based disabilities not only cope with their deficits, but they actually learn, and are taught, how to prevail over them magnificently. Their will to prevail over their deficits can usually be traced to an abundance of parental and professional support and love.

Even under the best of conditions, parenting can be a supreme test. Parents are expected to face this test with little or no formal training or preparation. It is simply assumed that they will rise to the occasion and figure out what they need to do. In many instances, the assumption proves correct. In other instances, however, parents may struggle and spin their wheels while trying to resolve problems and issues that they do not fully understand. Even highly intuitive and well-intentioned parents may not know how to deal with the learning disabled child's unique academic and emotional problems. This is especially true when the child appears to be locked into a cycle of failure and counterproductive behavior.

Parenting skills and intuition can be developed and improved. Parents desiring to do so must be willing to examine the dynamics of their relationship with their child. As they acquire insight, parents usually discover that they can either avoid or defuse many of the repetitive confrontations that produce anger, misunderstanding, ill will, defensiveness, and resistance. This insight can permit parents to transform inconsistent child-rearing practices into consistent practices. With effort and practice, they can learn how to replace manipulative scripts with communication that is authentic, productive, and pleasurable. Parents, however, must accept that they will make occasional errors in judgment regardless of insight, effort, and practice. The ability to learn from these mistakes is the key to acquiring more effective parenting skills.

All children have basic emotional needs that must be met. Love, appreciation, acknowledgment, structure, and support are at the top of the list. The unique pressures and stress experienced by the learning disabled child usually require that he be provided with more of these emotional nutrients than the typical child. He also will require more patience.

Parents who are concerned about their child's self-esteem must make a special effort to understand how self-esteem evolves. The factors that comprise and influence self-esteem are interrelated and overlapping. The interaction of these components is graphically represented here. The two cycles illustrate the reciprocal synergy of the components and their effects on the child's sense of himself, his abilities, and his identity.

POSITIVE SELF-ESTEEM CYCLE

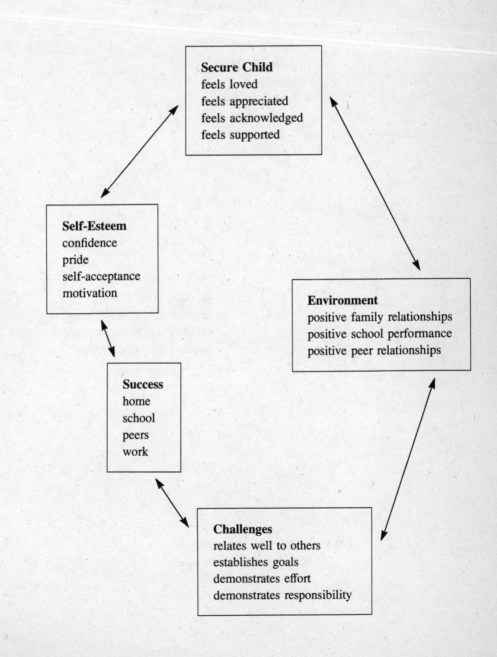

Secure Child
feels loved
feels appreciated
feels acknowledged
feels supported

Self-Esteem
confidence
pride
self-acceptance
motivation

Environment
positive family relationships
positive school performance
positive peer relationships

Success
home
school
peers
work

Challenges
relates well to others
establishes goals
demonstrates effort
demonstrates responsibility

NEGATIVE SELF-ESTEEM CYCLE

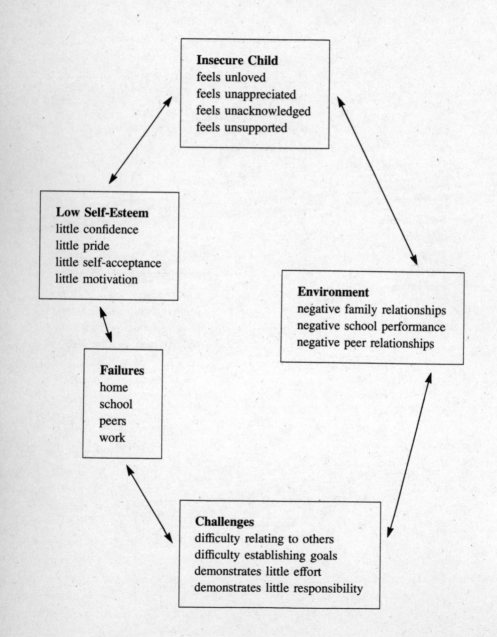

These graphic representations emphasize how the components that comprise self-esteem are linked in an interactive system. One single negative factor can potentially transform a positive self-esteem cycle into a negative self-esteem cycle. For instance, a nonlearning disabled and normally well-adjusted child may develop social problems. These problems begin to have a negative impact on his school performance and family relationships. His difficulty in school and the tension at home cause the child's confidence and self-esteem to suffer, and the child becomes increasingly insecure. He begins to feel unloved, unacknowledged, and unappreciated, and his self-esteem sinks lower and lower. Had the child not begun to experience social problems, he normally would have been characterized by a positive self-esteem cycle. By altering one single environmental factor, however, a domino effect is created, and the child is now characterized by a negative self-esteem cycle.

Another example of the reciprocal dynamics of the self-esteem cycles is illustrated by the case of the secure and capable student who enrolls in a highly accelerated gifted program. Although the child had been a good student in his regular class, he now finds that he is barely able to keep up. Despite continual effort, school becomes a monumental struggle. Experiencing little success, the child's confidence and self-acceptance begin to suffer. He becomes less and less motivated. He perceives for the first time that his parents are dissatisfied with his performance. A previously confident and secure child has now become a nonconfident and insecure child.

An examination of the two cycles reveals the four critical points at which parents and teachers can most successfully intervene and influence the evolution of a child's self-esteem. These four intervention points are *environment, challenges, support,* and *love.*

To intervene effectively, parents must draw upon their intuition, desire, and parenting skills. With skill and effort, they can intentionally structure the home environment so that communication and interactions are more positive. By procuring quality remedial support for their child, they can help their child acquire the skills he needs to succeed in school.

Parents can also influence the nature of the challenges to which their child is exposed. By diplomatically encouraging their child to select realistic challenges, they can significantly improve his chances of experiencing success. For example, they might encourage a sixth grader who is reading at the fourth-grade level to choose a book which he can read and enjoy. If they suspect that the material their child is being asked to read is too difficult, they can consult with their child's teacher and request that more realistic work be assigned. Reading a book that the child enjoys and can decode is far more important to the development of his self-esteem and attitudes about learning than reading a book at grade level. Although improving the child's reading skills is vital, helping him to experience success and begin to associate reading with pleasure is equally vital. Intentionally creating opportunities for success is instrumental in convincing the insecure child that he has the ability to succeed.

Parents who help their child establish realistic short- and long-term goals are training him to focus his energy on specific challenges. When they establish reasonable guidelines and performance criteria, they encourage effort, responsibility, and achievement.

Love represents the final intervening point. Parents desiring to improve their child's self-esteem must commit themselves to providing an extra measure of love, appreciation, acknowledgment, and support. Impressing upon a child that he is loved in spite of his performance is a crucial component in the process of helping the child develop self-esteem.

For teachers to intervene effectively in the self-esteem cycle, they, too, must draw upon their intuition, desire, and teaching skills. If they wish to build the learning disabled child's self-esteem, they must control the environment so that the child can be successful. Although the accomplishments of the learning disabled student may be quite modest when compared with the achievements of other students, these successes are crucial for the child. Being acknowledged and affirmed by the teacher is especially critical, and the struggling child's self-esteem can hang in the balance.

A teacher's performance criteria must be geared to a realistic assessment of the student's skill level. Expecting a fifth grader who is reading a year below grade level (and who would probably not qualify for learning assistance in many states) to do quality work in social studies is unrealistic. Unfair expectations invariably produce frustration and anxiety. Ideally, teachers will have a degree of latitude grading the work of children with learning problems. If, however, school policy or their own attitudes prevents them from being flexible, they might consider giving the struggling child two grades on his work. One grade would indicate his performance relative to the other children; the second grade would indicate the student's performance relative to his own previous performance level. In fairness to the other students, the score recorded on the child's transcript would be competitively derived.

It is unfortunate that in many school districts, mainstreamed learning disabled children are graded competitively. The primary educational objective for these students should be to build their self-esteem and help them overcome their learning deficits. Once this is achieved and they have mastered the skills they need to compete, their work can be evaluated in comparison to that of other students.

Teachers who are particularly sensitive to the special plight of the learning disabled student might urge such a child to do additional projects for extra credit. For example, a child with severe language arts problems who is studying the Civil War might be given the option to draw pictures or maps that would demonstrate his understanding. By urging the student to express his interest and knowledge in a medium in which he might have special talent the teacher provides the student with an opportunity to experience success and pride in his accomplishment, and to participate actively in his education. If the child's work is good, it can be held up as an example for other children to emulate. To be fair, the teacher should also give the other students in the class an opportunity to do additional projects for extra credit.

Perceptive and sensitive teachers intentionally create opportunities for the insecure, struggling child to feel appreciated and affirmed. They help the child establish short-term goals, and they encourage effort and responsibility, not with lectures, but by creating a context in which children can achieve and feel good about themselves.

The learning disabled child needs the support not only of his special education teacher, but also of his regular classroom teacher. (This statement assumes that the child is being mainstreamed into regular classrooms for a portion of the day.) Both teachers have a responsibility to apprise the child of how he is doing and what he still needs to achieve. The child must realize that his teachers are working as a team and that they expect him to attain specific objectives. He also must realize that they believe he can prevail and achieve these objectives. Finally, the learning disabled student must recognize that his teachers will not accept work below a reasonable standard and that they will not permit him to be irresponsible or manipulative.

Before parents and teachers can effectively influence and regulate the nature of the challenges a child experiences, they must determine accurately the child's current level of academic skills. Recent scores on the standardized tests administered in school can provide them with this information. Knowing the student's present skill level permits teachers and parents to measure subsequent improvement or regression.

Parents and teachers desiring to intervene effectively must strive to understand the nature and implications of their child's particular learning problems. Although positive expectations can be an inspiration for a child, unrealistic expectations can be a nightmare. To expect a learning disabled child who is two years below grade level to catch up in six months would be setting up the child and themselves for a major disappointment. If the child fails to achieve the objective, he will have suffered another defeat. For a child whose self-esteem is already tenuous, this defeat can have disastrous emotional consequences.

The most effective means for improving the learning disabled child's self-esteem is for parents and teachers to reduce the opportunities for failure and to increase the opportunities for success. Encouraging the learning disabled child to develop a special interest or talent could be instrumental in helping the child acquire pride and confidence. For example, parents might encourage the struggling child to collect something, to learn how to use a lathe, or to master needlepoint. The child who can see his accomplishments will be far more convinced of his ability than the child who is told he is smart and capable by well-intentioned parents. Nothing builds self-esteem more effectively than tangible success.

Teachers obviously play a pivotal role in establishing attainable goals for children. Like a child's parents, they, too, walk a fine line between expecting too much and expecting too little. That their level of expectations can have a dramatic impact on the child's level of achievement and self-esteem has been repeatedly documented by educational research.

An experiment that is purported to have occurred in the school of education at a well-respected university offers an excellent illustration of the effect of teachers' expectations on a child's level of achievement. A professor informed some graduate students that they were being assigned to teach a group of severely learning handicapped students with enigmatic learning problems. These children had not responded to standard learning assistance methods. Although the students were very bright, no teacher had ever succeeded in helping them master basic academic skills. The professor expressed complete confidence that the graduate students would be able to find the key that would help the children learn at a level commensurate with their intelligence.

During the next several months, the graduate students tried every conceivable teaching method. Although progress was slow, the children began to respond positively to their teachers' efforts and achieved relatively significant academic gains. Only after the graduate students had documented this achievement did the professor inform them that the children were marginally retarded. The test results confirmed that the children had progressed at a far faster rate than is customarily expected from students of their tested intelligence level.

Because the graduate students believed that the children were bright, they approached the challenge of teaching them with positive expectations. Undeterred by the fact that other teachers had been unsuccessful, they enthusiastically tried every conceivable teaching method. Knowing that others had tried and failed inspired them to make a breakthrough. Their efforts were prodigious, and the results provided direct testimony to their positive expectations, their innovative teaching strategies, and their extra effort.

Miraculous things can occur when human beings are motivated to test themselves and their capabilities. Human history is replete with instances of inspired men and women breaking records and overcoming limitations. For people to accomplish the seemingly impossible, they need only feel convinced that they can succeed and deserve to succeed.

This same axiom is especially applicable to learning disabled children. For them to overcome their problems, they must be motivated to learn, and they must become convinced that they *can* learn. Initially, their parents and teachers may have to provide the inspiration and the conviction. If they are skillful, they can begin to shift the responsibility for generating motivation to the child. The proof of the success of their efforts occurs when the child himself develops the desire to learn and achieve and when he himself becomes convinced that he possesses the ability to learn and achieve.

JODY: LEARNING TO BELIEVE IN HIMSELF

The third grader had made up his mind. He didn't want to be promoted to the fourth grade. He was convinced that he wouldn't be able to do the work.

Neither my staff nor the principal of Jody's school was as convinced as Jody about his limitations. During the five months that he had been attending our center, he had actually made remarkable progress, and there was every reason to expect that he would continue to improve during the remaining three months of the school term. We were all certain that by the end of the summer Jody would be reading at least one year above grade level. Given his remarkable improvement, retention could not possibly be justified.

As I chatted with Jody, I could sense his apprehension about being assigned to either of the fourth-grade teachers at his school. He had heard that they were both very demanding. He confided that he was afraid of being embarrassed in front of the other children if he made a mistake while reading aloud, or if he asked a question about something he didn't understand.

Jody's relationship with his third-grade teacher was excellent. She liked him and was very supportive. Because Jody felt very secure with her, he desperately wanted to remain in her class for another year.

Although I could understand the child's anxiety about fourth grade and his trepidations about being assigned to a more demanding teacher, I knew that retention would be a mistake. I felt certain that the ten-year-old would be able to handle fourth grade and would have a very successful year.

A child's fears and anxieties may appear irrational or unwarranted, but to the child these emotions are real and can have a paralyzing effect. We could not simply dismiss Jody's concerns about fourth grade as being silly. We were asking an insecure child to leave a safe and comfortable setting where he felt appreciated and successful and enter a setting where he feared he might experience failure and ridicule. Jody was understandably frightened. He needed more than simple assurances to feel confident about making a transition that could be emotionally traumatizing. Before his anxieties could be allayed, he would need tangible proof that he could succeed in fourth grade.

To reduce Jody's stress, I told him that no decision would be made until August. In the meanwhile, we would continue to provide him with learning assistance. Jody seemed greatly relieved to put off the decision.

During the next five months, my staff developed a series of tasks that challenged Jody's academic and reasoning skills. The tasks were sequential and were designed to become increasingly more difficult. Each task or test had been carefully selected so that the child would be able to succeed. Jody was very aware that the work was becoming harder. Because he was succeeding, he had become very involved in the process and eagerly looked forward to the next "test" of his ability.

In August, we informed Jody that the tests he was taking were at the seventh-grade level. He was stunned, and believed us only after we showed him the manual and the test booklets from which we had taken the material.

I called Jody into my office and told him that I had decided to skip him up to seventh grade the following year since he was clearly able to do seventh-grade work. Jody's mouth dropped open. I then smiled and told him that if he preferred I would agree to place him in the fourth grade. A big grin spread across his face. I asked him if we had a deal, and he nodded his head in agreement.

Jody made the honor roll in fourth grade. When he was tested with the other fourth graders in his class on national achievement tests, he scored at the ninth-grade level in both reading and math.

CHANGING PERCEPTIONS

Most children who are not successful in school expend a great deal of emotional energy protecting themselves from feeling inadequate. Guiding a child from behind the walls that guard a fragile ego demands strategic planning and careful execution on the part of both parents and teachers.

Jody was terrified of the dangers that he felt were lurking on the other side of the wall. If he remained in third grade, he was assured of success and nurturing. Beyond the wall, in fourth grade, he saw himself exposed to failure and embarrassment. Although his learning problems were subtle, they seemed monumental to him. Lacking self-confidence and convinced that he could not possibly succeed in fourth grade, he had pulled up the drawbridge and had barricaded the gate to his fortress. He would stay where he was safe.

The process of transforming Jody's expectations of disaster into expectations of success was carefully planned. The teachers challenged him with tasks which were difficult, but not too difficult. They provided acknowledgment and encouragement, but the feedback was honest and never so effusive that the child would begin to discount it. They provided intensive learning support, but were careful not to become so supportive that Jody would develop an emotional dependency on them.

The strategy proved successful. Jody discovered that he could succeed at virtually anything we asked him to do. He began to derive more satisfaction from testing himself and "winning" than he did from protecting himself and being nurtured by his well-intentioned third grade teacher.

Jody had been set up to succeed. His self-esteem had been cultivated like a carefully planned garden. As he experienced more and more success, he began to accept himself and appreciate his many talents. He also began to expect further accomplishments and to believe that he not only could achieve, but that he *deserved* to achieve. This attitude is the very essence of self-esteem and self-acceptance.

STRUCTURING SUCCESS

For most couples, producing a child is relatively easy. Helping that child become happy, self-accepting, and self-confident can be far more difficult. The process demands love, dedication, and much skillful parenting.

Helping the learning disabled child who has a poor self-concept can be one of the most difficult and emotionally demanding challenges that parents can face. But it can also be one of life's most rewarding experiences. What could possibly be more exciting and meaningful for a parent or a teacher than witnessing and participating in the transformation of a despairing and defeated child into a confident and achieving individual.

No wonder children who fail in school become children who hate school! Repeated failure and frustration must inevitably destroy the will to learn and the desire to achieve. Children who do not win their desperate battle with their learning problems are destined to discover that they lack the keys that open the doors to fulfilling careers, financial rewards, and self-esteem.

Once you acquire sufficient information and insight about the nature and implications of your child's learning problems, you can play a vital role in assuring that your child experiences success and not failure in school. If you are to affect the outcome, you must be willing to monitor your child's academic performance closely, and you must be willing to make certain your child receives the learning assistance he requires. The quality of your participation, your insight, your emotional support, and the quality of the education provided by your child's teachers will determine whether or not your child prevails and ultimately conquers his or her learning problems.

Appendix: Standard Tests

BERRY-BUKTENICA DEVELOPMENTAL TEST OF VISUAL-MOTOR INTEGRATION

Function: Measures visual perception and fine-motor coordination.
Age range: 2–15 years.
Scores: Age level.
Procedure: Students copy geometric forms that range from straight lines to complex designs.

BENDER VISUAL MOTOR GESTALT TEST

Function: Measures visual-motor integration, perceptual maturity, and emotional disturbances.
Age range: 5–11 years.
Scores: Age level, percentile.
Procedure: Students copy nine abstract designs.

BRIGANCE DIAGNOSTIC INVENTORY OF BASIC SKILLS

Function: Measures readiness, reading, language arts, and mathematics skills and pinpoints specific areas of academic strengths and weaknesses.

Age range: K–6th grade. Separate inventory for older children.
   Scores: Grade level.
Procedure: Examiner asks student questions and records the answers in a record book.

DENVER DEVELOPMENTAL SCREENING TEST

Function: Detects developmental delays in young children.
Age range: Birth–6 years.
   Scores: Age level.
Subtests: Personal/social (getting along with people).
   Self-help skills (dressing).
   Fine-motor adaptive (using hands to pick up objects, drawing).
   Language (following commands, speaking).
   Gross-motor (sitting, walking, jumping).

DETROIT TESTS OF LEARNING APTITUDE

Function: Measures general learning abilities.
Age range: 3–19 years.
   Scores: Mental age and I.Q. Test also indicates the student's strengths and weaknesses.
Subtests: Reasoning and comprehension.
   Practical judgment.
   Verbal ability.
   Time and space relationships.
   Numerical ability.
   Auditory attentive ability.
   Visual attentive ability.
   Motor ability.

GOODENOUGH-HARRIS DRAWING TEST

Function: Measures intellectual and emotional maturity.
Age range: 3–15 years.
   Scores: Standard, percentile, quality scale.
Procedure: The child draws a complete picture of a man, woman, and then of himself.

ILLINOIS TEST OF PSYCHOLINGUISTIC ABILITIES (ITPA)

Function: Measures visual-motor and auditory-vocal skills (listening, then responding by speaking).

Age range: 2–10 years.

Scores: Age level, scaled (scaled from 0–68 with a mean score of 36. Anything below 26 is considered to be a potential danger signal).

Subtests: Auditory reception—Measures how well the child understands verbal questions; Example: "Do caterpillars fly?"

Visual reception—Measures how well the child understands visual pictures; Example: matching similar pictures.

Auditory association—Measures how well the child links ideas that are presented orally; Example: A bird has wings; a dog has———.

Visual association—Measures how well the child links ideas that are presented visually; Example: finding a picture of a spoon that goes with a picture of a bowl of soup.

Verbal expression—Measures how well the child describes familiar objects; Example: a button is round, has four holes, etc.

Manual expression—Measures how well the child shows how objects are used; Example: the child makes a sawing motion when shown a picture of a saw.

Grammatic closure—Measures how well the child uses correct grammar; Example: Here is a house. Here are two ———.

Visual closure—Measures how well the child identifies pictured objects when parts are missing; Example: a child is shown a picture of a junkyard scene with many dogs in it, some partially obscured. The child must find all the dogs.

Auditory sequential memory—Measures how well the child remembers what he has heard; Example: the child is told a series of numbers and must repeat them in order.

Visual sequential memory—Measures how well the child remembers (in order) what he has seen; Example: the child is shown a series of shapes and must reproduce them in order.

Auditory Closure—Measures how well the child identifies a word when a part of it is not said; Example: —asketball.

Sound blending—Measures how well the child blends individual sounds into a word; Example: "c," "a," "t" into "cat."

KEY MATH DIAGNOSTIC ARITHMETIC TEST

Function: Measures a wide range of mathematical skills.
Age range: K–6th grade.
Scores: Grade level.
Subtests: Numeration, fractions, geometry and symbols, addition, subtraction, multiplication, division, mental computation, numerical reasoning, word problems, missing elements, money, measurement, time.

MARIANE FROSTIG DEVELOPMENTAL TEST OF VISUAL PERCEPTION

Function: Measures visual perception and visual-motor skills.
Age range: 3–8 years.
Scores: Age level, scaled (ranging from 0–20, with 10 as average), and perceptual quotient (scores lower than 90 suggest high risk of learning disabilities for children entering first grade).
Subtests: Eye-motor coordination (tracing within boundaries).
Figure-ground.
Constancy of shape (picking out one shape from other similar shapes).
Position in space (finding identical figures).
Spatial relations (copying designs by connecting dots).

MEETING STREET SCHOOL SCREENING TEST (M.S.S.S.T.)

Function: Identifies children with potential learning disabilities and identifies developmental maturity.
Age range: 5–7½ years.
Scores: Scaled scores (for each subtest, from 1–19; total test score from 20–80. Cutoff for kindergarten children is 39, for 1st grade, 55).
Subtests: Subjective behavior rating scale.
Motor patterning (hopping, clapping).

Visual-perceptual-motor (matching shapes, copying forms, remembering forms and letters).

Language (repeating words and sentences, telling a story).

PEABODY PICTURE VOCABULARY TEST

Function: Measures understanding of word meanings.

Age range: 2–18 years.

Scores: Mental age, percentile, IQ equivalent.

Procedure: The examiner pronounces a word. The child must select the picture that represents that word.

PURDUE PERCEPTUAL-MOTOR SURVEY

Function: Measures perceptual-motor, gross-motor, and fine-motor skills.

Age range: 6–10 years.

Scores: None, profile only.

Subtests: Balance and posture, body image (knowledge and movement of body parts).

Perceptual-motor match (rhythmic writing and chalkboard tasks involving directionality and laterality).

Ocular control (visual tracking activities).

Form perception (copying geometric forms).

SLINGERLAND SCREENING TESTS FOR IDENTIFYING CHILDREN WITH SPECIFIC LANGUAGE DISABILITIES

Function: Measures visual, auditory, and kinesthetic skills which are related to reading and spelling.

Age range: 6–12 years.

Scores: None, provides guidelines for prescriptive teaching.

Subtests: Copying, visual memory, visual discrimination, auditory memory, initial and final sounds, auditory discrimination, following directions, word finding, story telling.

SLOSSON INTELLIGENCE TEST FOR CHILDREN AND ADULTS

Function: Measures mental ability.

Age range: 5 months–adult.

Scores: Mental age, IQ.

Procedure: The examiner asks the student a variety of questions dealing with general knowledge, mathematical reasoning, vocabulary, and auditory memory.

SPACHE DIAGNOSTIC READING SCALES

Function: Measures a wide range of reading skills.

Age range: 1–8th grade, 9–12th grade for students with reading problems.

Scores: Grade level.

Subtests: Word recognition, oral reading, silent reading, auditory comprehension, and phonics.

STANFORD-BINET INTELLIGENCE SCALE

Function: Measures general intelligence.

Age range: 2 years–adult.

Scores: Mental age, IQ.

Procedure: The examiner asks the student to answer questions or perform tasks which assess a variety of abilities including vocabulary, memory, abstract reasoning, numerical concepts, visual-motor skills, and social competence.

WECHSLER INTELLIGENCE SCALE FOR CHILDREN REVISED—(WISC-R)

Function: Measures general intelligence.

Age range: 6–17 years.

Scores: Verbal IQ, performance IQ, full scale IQ, scaled score, test ages.

Subtests: Verbal section.
Information (What day comes after Tuesday?)
Similarities (How are a shoe and a boot alike?)
Arithmetic (word problems involving mental computation).
Vocabulary (What is a stadium?)
Comprehension (What should you do if you cut yourself?)
Digit span (remembering a series of numbers).

Performance section

Picture completion (identifying what's missing from an incomplete picture of an object).

Picture arrangement (putting pictures in a logical order).

Block design (copying a design with blocks).

Object assembly (putting puzzle pieces together to form a familiar object).

Coding (associating a symbol with a particular shape).

Mazes (following a maze without lifting the pencil).

WEPMAN AUDITORY DISCRIMINATION TEST

Function: Measures auditory discrimination.

Age range: 5–8 years.

Scores: Rating scale ranging from "very good development" to "below the level of the threshold of adequacy."

Procedure: The examiner pronounces two words and the child must determine if they sound the same or different. Example: "bad-bat."

WIDE RANGE ACHIEVEMENT TEST

Function: Measures achievement in reading (word recognition only), spelling, and arithmetic.

Age range: 5 years–adult.

Scores: Grade level, standard, percentile, and stanine.

Procedure: The student reads word aloud, writes down dictated spelling words and writes down the answers to printed arithmetic problems.

WOODCOCK READING MASTERY TEST

Function: Measures a wide range of reading skills.

Age range: K–12th grade.

Scores: Grade level, percentile, relative mastery, achievement index, reading range.

Subtests: Letter identification, word identification, word attack, word comprehension, and passage comprehension.

Glossary of Educational Terms

Aphasia: A complete inability to use language to communicate effectively. (This communication disorder is not the result of a physical impairment such as damage to the vocal cords or larynx.) (See Dysphasia.)

Apraxia: Complete inability to make purposeful motor movements when there is no paralysis (See Dyspraxia.)

Associative Skills: The ability to relate a new concept or new material to previously mastered material. *For example:* A child seeing the word "cat" must associate the letters that make up this word with the furry animal that purrs.

Ataxia: An inability to coordinate muscles. (See Dystaxia.)

Auditory Discrimination: The ability to hear the difference between sounds. *For example:* "pig" and "peg."

Auditory Memory: Remembering what is heard. *For example:* A teacher tells the class to get out their science books, turn to page 145 and do problems 1–6. The student is expected to remember all three directions. If a child is unable to remember this information, he may have auditory memory deficits.

Auditory Perception and Processing Skills: The ability to recognize and interpret things that are heard. This term includes auditory discrimination, auditory memory, auditory sequencing, and figure-ground discrimination.

Auditory Sequencing: Remembering the proper sequence in which things are heard. *For example:* 12345 and not 12435.

Behavior Modification: A technique used to change a child's behavior by setting up a system of positive rewards and/or negative consequences. The positive rewards might consist of food, money, or tokens, while the negative consequences might consist of punishment or denial of privileges.

Blending: The ability to "sound out" and put together the separate sounds that make up a word. *For example:* A child would blend the "c" sound, the "a" sound and the "t" sound to form the word "cat."

Closure: The act of bringing an experience or a concept to a conclusion. When everything is stated and the child understands and has integrated the information into his store of knowledge, then closure has been achieved. Some material (such as grammar or syntax) may require months or even years before a child fully understands the concepts involved and is able to achieve closure.

Convergence: The ability of both eyes to coordinate their movement and focus on an object or a written word.

Decoding: The basic process of responding to auditory or visual symbols. An example of decoding is reading words aloud; that is, using the knowledge of the sound that each letter makes to figure out how to pronounce a word.

Differential Diagnosis: A relatively comprehensive testing procedure designed to pinpoint areas of strength and weakness and, where possible, to locate the exact cause of the child's learning difficulties.

Directionality: Being aware that there is a right and left side to the body and being able to relate this internal awareness to external objects. Children with directionality problems will frequently reverse letters and/or numbers ("b" for "d") because they cannot perceive that the letters are pointed to the right or to the left.

Discrimination Skills: Skills that help a person tell the difference between two or more things. (See Auditory and Visual Discrimination.)

Dyslexia: Generally, a visual perception problem commonly characterized by letter and word reversals ("p"/"q" or "saw"/"was"). Dyslexic children frequently have directionality problems (right/left confusion) and visual tracking problems (difficulty seeing letters and words accurately when reading). Sometimes the word "dyslexia" is used simply to describe a reading problem.

Dysphasia: Difficulty in using language to communicate which is not the result of a physical impairment such as damaged vocal cords or larynx.

For example: A child may have difficulty finding the appropriate word to complete a sentence or a thought even though the word is part of his everyday vocabulary. (Aphasia is more severe).

Dyspraxia: Great difficulty in making purposeful motor movements when there is no paralysis. *For example:* A child playing hopscotch may remain poised on one square trying to make his muscles work correctly in order to hop to the next square. Less severe than apraxia.

Dystaxia: Difficulty in coordinating muscles. The condition is less severe than ataxia.

Encoding: The process of writing or speaking by retrieving the written and spoken symbols (or words) from memory and using those symbols to express oneself.

Far Point Deficits: Difficulty copying or reading something in the distance. *For example:* Difficulty copying from the blackboard.

Figure-Ground Deficits: Difficulty in distinguishing a specific shape or sound from the background. *For example:* A child may be unable to screen out distractions and background noises when trying to listen to the teacher talking.

Fine-Motor: Referring to the specialized muscles in the hands. These muscles develop more slowly than the large skeletal muscles and are needed specifically for good handwriting.

Gross-Motor: Referring to the large skeletal muscles used for crawling, walking, lifting, balancing, etc.

Hard Neurological Signs: Specific measurable deviations in brain functioning that usually indicate organic brain damage. Hard signs are usually revealed by an EEG exam that is performed by a neurologist.

Kinesthetic Techniques: Methods of teaching reading that involve movement of the fingers, arms, or whole body. Children who are taught by this method receive input from the muscles which is intended to reinforce the association of the visual symbol with its sound. *For example:* A child learning the letter "b" might trace over a "b" with his fingers on sandpaper, trace a giant "b" in the air, or form a "b" with his whole body.

Language Disabilities: Difficulty expressing oneself in either written or spoken form. *For example:* A child who knows the answer to a question but has trouble finding the words to express it may have a language disability. (See Encoding.)

Laterality: Being aware of and being able to use both sides of the body.

Linguistic Approach: A teaching method that emphasizes learning to read whole words and word families. *For example:* if the child can read "dog," then he should be able to read "log."

Math Skills: The ability to use numbers effectively to solve problems. Math skills involve 1) the ability to do basic computations (adding, subtracting, multiplying, dividing); 2) the ability to apply those skills to everyday situations (word problems); 3) the ability to understand the mathematical concepts involved in the computations (adding mixed fractions).

Mental Retardation: A condition in which a child's IQ is determined to be below 70 and where the child has deficits in adaptive behavior, motor coordination, communication, self-help, and/or socialization skills.

Mid-Line: An imaginary vertical line which divides the right and left sides of the body. The left half of the brain controls the right side of the body, and the right half of the brain controls the left half. Skipping, or drawing a line from the left side of a paper to the right side involves crossing the mid-line. Difficulty crossing the mid-line (*for example:* difficulty coordinating both sides of the body) can be a symptom of a perceptual or neurological problem.

Minimal Brain Dysfunction (M.B.D.): A medical term applied to children who show "soft" neurological symptoms of perceptual deficiency but who show no organic evidence of brain damage as measured by an EEG. (See Perceptual Dysfunction.)

Motor-Coordination: The ability to perform with dexterity tasks involving movement of the body, such as walking or swimming. Specific components of coordination include: balance, synchronized upper-lower body movement, fine-motor skills, eye-hand coordination, and depth perception.

Motor Planning: Thinking through the movements that the body must make to perform a task before attempting the action. An example of basic motor planning is a child thinking of how to move his muscles in order to jump over a rope. More complex motor planning might involve looking at a set of instructions for building something and then purposefully planning how to move one's hands to follow the directions.

Motor Skills: Skills which involve the coordinated movement of the body, such as jumping, balancing, or drawing. (See Gross-Motor and Fine-Motor.)

Near Point Deficits: Difficulty copying or reading something that is close at hand. *For example:* Copying from a book on the desk.

Neurological Disorders: A condition resulting from damage to the brain or central nervous system. The damage may be so slight that there are no observable symptoms or there may be more serious damage that can be measured by neurological tests. (See Soft Neurological Signs and Hard Neurological Signs.)

Neurological Impress Method: A reading method in which the teacher and student read out loud simultaneously at a fairly rapid pace while the student follows the printed word with his finger. The child has input from the printed page, and the movement of his finger and the sound of the two voices reading help him master the words.

Perceptual Decoding: See Decoding.

Perceptual Learning Disabilities: An inability to process sensory data efficiently resulting in specific learning problems such as letter reversals, spelling problems, and reading comprehension problems.

Perceptual-Motor Activities/Perceptual-Motor Training: Activities designed to train the child to process information coming from the senses efficiently and to make appropriate responses to that sensory information. *For example:* A physical activity which requires children to follow a series of command strains them to listen carefully to the directions and remember what was said.

Perceptual Processing: The instantaneous sorting and analysis by the brain of sensory data from the five senses and the association of this data with past sensory experiences. *For example:* A child sees a "b," recognizes it, associates it with the letter "b" and says, "This is a 'b.' "

Phonics Approach: A method of teaching reading which emphasizes learning the sound of each letter and then blending the sounds together to say words. To read "hen," the child would first say the sounds "h," "e," and "n," then put them together to say "hen."

Reading Comprehension: The ability to understand and remember what one has read.

Self-Concept: A person's view of himself. Children who have good self-concepts see themselves as generally able to succeed in many areas. Children who have a poor self-concept often perceive themselves as unpopular or inadequate.

Sensory Impairment: Physical damage to one of the sensory receptors (*for example:* the eyes) resulting in partial or complete loss of the use of that sensory receptor. Blindness and hearing loss are two examples of sensory impairments.

Sensory-Motor Integration/Sensory Integration Therapy: A procedure designed for children with relatively severe perceptual problems, in which perceptual processing skills are enhanced by means of activities and exercise which stress central nervous system development. This procedure is usually implemented by trained occupational therapists.

Sight-Word Approach/Sight-Word Recognition: In reading, learning to recognize words by memorization. There are many words, such as "thought," which do not follow phonic rules and which must be learned "by sight."

Soft Neurological Signs: Deficits in gross-motor and fine-motor coordination, balance, and concentration which are associated with minimal brain dysfunction and perceptual learning disabilities. "Soft signs" involves less severe neurological symptoms and can be distinguished from "hard signs" which generally indicate a neurological disorder involving organic brain damage.

Sound/Letter/Word Retrieval: In reading, the ability to remember a previously learned sound, letter, or word.

Spatial Judgment/Spatial Concepts/Spatial Skills/Spatial Relationships: The awareness of one's body in space and its relationship to other things around it. Judging distance, size, and location all involve spatial skills. A child may have difficulty with prepositions (such as "above," "next to," and "behind") because he has difficulty understanding spatial concepts.

Tracking: See Visual Tracking.

Visual Decoding Skills: See Decoding.

Visual Discrimination: The ability to tell the difference between things one sees (*for example:* differentiating "b" and "d". Poor visual discrimination is frequently responsible for poor reading skills.

Visual Memory: Remembering what one has seen. *For example:* A child with poor visual memory who is shown a series of numbers will have difficulty repeating the numbers from memory.

Visual-Motor Skills/Visual-Motor Integration: Skills that involve making a motor response (speaking, writing, or moving) to a visual stimulus. A child copying or reading from the blackboard or following written directions is using visual-motor skills.

Visual Perception/Visual Processing Skills: The ability to recognize and interpret the things one sees. This includes figure-ground discrimination, visual discrimination, visual memory, and visual sequencing. *For example:* Finding matching pictures or letters.

Visual Sequencing: Process of remembering and then placing what one has seen in the correct order. *For example:* When copying the word "milk" from the board, a child with poor visual sequencing skills might remember all the letters but put them in the wrong order and write "mlik."

Visual Tracking Problem: Difficulty reading with precision the letters and words which make up printed text. Typically, children with visual tracking problems will confuse "b" and "d" (a static tracking problem) and/or will omit syllables, mispronounce words, and drop word endings (a kinetic tracking problem). Children with visual tracking problems often lose their place when reading and may skip words, phrases, or entire lines.

Word Attack Skills: Skills that help a child to pronounce and understand words that are read. These skills primarily involve phonics, but also include recognizing context clues (how was the word used in the sentence) and structural clues (prefixes, suffixes, syllables).

Glossary of Testing Terms

Ability Test: A test designed to measure what a person can do.

Achievement Test: A test designed to measure how much a person has learned after instruction in a specific content area. Generally, these tests are standardized and normed.

Aptitude: An ability, capacity, or talent in a particular area such as music or mathematics. Aptitude is a specialized facility to learn or understand a particular skill.

Criterion-Referenced Test: A test, usually designed by a teacher or publisher, which measures the student's mastery of a specific subject he has studied. The scores are not standardized but can provide the teacher with useful information about what the child has and has not learned.

Diagnostic Test: A test that pinpoints a student's strengths and weaknesses. The results are generally used in planning specific strategies designed to correct the weaknesses.

Grade Equivalent: A statistical ranking of a child's performance based on his raw score which compares the child's performance level to the score which could be expected statistically from an average child at that same year and month in school. This score is expressed in terms of years and months, (9 months making up each school year). *Example:* a score of

2.8 would mean that the student's score is the same as an average child in second grade, eighth month.

Intelligence Quotient (IQ): An index designed to predict academic success. The IQ test compares a person's intelligence (or learning potential) with that of others the same age. This comparison yields a derived score called IQ. The score does not measure creativity, talent, or motivation. Any IQ score between 85 and 115 is considered to be in the average range. A score between 70 and 85 is low average, while 115 to 130 is high average. A score below 70 indicates possible mental retardation and a score above 130 indicates possible giftedness. These scores may vary slightly depending on the IQ test that is administered and the scores can be influenced by emotional, cultural, and perceptual factors.

Mastery Test: See Criterion-Referenced Test.

Mean Score: The mathematical average of all students' test scores in a particular test.

Mental Age: A score on a mental abilities test which ranks the performance level of a child in relation to the score which could be expected statistically from a child at that same age. The mental age score is used to distinguish between a child's chronological age and his actual performance. *Example:* If a child's chronological age is 10-6 (10 years, 6 months) and his mental age is 11-4, then his performance on the test is comparable to the average performance of children whose chronological age is 11 years, 4 months. The child's mental age would thus be "above average."

Norms: A frame of reference for a standardized test which shows the actual performance on the test by pupils of specific ages and grades. Through the use of norms, the score of an individual student can be compared to the scores of other students of a similar age or grade across the country.

Percentile: A score which states a student's relative position within a defined group by ranking all students who have taken a particular test.

Personality Test: A test that measures character traits and the way a person acts rather than specific knowledge or intelligence.

Power Test: An untimed test with items usually arranged in order of difficulty that determines a student's level of performance in a particular subject area.

Raw Score: The total number of correct answers on a test.

Readiness Test: A test that measures a student's maturity or mastery of prerequisite skills which are needed before going on to a new content area. This kind of test is typically used in preschool or kindergarten to determine whether the child is academically and developmentally prepared to function effectively at the next academic level.

Reliability: How well a test consistently produces the same results.

Scaled Score: A ranking system, chosen by the publisher of the test, which is derived from the raw scores obtained on that test. A different scale is established for each test. For example, one test could have a scale from 1 to 19 while another might have a scale from 1 to 70. In order to interpret a scaled score, you must know the mean score and the standard deviation for that test.

Standard Deviation: A measure of how much one student's score varies from the mean score of all the students taking the test.

Standard Score: A statistical ranking, with respect to the performance of a large sample of students of the same age and/or grade level, of a child's performance on a standardized test, based on the raw score he achieved on the test.

Standardized Test: A test that has specific and uniform instructions for administering timing and scoring. It is given to large numbers of children at one time and statistically compares one student's performance with that of a large sample of students of the same age and/or grade level. The norms established by the standardization process are used by teachers and school psychologists to determine a child's relative level of performance or achievement.

Stanine: A statistical ranking of a child's performance on a standardized test on a scale of 1 through 9. A mean score is 5 and any stanine score from 3 to 7 is generally considered to reflect average performance. Frequently, the results on a standardized test will be given by means of both a stanine score and a percentile score. The higher the stanine score, the higher the percentile score will be.

Survey Test: Test which measures general achievement in an academic area. It is not as comprehensive or specific as a criterion-referenced test.

Validity: The accuracy with which a test measures what it has been designed to measure.

Bibliography

Bannatyne, A. *Language Reading and Learning Disabilities.* (2nd ed.) Springfield, Ill.: Charles C. Thomas, 1971.

Compton, C. *A Guide to 65 Tests for Special Education.* Belmont, Calif.: Pittman Learning Inc., 1980.

Durkin, D. *Teaching Them to Read.* (2nd ed.) Boston: Allyn & Bacon, Inc., 1974.

English, H. and English, A. *A Comprehensive Dictionary of Psychological and Psychoanalytical Terms.* New York: David McKay Company, Inc., 1958.

Greene, Lawrence J. *Getting Smarter.* Belmont: David S. Lake Publisher, 1985.

_____. *Kids Who Underachieve.* New York: Simon & Schuster, 1986.

_____. *Smarter Kids.* Tuscon: H. P. Books, 1987.

Hinsie, L. and Campbell, R. *Psychiatric Dictionary.* (3rd ed.) New York: Oxford University Press, 1960.

Johnson, D. and Myklebust, H. *Learning Disabilities.* New York: Grune & Stratton, 1967.

Kauffman, J. *Characteristics of Children's Behavior Disorders.* Columbus: Charles E. Merrill Pub. Co., 1977.

Lerner, Janet, *Learning Disabilities*. (3rd ed.). Boston: Houghton Mifflin Co., 1981.

Levinson, Harold N. *A Solution to the Riddle of Dyslexia*. New York: Springer-Verlag, 1980.

MacMillan, D. *Mental Retardation in School and Society*. Boston: Little, Brown & Co., 1977.

Mercer, C. *Children and Adolescents with Learning Disabilities*. Columbus: Charles E. Merrill Pub. Co., 1979.

Olson, J. and Dillner, M. *Learning to Teach Reading in the Elementary School*. New York: MacMillan Pub. Co., Inc., 1976.

Telford, C. and Saurey, J. *The Exceptional Individual*. (3rd ed.) Englewood Cliffs, N.J.: Prentice-Hall, Inc., 1977.

Test Service Notebook. "A Glossary of Measurement Terms." New York: Harcourt, Brace Jovanovich, Inc.

Wiig, E. and Semel, E. *Language Disabilities in Children and Adolescents*. Columbus: Charles E. Merrill Pub. Co., 1976.

Index

About the Author

After completing his graduate studies in the School of Education at Stanford University, Lawrence Greene pursued his clinical training in learning disabilities in Chicago. During the last seventeen years he has been Executive Director of the Developmental Learning Center in San Jose, California, where he and his staff have treated more than 7,000 learning disabled and underachieving children. In addition to his clinical, counseling, and program development responsibilities, Lawrence Greene is a school consultant and teaches courses for parents in the Child Study Department at West Valley College. He has taught at the Esalen Institute in Big Sur, California, and has trained teachers and learning disabilities specialists as part of the Continuing Education Program at San Jose State University. He is currently teaching graduate courses in education through the Extension Program at the University of California, Santa Cruz.